REVOLUTIONARY TRACINGS

REVOLUTIONARY TRACINGS

JAMES E. JACKSON

50 YEARS 1924-1974

INTERNATIONAL PUBLISHERS · NEW YORK

209

Library of Congress Cataloging in Publication Data

Jackson, James E
Revolutionary tracings.

1. Communism—United States—1917—   2. Communism.
3. Negroes—Social conditions—1964—
4. Black power—United States.   I. Title
HX86.J18   335.43'0973   74-23242
ISBN 0-7178-0451-8
ISBN 0-7178-0452-6 (pbk.)

To Esther

and

to the memory of

Louis

and

Ed

Contents

Preface

In a certain sense this volume is like a book of matches.

The glow from a match will not light a room, but it can serve to locate the light-switch.

This writer will be happy if the contents of this volume fulfill the function of discovery lights revealing the switches which may turn the bright lights of Marxist-Leninist illumination upon the urgent realities and tasks of our times.

Part I offers analysis and commentary on the politics of international and national questions of continuing concern. Part II deals with questions of theory and practice in respect to the Black liberation struggle in the United States. The two parts are as connected as is *the general* and *the particular* in all living reality.

A lot of the documentation and statistical data which were contained in the original versions of some pieces have been eliminated in the interest of greater readability and because developments have confirmed the conclusions and projections made. Where called for, more recent figures have been inserted in lieu of those used initially.

This volume was produced with the encouragement of my comrades in the Central Committee. Especially am I indebted to the National Chairman of our Party, Henry Winston, whose outstanding book, *Strategy For a Black Agenda,* is the classical statement of our Party on the vital problems of Black liberation. And, to the General Secretary of our Party, Gus Hall, whose major study of *Imperialism Today* provides the ideological and political guidelines for the ongoing theoretical and practical work of the Communists of the United States.

JAMES E. JACKSON
New York, 1974

part *I*
World Politics

. . . the true lover of his country is not he who would consent to lose it unjustly rather than attack it, but he who longs for it so much that he will go to all lengths to recover it.

Alcibiades of Sparta

1 The Meaning of Watergate

Watergate is an infield error in a carefully designed game-plan to administer a crushing defeat to what remains of democratic government in order to insure the unbridled political domination of the monopoly capitalist class over the state.

Nixon is not to be explained as simply some unfathomable, evil and corrupt individual. Nixon is a committed servant of the general interests of the monopoly capitalist class as a whole. The game-plan was to effect basic changes in the political superstructure and elaborate a regime of personal power. He wanted to concentrate unshared power in the executive leadership of government and nullify the possibilities for popular intervention in the decision-making processes. If this plan has gone askew, has been temporarily aborted by the Watergate disclosure, it cannot be concluded that his effort in this direction has no relationship to the grand designs and strategic domestic political purpose of the master class of monopolists to whose service he is so scrupulously committed. We must seek the meaning of Watergate in other than the tricky character of the personality of a Nixon; it lies in the nature and fundamental political tendency of the capitalist system in its state monopoly stage.

Under the aegis of the Nixon Administration, the military-industrial complex forged to the forefront as the dominant category of the monopoly capitalist class. The union of personnel between the giants of industry along with aides from the military and the intelligence branches of the police—especially of the Central Intelligence Agency (CIA) and Federal Bureau of Investigation (FBI)—and the state apparatus distinguishes the Nixon administration from its predecessors. The domination of the state apparatus by the personnel of the monopolists has been brought to a high point of development. The narrow class interests of the monopolists have been given free rein to determine both foreign and domestic policies. The biggest corporations and the government interchange executive and administrative personnel in shifts, like a game of musical chairs. Under this order of state monopoly capitalism, the monopolists constantly strive to "streamline" the government, eliminate all democratic frills and encumbrances to its functioning exclusively for the maintenance and strengthening of their economic, social and political positions.

The undermining of the already limited bourgeois democracy is a continuing operational tendency of the capitalist society in its state-monopoly stage. The economic basis is established for it and the social and political roots of right-wing tendencies are nurtured by state-monopoly capitalism. The distinctive features of this ultimate socio-political formation of the capitalist epoch continually reproduce the striving toward a fascist type of state governmental structure of class dictatorship.

That the bourgeoisie wishes for a restructuring of the governmental system to better accord with the narrowest class interests of the monopolists is given expression—even if inadvertently—in a statement made on television by one of the members of the select Senate Committee during the hearings on Watergate. Senator Howard Baker Jr. (R. Tenn.) said: "Democracy is an uncomfortable process . . ."

The odorous pus-flow from the ruptured boil on the body-politic that is Watergate is a manifestation of a malignant systemic illness of capitalist society, a condition that is not temporary. On the contrary, it is terminal.

Watergate is the exposed fragment of a comprehensive and long-range strategic class conspiracy on the part of finance capital, on the part of the dominant section of the monopolists, to secure its total control of the state apparatus, to insure its dictatorship over the masses, under contingent circumstances when it would find that the "old methods of bourgeois democracy and parliamentarism" no longer sufficed.

Watergate was designed to be a substantial stride down the road toward a neo-fascist state, not in its classical well-known form, but in a modern, modified and "original" design to correspond to unique current U.S. and international circumstances.

Watergate reveals that a considerable contingent of ultra-rightist, neo-fascist types—largely drawn from the front offices of huge monopoly corporations, the military and police forces, especially the intelligence services, the CIA and FBI—have been given command of wide areas of administrative and executive power in the government by the White House. Watergate has disclosed that the process of fascization of the government apparatus has been under development for a considerable period of time. The President has arrogated to the executive branch more and more unchecked power at the expense of the legislative and judicial branches and at the expense of the citizens' Bill of Rights, that is, constitutional rights and privileges. Nixon has packed the Supreme Court and the Federal District and Appellate courts with men of his own type.

The secretive route toward a radical change in the form of class rule taken by the monopolists, via the subversion of the norms of bourgeois democracy and the transfer of effective power to the President and his appointed surrogates, was determined by a number of particular circumstances.

The monopolists confront a cluster of problems in their efforts to fit a fascist or neo-fascist strait jacket over the state structure in the United States at this time. First of all, the reactionary war-of-aggression against the peoples of Vietnam, Cambodia and Laos, with its high cost in lives of our drafted soldier-youth, its well publicized massive atrocities committed against the Vietnamese and Indochinese peoples as at My Lai, the carpet-bombing of Hanoi and areas of Cambodia, resulted in a massive movement demanding peace. The resistance to the war was a politicalizing influence upon millions, leading them to view the government with suspicion and sharply criticize its policies.

The economic consequences of the disastrous war adventure, the inflationary rise in prices and loss of jobs, the rise in taxes and curtailment of expenditures for meeting the social needs of people, have brought tens of millions into conflict with the Administration. The government's policy of "benign neglect" of social programs in general, and the equality needs of Black Americans in particular, has intensified the social criticism by masses and strengthened the hostility of Blacks against the regime.

Secondly, the people of the United States still retain the livid scars from the bludgeoning of popular liberties and the recourse by government to naked police terror against real or alleged critics of its policies which were characteristic of the McCarthy years. Masses have not forgotten the lesson of those years: that when tyrants jail the Communists they fit handcuffs for the whole nation. Therefore, they have to pursue their aims by a different route than McCarthy took. For the same reason, history does not permit the ruling class to repeat the same pattern of the classical fascist ascent to power as it occurred in Germany. Our people and the world's peoples are endowed with memory of the ghastly consequences of fascism in power following the German nazi model. It would easily detect and reject such a brand. Imperialist war for national aggradizement is an indispensable accompaniment of fascism of the German nazi model. For, with the loot of the conquests, the masses at home are to be bribed into no resistance to the surrender of their civil liberties and democratic rights, and accept the exclusive leadership of the annointed surrogate of the most powerful and reactionary sector of the monopolist capitalist class.

A determined center of the ruling monopoly capitalists plotted an underground route to the institutionalization of a particular Americanized modern version of fascism as the effective governmental form. This Trojan-horse route to fascism was to be accomplished without fascists and without a fascist party.

To accomplish it required the cooperation and good offices of the President himself. It required also an extensive operating center within the old guard Republican Party, now the governing party, but a presence within the Republican Party that left the neo-fascists with a freedom of operation unrestricted by the rules and traditions of the old bourgeois democratic "party of the establishment."

The Committee to Re-elect the President (CREEP) provided just the "wheel within the wheel" that the fascist conspirators needed, and they took full charge of it. One task they set themselves was that of insuring that no liberal challenge would be able to rise again against them from out of their rival party of Big Business, the Democratic Party. This would be accomplished in two ways: first through the accumulation and elaboration of blackmailing material for character assassination and scandal campaigns for use in destroying candidates who may challenge for membership in Congress or as presidential opponents in the future; and second by elevating people like Robert Strauss and other reliable conservatives into the leadership of the party.

The neo-fascist conspiracy of monopoly capital to erect a contingency structure within the government, to insure a permanency for their unbridled class rule after the Nixon term of office expires in 1976, was timed to take advantage of the Nixon "landslide" success in the 1972 elections. Under cover of his prestige and relying on his authority "to carry it off" undetected and without serious challenge, they expected to execute the key steps in their ongoing conspiracy to change the form of government, to fulfill the fascist function of insuring the permanent domination of the monopolists. The operatives in the plot worked from safe havens of appointed posts in the executive controlled governmental bureaucracy. These technicians of the fascist coup were drawn from the CIA, FBI, metropolitan police departments, the Army, Marine Corps, Naval and Air Force intelligence services. From this motley brigade, a cadre from an undercover political array was formed into a special secret "Security Agency" force solely beholden to and accountable to the President's chosen surrogates—Mitchell, Dean, Haldeman, Ehrlichman—and under the field command of men of a genuine fascist ideological persuasion such as E. Howard Hunt and G. Gordon Liddy, Jr. In place of an organized popular base they would make exceptional use of the latest scientific and technical developments in electronic equipment for spying, infiltrating, forgeries, deception and manipulation of the media of mass information to impose their will upon the country.

Watergate signifies that the ruling monopolist class has no confidence in its ability to meet the rising demands of the masses for relief from the burdens of capitalism's deepening crisis which is being shoved onto their shoulders. Joblessness and high prices soar, taxes increase and social services are retrenched; all down the line the quality of life of the masses declines while the fortunes of the ever narrowing circle of the rich multiply. Funds are withdrawn from meeting the educational needs of the people, while the fires of racial bigotry are stoked with new combustible savageries against the Blacks and other non-white national minorities.

Watergate signifies that the ruling class anticipates an upsurge in the struggles of the working class accompanied by the militant action of broad strata of the people currently burdened by the reign of the monopolists. Watergate signifies that the capitalist class has no confidence that it can cope with coming struggles of the masses to secure their livelihood, and enlarge their political power and win for themselves a new birth of freedom from the yoke of exploitation and discrimination which the monopolists have imposed upon them. That is, they have no confidence they can meet the rising tide of challenge from the masses through the bourgeois democratic forms of exercising their class rule. They fear that they would be beaten in class battle waged on the plain of even the limited democracy that obtains presently. Therefore, they have made up new rules for a new "game plan" to deal with the anticipated forthcoming struggle of the masses against them. They are bent on realizing a new U.S. neo-fascist form for securing their domination and control of the state power to safeguard their grip upon the economy. Such is the essence, the real meaning of Watergate.

The measures taken by the Nixon Administration aim to disembowel the rival party of the monopolists, the Democratic Party; to suppress in its infancy any moves toward the rise of a genuine mass anti-monopoly party; and to penalize and prevent the radicalized advanced masses from following the logical course of their developing political consciousness into joining the Communist Party. It constitutes a new style in approach to the accomplishment of the goal of the oldest political tendency of capitalism in its imperialist stage, absolute control of the state power by the monopolists—which is equivalent to the political function of fascism.

That the real rulers of the country are the monopoly capitalists and that their influence has always been dominant in the determination of government policies has been long established.

What is new is the brazen use of the office and executive powers of the presidency to circumvent and undermine the established democratic processes.

A very special feature of the present operational tendency to fascization which Watergate reveals to a degree, a feature which is distinct from the classic pattern of the fascist bid for power, is this: the Nixon government represents and basically speaks for and acts in behalf of the main sections of the monopolist ruling class, the decisive majority of that class, not simply the ". . . most reactionary, most chauvinistic and most imperialist elements of finance capital." (Georgi Dimitrov, *The United Front*, New York: International Publishers 1938, p. 10) This important difference explains the speed with which large sections of the class declared their opposition to the exposed features of Nixon's political police methods.

The Watergate disclosures are dramatic evidence of a permanent tendency inherent in state monopoly capitalism to effect neo-fascist alterations in the political superstructure on the part of the main forces of the ruling class. This tendency, however, is increasingly countered by another, that of making some accommodation to the new reality of the changed relation of forces as between the two world systems, socialism vis-a-vis capitalism, in international affairs, and to yield concessions to the rising tide of popular democratic struggles of the anti-monopoly forces at home which are generated by the working class, the militant actions of Black people's freedom and equality movements and the demands of Chicano, Puerto Rican, Native American and other oppressed national minorities.

Both tendencies of modern capitalism at the present stage, the one toward more repressive and dictatorial government, and the other toward yielding concessions in hope of moderating the class struggle, stem from capitalism's deepening general crisis. Watergate sharpens and brings to the crisis point these two tendencies operating in U.S. capitalism. The tendency for policies of realism related to coexistence requirements is supported by the dominant world political trends and economic developments. The conspiracy of the neo-fascist tendency which is being unmasked in the Watergate affair has every chance of being beaten by the mass actions of an informed and rallied people who cherish their hard-earned democratic rights.

What is to be done to meet the arrogant challenge of Watergate?

The fascist menace formulated in the White House underground can be effectively fought and defeated only in the general context of forwarding the anti-monopoly, anti-imperialist struggle in which the working class comes up front and takes the lead. The crisis of Watergate cannot be overcome by a simple change of the guard of the class interests of the monopolists, nor by restoring the balance of the rival party of the monopolists, the Democratic Party, to its pre-election "prestige." At this point in history and the general decline of world capitalism, the anti-fascist struggle cannot be conceived of as a different cause from that of the anti-monopoly, anti-imperialist struggle. It rallies all supporters of democracy and believers in freedom to the working class cause of curbing the monopolists, removing them from government and placing genuine representatives of the people in command of the state.

Watergate opens new political opportunities before the U.S. working class to be about the business of preparing and bringing into being a genuine mass anti-monopoly labor-people's party.

Watergate raises the crying necessity for a real change of system; the masses seek the way forward; we must show why socialism is the answer and how to get it.

Watergate is the instant point of reference to expose and teach the anatomy of monopoly capitalism to the millions.

Watergate is a profound ideological propaganda and agitational chal-

lenge to and opportunity for the Communist Party to raise the consciousness of millions as to the nature of capitalism and the necessity of
the socialist alternative. This we must do if the bell of freedom is not to
be silenced and if the quality of life for the masses is to rise to the lofty
heights that modern scientific and technical attainments have made
possible.

World Magazine, New York. June 16, 1973

2   Beware the Tigers of U.S. Monopolies

Among the good things done for us during our visit to always
make it a cherished memory, was the organization of an excur-
sion to Kerala's beautiful tourist resort—Teakgari. There, for the pleas-
ure of visitors, are elephants and other species of wild animals living as
in their native habitat.

However, it was not my first encounter with jungle animals. Indeed,
it is no fable but harsh truth to speak of the America of the U.S.
imperialist ruling class in terms of a jungle. You all know that in our
country our cities have skyscraper buildings which soar upward like
trees in a forest. But in the asphalt and concrete jungles of these forest
cities of the United States prowl the man-eating tigers—rapacious profiteers, elephantine corporations and trusts which crush the lives and
bleed the bodies of the working men and women. The robber barons
who own these cities leave one-third of the whole population ill-housed,
and the exploiters of the labor of our toilers have kept 35 million in
poverty, while another 6 million seek jobs in vain.

Glittering "golden America" is a North America of avaricious,
greedy monopolists with fangs bared and claws curled against the independence and well-being of the peoples of the East, the Middle East,

Latin America and Africa. The wildest elephant in the asphalt jungles of America is the ruling Republican Party's leader, Richard Nixon. Let the peoples of India and Asia beware of the seductions and blandishments of this clever elephant with the snake-like trunk. He is the elephant that tramples into the dust the lives of hundreds of thousands and the peaceful pursuits of millions of people of Vietnam, Laos and Cambodia. When he draws near to you, India, it is not to offer his strength to serve your needs, but to crush you under his brutal bulk. Be vigilant against the hand that drips with the blood of the slaughtered children and women and old people of Vietnam's My Lai villages.

But the people of India, as of the whole world, have come to know and cherish the fact that the United States of America is more than the mad animals of the Wall Street canyons and skyscraper forests; it is also a nation of hard-working and peace-loving people who are engaging the monopolist ruling class that preys upon them, and all mankind, in steadily mounting battles.

Today, as never before, the plain people of my country are rising in struggle against the capitalist man-eaters who would devour them and hold the peoples of the world under the threat of their aggressive violence. The workers have taken the path of increasingly sharp strike actions to uphold their living standards against the collapse of capitalism's prosperity boom.

The Black Americans are in continuous battles on a wide front in unrelenting demand for an end to all manner of discrimination and racist indignities, and for full economic, social and political equality. The youth and women demonstrate their militant will to secure radical social reforms in mass actions for full equality and the material means for the satisfaction of their urgent social, educational, cultural and employment needs.

Such major forces in the arena of social action and political struggle constitute the main armies of the fighters against the Nixon government for ending the criminal war against the peoples of Vietnam, Laos and Cambodia, for respecting the independent sovereignty of all countries, and for ceasing the practiced hostilities and interventions of U.S.-sponsored aggressions in the Middle Eastern and Latin American countries; and for the liquidation of U.S. military bases in Europe and the vacating of its outposts of aggression around the world.

The incendiaries of the CIA and Pentagon are probing an opportune opening to add to the conflict and tensions on India's eastern frontier.

The savage mass atrocities carried out by the troops of the Yahya Khan government of Pakistan against the peoples and national democratic movement of East Pakistan (Bangladesh) have evoked world-wide protests and condemnation. We join with all who demand that an end be put to the criminal acts of military repression being carried out against the national movement, and call for the right of the Bangladesh people to be secure in the exercise of their rights and the democratically determined course they have chosen for their national formation of Bangladesh.

World public opinion, which has rallied to the cause of heroic Vietnam, comes to the aid of the victims of the wrath of the Yahya Khan of (West) Pakistan. And so it is that the peoples of India, as of the whole world, are indignantly demanding that the President of the United States and Ronald Reagan, the Governor of California, take immediate actions to free Angela Davis from prison. The suffering and imprisonment of this valiant young Communist woman at the hands of the police and prison authorities in the United States have tugged at the heartstrings and roused the anger of the people in all lands.

The days of the great Ninth Congress of the Communist Party of India coincide with the celebrations of the affirmation of a new birth of friendship between India and the Soviet Union and pledges of cooperation and mutual aid for the solution of weighty problems of national development and the maintenance of world peace. Modern history for the entire Orient may some day be dated from the signing of the Indo-Soviet Treaty of 1971.

How fortunate it is for great India to have at this hour, marching in the first ranks of its patriotic national democratic front of fighters for her advancement along the chosen path of anti-imperialist, anti-monopolist, democratic line of socio-political development—the tested and powerfully organized Communist Party of India!

This Party, armed with the science of Marxism-Leninism, and girded about with the international solidarity and experience of the movement of the masses of all the capitalist and socialist countries, serves India and the cause of progress, peace and socialism in the whole world. May India make great successes along the way of unity of all that is progressive in the nation, along the path of militant struggle against all that is backward-looking and reactionary, along the path that leads through democracy to socialism—the line of march set forth by the great Ninth Congress of the Communist Party of India.

The way forward as set forth by the Communist Party will fulfill the national patriarchs' fondest dreams for the development of the Indian peoples. India will be done forever with all communal prejudices, caste divisions and class distinctions as the workers, in alliance with the peasants and progressive intellectuals, more and more come to the fore in the leadership of the nation.

Speech in Cochin, Kerala, India. October 10, 1971

3   Chile's Cause is Ours

The most important battle against imperialism in the whole hemisphere of the Americas is joined on the soil of Chile today. The gallant working class of Chile mans the front lines of the struggle against imperialism for democratic advance, national liberation and social progress. Working class and popular democratic struggles in all other countries of the Americas, at this hour, relate to the Chilean front as supportive actions of the rear base. The valiant working people of Chile are calling on us, their class brothers and sisters, for support to their struggle, which has entered a crucial stage.

The Chilean masses have won vital advance positions in their battle against the national reactionaries and U.S. imperialism. They have broken the stranglehold of the imperialist-monopolists over their country, and smashed the old home-grown oligarchy of the wealthy parasites. The people of Chile, with the working class at their head, have placed in power a government of popular union, with the Socialist and Communist Parties as its leading components. Important reforms have already been enacted to restore the natural resources to the people and to nationalize foreign enterprises and basic industries which were created out of decades of exploitation of Chilean labor. Under the Popular Unity Government, headed by Salvadore Allende, national independence has been advanced, democracy made meaningful, and the way opened for the enrichment of the quality of life and satisfaction of the urgent needs of the Chilean people.

But now a critical moment has emerged in this historic fight of the common people of Chile to win a new life for themselves and a free status of honor for their nation. The imperialists and defeated forces of the old oligarchy have mounted a ferocious counterattack. Their objective is nothing less than that of the overthrow of the Allende Government of Popular Unity, and the restoration of the tyranny of the domestic and foreign monopolists upon the backs of the Chilean masses. The rallying cry of the counter-revolutionary thrust against the popular democratic government of Allende is that of "free enterprise," that is, for freedom to destroy the democratic and social achievements of the Chilean working class and popular masses.

Such giant U.S. monopolies as the International Telephone and Telegraph Corporation (ITT), Gulf Oil, Kennecott, Guggenheim Nitrates, along with other notorious robbers of the wealth of nations and exploiters of the working peoples of the hemisphere, are the backers and financiers of the counter-revolutionary insurgents. Along with the Wall Street monopolists, the Washington-Pentagon imperialists are making use of their CIA manipulated fifth-column of neo-colonialist agents inside Chile in the organization of counter-revolutionary assaults upon the lives, liberty and legality of Chile's popular government.

With the brazen intervention of the international fraternity of robbers and plunderers headquartered in Washington and Wall Street, the reactionaries are striving to plunge Chile into a civil war. They are hoping thereby to drown the revolutionary cause of the Chilean people in their own blood and bring about a reversal of the progressive course already commenced toward social and political fulfillment of the aspirations of the masses.

The cause of Chile is our own cause. The Chilean masses hold the pivotal sector of struggle on our common front. We are called upon to take extraordinary measures to come to the aid of the embattled Chilean working class. Let no efforts be spared in making known the solidarity and common interests of the broadest masses of our countrymen with the struggle of the Chilean people.

It is urgent and necessary that a sense of emergency activate our efforts to secure thousands of telegrams of solidarity and support from the most representative strata of our citizens, to be sent to President Allende. It is imperative that every organization, trade union, church congregation, cultural group and individual be contacted and urged to enact resolutions of solidarity and support to the chosen government of the Chilean people, to express their indignation and outrage at the conspiracy of the imperialists to nullify the Chilean people's governmental choice. Let meeting halls and street rallies ring with the demand that the U.S. corporate giants and CIA conspirators keep *Hands Off Chile!*

The foes of the people's government of Chile are our enemies.

The freedom struggle of the Chilean working people is our common cause.

Daily World, New York. June 1, 1973

4 Our People Want and Need Peace, Friendship and Cooperation with the Soviet Union

Leonid Ilitch Brezhnev's visit is another historic milepost along the way to the consolidation of good relations between our two countries, a matter which holds the promise of such great mutual benefits to our two peoples and corresponds to the best interests of the progress, peace and well being of the peoples of all countries of the world.

Brezhnev's visit is in accord with the spirit and is a continuation of the work begun at the memorable Moscow Summit meeting of May of last year. There, the government leaders of our country and the USSR solemnly resolved to bring into force a full turn from the hostile relations of the long years of cold war. They charted a new course based upon the principles of peaceful co-existance of the two states whose social systems are of a fundamentally different order — the U.S. being the major imperialist country in the world, the Soviet Union being the foremost socialist state power — for the promotion of mutually beneficial cooperation and for the relaxation of international tension.

In the two years since the 24th Congrress of the Communist Party and the Supreme Soviet of the government of the Soviet Union adopted the Peace Program, the world has come to admire Brezhnev's work and that of the Soviet Union in behalf of peace and friendship between the nations, in the service of the social progress and freedom of peoples. Leonid Brezhnev's personal contribution as an extraordinary emmisary in "the promotion of peace among nations" has been recognized in the award made to him of the International Lenin Prize. Looking forward to his visit to our country, he said: "On our part we are prepared for a continuation of the improvement of Soviet-American relations that has already started, for a further development of mutually advantageous cooperation in various fields on the basis of the principles of peaceful coexistence. We hold that such a development accords with the interest of the peoples of both countries and at the same time is an important part of the general process of the improvement of international relations and strengthening of universal peace."

We are confident that such sentiment will find a welcome and reciprocal response from all thoughtful citizens of our country.

The consolidation of world peace is heavily dependent upon the further development of relations of peaceful coexistence between the U.S. and the USSR. Every step forward taken in this direction will benefit the masses not only by diminishing the danger of thermonuclear war between these great powers, but will open the door to many rewards that flow from peaceful cooperation in the areas of trade, scientific and cultural exchange and relief from the burdens of taxes which flow into the murderously wasteful enterprise of arms-making and armies.

May the consultations which will attend the visit of Leonid Ilitch Brezhnev, the outstanding statesman and leader from the Soviet Union, the socialist land where the working class is the ruling class, be highly productive of new advances along the necessary road of peace and disarmament and of strengthening cooperation between our two peoples and countries for the betterment of the condition of life of all mankind.

Daily World, New York. June 1, 1973

5   Vietnam: The Number One Front Against Imperialism

There is nothing ahead for the expeditionary force of U.S. imperialism in Vietnam but death for its soldiers by the tens of thousands.

Already the U.S. ruling circle has suffered an irreparable defeat. Its sinister design to crush with military might the social emancipation and national liberation movement, to establish South Vietnam as a new-type U.S. colony and a strategic base upon which it could rest the lever of its military power for domination of the whole of Southeast Asia, has failed.

Its neo-colonialist puppet government in Saigon is now utterly without authority or resources. As this is written, the range of its control is limited to a few main boulevards during daylight hours in the capital city of Saigon. And Saigon itself is under continuous fire by the Peoples Liberation Armed Forces (PLAF). Admitting that no place in South Vietnam is completely safe anymore, and that no military position can be said to be permanently secured, on the day of his retirement after more than four years as commander of the forces of U.S. aggression in Vietnam, General William C. Westmoreland admitted that "classic victory" in Vietnam is "beyond our grasp." In other words, the United States has failed to make South Vietnam politically "secure" by imposing a neo-colonialist regime and destroying the patriotic liberation movement in order to make the country into a vast U.S. military base.

Today, after years of escalation of the war under Commander-in-Chief Lyndon Johnson, and 11 years of American military presence and large scale aid to various puppet regimes in Saigon, the Peoples Liberation Armed Forces of South Vietnam are everywhere on the offensive. The U.S. command with 550,000 American troops, the entire Seventh Fleet and what is left of 5,000 planes, plus an additional 700,000 Saigon puppet troops, is staggering from defeat to defeat.

The U.S. expeditionary army has suffered a loss of some 85,000 casualities, including over 10,000 deaths, during the first 15 days of the PLAF general offensive, which began on May 5 of this year and continues without pause.

In the last week of May some anti-aircraft gun crews became national patriotic heroes or heroines of great "collective exploit"—for, in that week the 3,000th U.S. plane was shot down over North Vietnam.

The current casualty rate of U.S. soldiers in Vietnam is in the neighborhood of 400 dead and 4,000 wounded a week. This will mean that some 30,000 American men will be killed in Vietnam, and another 120,000 will be wounded, in the current year alone.

Increasingly our soldiers and officers are asking the question: "Why are we here? For whom and for what are we wallowing in this mud with the explosion of death thundering in our ears?" These are the questions behind the greatest demonstrations of militant opposition to Washington's war policies in our history. On such questions the consciousness and the conscience of the nation have been focused during the campaigns of such peace candidates as Senator Eugene McCarthy for Presidential nominee, and candidate for election to the Senate, Paul O'Dwyer of New York.

The hawkish *U.S. News & World Report* was compelled to devote an article in its June 24th issue to the "mood of Americans in Vietnam." It found the "mood" below the top echelon of officers to be bitter, cynical, pessimistic. The magazine states that enlisted men and lower echelon officers refer to the U.S. effort in Vietnam "openly and frankly as a lost cause . . . the career soldiers are looking for the diplomats in Paris to end America's agony in Vietnam. They are almost cheering them on to find some solution."

Yet, while chief warhawk Westmoreland discloses his conclusion that there is no win possible in Vietnam for the United States, despite the disclosure that the morale of the U.S. troops in the field is at an all-time low, and in defiance of manifestations of the sentiments and appeals for an end to the bombing and for withdrawing the troops on the part of millions of Americans and tens of millions of peoples around the world, President Johnson and the Pentagon persist in their war of aggression and destruction against the people and populated places in Vietnam, North and South.

I have just returned from a 21-day intensive tour of North Vietnam——the Democratic Republic of Vietnam (DRV)— and I bear witness that the government of the United States, with unconscionable motive of vengefulness for the frustration and defeat of its war aims, is bending every effort to accomplish the *genocidal obliteration* of a sovereign state, an independent people and their distinctive social system—that is, to *physically destroy the DRV,* before the people of the United States can replace LBJ's government by another, and before world public opinion compels it to cease its aggression and withdraw its armed forces.

In its *war of aggression* in the South, and its savage *war of destruction* in the North, the U.S. imperialist ruling class has plumbed a new depth in infamy. North and South, its bombers fly and its tanks roll forward, under the injunction to "burn all; destroy all; kill all."

I have seen its handiwork, not only in Hanoi's suburbs and Haiphong harbor's factory districts, but in rural Thanh Hoa province— in the ruins of hospitals, workers' new housing-blocks, in the crater pock-marked school yards of bomb-fractured dormitories. Where are the graceful lacework of the hundreds of bridges which once arched across this land of rivers from one end to the other? And the American bombers have blown up a thousand miles of railroad tracks.

But as the invaders have descended to a new depth in bestial behavior against their fellow men in this war against the Vietnamese, the Vietnam fighter-citizens have added a new stature and grandeur to the name and glory of man. With a sustained valor and heroism, against odds unprecedented, this people—the Vietnamese—have fought, and yet fight on, with unconquerable will and confidence in the certainty of their victory.

In the South, the general offensive, which was launched on May 5th by the PLAF, supports and inspires popular uprisings in the rear and in the center of the "positions of strength" of Saigon's puppet rulers and U.S. military bases. All cities are now battle-grounds in the South. Recruits are flocking to the Peoples Liberation Armed Forces. At the same time, as the *U.S. News & World Report* article previously referred to admits: ''The desertion rate among South Vietnamese soldiers, always an indicator of troop morale, has shot up—while the defection rate among Communist soldiers has plummeted.''

The Vietnamese refer to the North as ''the great rear base of the South.'' The people of the North will render every possible aid to their embattled kinsmen of the South, so long as a single alien boot remains on their soil. The war of national liberation, which their brothers to the South are waging against the U.S. armies of aggression and their puppets, is in the common cause of reunification and national salvation.

However, the role of the North in the struggle against the expeditionary forces of U.S. imperialism is much more than that of a fraternal source of solidarity. U.S. imperialism is waging the most savage air and naval *war of destruction* against the sovereign Democratic Republic of Vietnam. And the entire people of the DRV have risen like one man to fight back against the invaders.

Under the compulsion of defending their country against the merciless invaders, and relying upon the material-technical aid rendered by members of the commonwealth of socialist countries—especially the Soviet Union—the DRV people have built a formidable up-to-date armed power, capable of confronting and defeating any attack upon their territory from any direction. Already, their military excellence has been proven in the air war: three thousand of the five thousand planes sent against the DRV have been shot down, their pilots killed or captured. The principles of peoples' war, as elaborated by Ho Chi Minh and General Giap, are based upon a total involvement of the entire people. The army regulars have the regional militia as organized auxiliaries and reserves. These in turn are able to rely upon locally organized but nationally integrated guerrillas and irregular units. All who work also train to fight and are organized to do so effectively. All who study also learn to fight. Even old folk and children organize themselves to aid the national defense and attend to the needs of the victims of aggression.

The armed forces of the Democratic Republic of Vietnam have been supplied with the most modern weapons and in abundant quantity. This army of peasants has become master of the most complicated arts of rocketry!

While every Vietnamese keeps his eye sharp on his gun, neither the people nor their government are neglecting the vital work of construction and development of the socialist economy. In industry, in agriculture, in transportation, in public health services, in mass and higher education and in culture—in all of these—expansion has outpaced the destruction wrought by the U.S. bombers. The heart-breaking problems posed by the wide-ranging bombing destruction have been met with brilliant improvisations, creativeness and astounding feats of organization. What miracles of organization lie behind the matter-of-fact statement which Minister of Transportation Phan Trong Tue made to me in the course of an interview:

McNamara boasted that he would destroy communications in North Vietnam in six months. In respect to the amount of destruction his bombers caused he did not exaggerate, but our people coped with the problems of miles of bombed roads, railroads and hundreds of downed bridges. We have kept the transportation moving. We are now transporting at least double the amount we were moving before the war. This in the face of continuing bombardment—last year 36,000 air attacks were made upon our roads and bridges and trains; some 660,000 tons of bombs were dropped.

For every bridge they have destroyed, we have built two. For every mile of railroad they have obliterated, we have built seven. When transport goes well all other branches of economy does well.

The extraordinary feats of organization in bridge and road repairing; in dismantling and resettling factories, hospitals and schools; in covering the country with a network of district hospitals and first-aid stations; in the construction of 20 million air raid shelters; in liquidating malaria and reducing to a fraction the cases of smallpox and other former mass killer-diseases—all these accomplishments attest to the solidity of the bonds of the people with their government.

The unity of the Vietnamese people with the leadership and the Vietnam Workers Party is mirrored in the high morale of all. It is attested to in the exploits of rank-and-file fighters, workers and peasants. One reads almost a joyfulness in the faces of these unbeatable men and women as they go about their daily chores amidst battered and bombed buildings.

The women, the youth and the old folk—in their special organizations—join the workers, peasants and intellectuals in the often expressed national resolution of President Ho Chi Minh that the aggressors can destroy their cities but not their will; that "we shall never bend nor bow before you, and we shall win the victory in the end."

The struggle between the world's progressive, democratic and re-volutionary forces and the global gangsterism of U.S. imperialism is joined in the war in Vietnam. No one of conscience, nor anyone who entertains a progressive social outlook for any section of humanity, can afford not to be involved in active support of the noble struggle which the Vietnam patriots are waging in the interest of all who honor peace and freedom.

Americans in great mass actions have manifested their abhorrence of the criminal war which the government wages against the Vietnam people in their name. This pressure has left some mark upon some officials. Yet, it has not brought about a serious diminution of the bombing nor an end of the acts of war against the DRV nor the Libera-tion Forces in the South. But the fact that Washington had to agree to the Paris talks, and that Johnson, facing the anger of the people over his disastrous escalation of the war, felt compelled to announce his absten-tion from seeking reelection as President in the fall; all this suggests that with even greater exertion of the pressure of public opinion, the gov-ernment can be compelled to put an end not only to the bombing but the war itself.

What is required is a powerful new and tougher anti-Vietnam war opposition of a mass character, focused at the point of production of the material for war—at the factories and docks. What is required is for everyone who has ever before acted out a demand for the ending of the U.S. aggression in Vietnam to do so again and again in company with new millions who have not spoken or acted for peace heretofore. Above all, it means carrying the message to the trade unionists, that they will join in fully with the Black people in seeing that their special class and material self-interest can best be served by doing all that is called for to force an end to the anti-human war which Washington wages against Vietnam.

Political Affairs, New York. July, 1968

6 An Appeal Whose Time Has Come!
Citizen-Soldiers!
Remember the Fourth of July!

I address these words to my fellow Americans who are far from home.

You were citizens before you were soldiers. Citizens born with certain inalienable rights, rights which you surrender to no command, rights which do not cease to be yours simply because you have been drafted into the armed forces and put into a uniform. Your birth-right heritage of citizenship rights include the freedom of thought and the right to freedom of expression and freedom of association—that is, freedom of organization.

These rights are the cornerstone of manhood, that liberty which marks the distinction between a free man and a slave.

Slaves to tyranny cannot fight for another's freedom.

To fail to exercise your right to speak out your mind, to think about your condition, to discuss with your fellow soldiers the situation you find yourself in, what the people back home are thinking about and doing about this war, to forfeit your right to think and speak out as a man is to surrender your freedom, is to cease to be a man, is to be a slave.

It's thinking and talking time, citizen-soldiers.

The time has come for taking those decisions that can save your lives and at the same time salvage something of the honor of our country.

No one knows better than you that there is nothing honorable or decent or just in the war being waged with your blood and bodies against a people who have never seen the United States as tourists much less sent planes and soldiers and ships to bombard its cities, burn its farms and slaughter its citizens.

Citizen-soldiers, the judgment of world public opinion rests heavily upon the troubled conscience of every American in this world who hasn't already buried his soul in a common grave with the corpse of some innocent Vietnamese woman, infant or old person burned to death by your flame-thrower, your "lazy-dog" anti-personnel pellet bomb, your napalm, your phosphorus.

The judgment of world public opinion, the decision of God and all decent mankind is in, and it is that the expeditionary forces of the United States, the government of Lyndon Johnson, of Washington, U.S.A. is the aggressor, the guilty party in this war.

It is the United States that has committed a half million soldiers, airmen and sailors and every conceivable vehicle, gun and machine of death to the savage, the bestial business of destroying the creations of generations of Vietnamese workers, farmers and cultural artists. It is the United States that is killing the inhabitants of this little country which for two thousand years has been minding its own business and embroidering its own ways, its gentle-spoken language and its open-armed and soft-smiling manners. This little country, ten thousand miles from the shores of the United States, has never possessed a single battleship, much less had an ambition to invade the United States.

The vast majority of the people of the United States have come to the conclusion that Lyndon Johnson and his generals have betrayed the honor and national interest by taking the country into this military adventure, and tens of millions have expressed themselves so sharply Johnson himself has become convinced he would suffer a most humiliating defeat if he ventured to run for reelection as President in November. So, he has announced his retirement.

Lyndon Johnson is the Commander-in-Chief of the Armed Forces. What is more, this war against the Vietnamese people—North and South—is a war never approved by Congress or by the voters. This is a sneak war, sneaking in behind a rolling barrage of lies about "stopping communism" put out by Johnson and the clique of career military men and merchants of death and profiteers, who are growing rich making and selling planes and napalm and bombs while you bleed and scratch and hug the muddy earth and wait to die.

Lyndon Johnson has repeated the crime against our country and our people that Jefferson Davis and his generals committed over a century ago. Then Davis split our country and forced it into a civil war to continue the enslavement of the Black people, of Black Americans.

Jefferson Davis, like Johnson, sent men into battle to die in an ignoble cause, to kill and be killed in a vain attempt to impose human slavery.

But the Black people rose up as one man, striking the Confederate soldiers in the rear and opening the way to victory for Abraham Lincoln's armies of liberation and national union.

The Black slaves of America's Civil War of a hundred years ago have given to the Vietnam National Liberation Forces, the Vietnamese people's own Lincoln—President Ho Chi Minh—the heritage of their glorious motto: *"Before I'd be a slave, I'll be buried in my grave."*

Man for man, the Southern white soldiers of the Confederacy were not cowards. Some were brave men with human instincts in the family circle. They said their prayers and loved their mothers. But they fought—*not* to set men free—but to keep them chained in slavery.

This is the main thing history remembers about the soldiers who fought Jefferson Davis' war. Many died.

All died without honor in a shameful cause.

What will they say about the gunmen who killed for L.B. Johnson? (For never has there been a more *personal* war waged by Americans.)

But even Johnson is deserting the battlefield. The Commander-in-Chief is heading back to Texas come November and there he will cool it in the shade, sipping mint juleps under the cottonwood trees at his ranch on the Perdenales River and watch the cowboys brand his initials, "L.B.J.," on the backside of his quarter-ton black Angus beef.

But how did President Johnson's grandfather and kinfolk get out of the swamp the Confederate states' President Jeff Davis and his generals, Robert E. Lee, Beauvegard, Johnston and others, had led them into?

I will tell you what they did. They acted in the tradition of Americans who pride themselves on being able to recognize when they have "been taken." They asserted their common sense. They didn't stand on ceremony but turned around and got the hell out of that swamp.

The whole world knows Johnson has committed a colossal, a disastrous mistake in undertaking to enslave this Vietnamese people. His war of aggression against the people of South Vietnam and his air and naval war of destruction against the sovereign and independent Democratic Republic of Vietnam in the north, has dismally failed.

Citizen-soldiers, the time has come to rejoin the American people. It is time to catch up with the folk back home. In the States, every day is witness to new great manifestations of hatred expressed by the people for this war and its terrible effects upon their lives and conditions. Every section of your fellow citizens has been heard from.

The draft-age students supported by 9,896 college professors have vowed never to answer the call of their draft boards. They participate in militant rallies and strikes, at Columbia University, for one, occupying the school for days on end.

The war has not brought jobs for the unemployed at home but more of your fathers and brothers have already lost their jobs because the big companies are making everything automatic now with government money to pay for the new-fangled machines to replace the men and women workers. As a result strikes are sweeping the country.

The thing that has Washington too nervous to sleep these nights is the seemingly endless march-in of column after column of hungry and jobless poor pepole who have set up a vast encampment near the Washington monument and just behind the White House and across from the Congress. This "Poor Peoples March On Washington" demands that the Government: *Stop the War in Vietnam and Start a War Against Poverty and Racism at Home!* This great crusade of the poor and jobless was projected and planned by the beloved Reverend Dr. Martin Luther King; then they killed him. They shot him dead in Memphis, Tennessee on the night of April 4, 1968—this year.

Martin Luther King was murdered not only because he was a Black man telling Black people they ought to be free *even in* Memphis, Tennessee, but he was assassinated by a *killer-unknown* (sic!) because his was the most eloquent and authoritative voice in the United States demanding an immediate end to the bombing and all acts of war by the United States against Vietnam—North and South. He called for the immediate withdrawal of all U.S. armed forces from Vietnam, leaving the Vietnamese to settle peacefully among themselves their own solution to all problems remaining between the North and South.

But the Black people of the United States have rallied around the legacy of Martin Luther King. In the streets of cities from coast to coast they are fighting like tigers to gain for themselves the full rights of equality in deeds and not just words, and their slogan is: *"Get Out of Vietnam and Join the War Against Racism and Poverty Now!"*

This slogan of the Black masses–still battling to be free in their own country after a hundred years of broken promises—should become a challenge and stimulant for thought to every soldier—Black or white, Northerner or Southerner, whether from the rural areas or the big city.

Citizen-soldiers, you have rights—the rights of the First Amendment of the Constitution which gives you freedom of speech, of conscience, of assembly.

More than this: *every man has the right of self-defense, to act to save his life and his honor as a human being.*

What is more, *there is a law higher than that of your superior officer: It is called the Nurenberg Judgment.* That is the international law by which the Hitler generals and others were tried for crimes against humanity committed in acts of wanton destruction, burnings, killings during World War II. Citizen-soldiers, all sections of our people have been heard from. In their overwhelming majority they demand an end to this cynical, mercenary, dirty, immoral, un-American and racist war of destruction, genocide and arrant aggression against the bravest and most patriotic small nation of peoples that the world has ever seen. Already U.S. national honor and pride and standing among her former allies have been lost to her—a casualty of this cruel and unjust war which she wages against a small country like some bully of a Goliath against the little Biblical David.

Already tens of thousands of young lives of American youth have been sacrificed on this burning cross that Johnson's orders have made of Vietnam.

Soon we will celebrate the most patriotic of our national holidays——the *4th of July.*

It was on this day that our country's freedom from British colonial slavery was proclaimed in the famous freedom charter, The Declaration of Independence. (Ho Chi Minh, the father of his country, like George Washington was of ours, cited the words of our Declaration of Independence when the Democratic Republic of Vietnam was proclaimed independent of French colonial domination.)

July 4th *could become* a date with a new patriotic significance if by this date the soldiers of the expeditionary armed forces invading Vietnam should come to a decision that they will withdraw their support to so patently a criminal, un-American and unmanly enterprise as this aggressive imperialist war against the peoples of Vietnam.

Soldiers, the hour has come when decision must be made to join the movement of the masses in the United States who come out boldly and openly for stopping the war, ending the bombardments and withdrawing the troops. *In unity there is protection when the cause is just.* The choice to live can be a collective, a united, a mass choice arrived at through discussions at the platoon, company, battalion level.

Death is no choice at all. *It is a personal and lonely agony in an ignominious cause.*

Citizen, soldiers! *Celebrate* the 4th of July *in a glorious mass affirmation of resolve and action not to tread on others as you would not have them tread on U.S.!*

Soldiers! *Join the millions of your countrymen* this July 4th and come out for peace! *Withdraw from the dirty war!*

Speech at a Peace rally, May 23, 1968

7   On the Death of Ho Chi Minh

Mankind has lost a great revolutionary leader, a brilliant Marxist-Leninist teacher.

So much of the poetic longing in the heart of man for a kind world gentled with the perfumed beauty of flowers and the joyful sounds of children's laughter entered into the all-sided humanism of the personal life he lived, the prodigious works he performed, and the cause he served throughout his lifetime. The name of Ho Chi Minh will ever be associated with the noblest deeds and loftiest dreams of mankind to achieve on the earth a truly fraternal community of the peoples: all enjoying equality and full satisfaction of their material and spiritual needs; for a world without war, tyranny, poverty or prejudice.

The father of the Democratic Republic of Vietnam, the creator and leader of the Lao Dong (Communist) Party, this man of consummate patriotism—three times the liberator of his country from the successive waves of imperialist invaders from Japan, France and the United States—was at the same time an international revolutionary of the highest purity. He fought for the brotherhood of man, for the freedom and advancement of the peoples of all lands and climes and colors no less ardently than he fought for the liberation of his own homeland from the heel of the invaders.

This great fighter against U.S. imperialism's savage assaults upon the peace, lives and land of the Vietnamese peoples, North and South, always displayed the greatest solicitude and manifested the firmest confidence in the growing strength of the peace forces in the United States. One of his last political acts was to address a greeting to the Communist Party of the United States on the occasion of its 50th anniversary. He applauded the struggles of the working class, Black liberation and peace forces in our country and expressed confidence in the triumph of their sacred cause.

The great example of Ho Chi Minh's life of selfless struggle in the service of his people, the workers of the world and all oppressed mankind will always inspire the hearts and guide the thoughts of fighters for peace, for freedom and for communism.

We like all who honor his great service to mankind, pledge redoubled efforts to help bring peace to the people of Vietnam through struggle for the immediate and total withdrawal of all U.S. armed forces from the soil, the seas and the air-space of Vietnam.

Plain people everywhere called him Uncle Ho and he refered to us all as "his dear nephews."

In an article written in commemoration of the 90th anniversary of Lenin's birth (April 22, 1960), Comrade Ho Chi Minh wrote:

"There is a legend in our country on the miraculous 'Book of the Wise.' When facing great difficulties, one opens it and finds a way out. Leninism is not only a miraculous 'book of the wise,' a compass for us Vietnamese revolutionaries and people; it is also the radiant sun illuminating our path to final victory, to Socialism and Communism." Let these, his words in the main, be our tribute in memorium.

Ho Chi Minh's star is one of the brightest in the firmament of mankind's great achievers. He lived long and worked arduously for the happiness and the freedom of the peoples, on many fronts, at many levels. His light is a composite of many talents and contributions but above all it radiates the illumination of Leninism: the science of struggle for the self-liberation of the toilers from the tyranny of their exploiters.

Ho Chi Minh, our comrade, had confidence and unwavering hope in us. He expected that the American masses would win a moral victory over the war gang here at home even before the Pentagon's forces were finally driven off Vietnam soil by the unvanquishable Vietnam patriots. This was his great expectation for us in life. It is his charge and the testament of his last will for us to execute for the sake of peace in

Vietnam, the relief of grave war danger in the world and for our own future as a nation, as a class, and as a Party.

Ho Chi Minh: may the noble example of his life burn in our hearts as an eternal flame.

Speech at Memorial Meeting, New York. September 18, 1969

8   Behind the Changing Chinese
and U.S. Attitudes

Currently, the crisis of leadership which grows out of and reflects the long maturing crisis of policy created by the "Great Leap" (economic scheme of 1957-58) has made China the object of new attention from within the ruling circles of U.S. imperialism.

Washington's South Vietnam puppet Premier Nguyen Cao Ky made himself spokesman for the preventive war hawks within the Pentagon and the Administration in regard to China when he said, "Sooner or later we have to face the Chinese Communists. And I think it's better to face them right now than in five or ten years."

On the other hand, Secretary of State Dean Rusk has been described as interested in softening the Administration's policy toward China somewhat—with more stress on "reconciliation" and less emphasis on "containment." He feels that it is opportune to open channels of contact and, hopefully, to exert an influence upon China, now that the country is locked in the throes of a massive internal struggle over the decisive question of direction of the revolution.

There can be no question that the chaotic political situation in the leadership of China constitutes a major diversion of the political and moral forces of the Chinese masses, preventing them from expressing their full solidarity with neighboring Vietnam which is so heroically withstanding the waves of bombing planes and the hundreds of thousands of invaders U.S. imperialism has sent against her.

The crisis of leadership and the chaos in policy inside China have been accompanied by a growing crescendo of wild declarations of vituperation against, and hatred of, the Soviet Union's party and leadership.

The spectacle of a Communist Party leadership out-distancing even the sworn class enemies of communism in vilification and abuse of a sister party, certainly does not escape the strategic planners for prolonging the existence of imperialism.

The virulent campaign of anti-Soviet defamation as currently being broadcast worldwide by the prominent Chinese leaders is something of great value to the world imperialists. Anti-Sovietism is the cause in common which the followers of Mao and the imperialists are pursuing relentlessly.

Is it this common cause which Rusk has in mind for further development that leads him to speak of softening his China policy?

The "Great Decisions" background brochure of the Foreign Policy Association quotes the Secretary of State as saying in regard to China contacts: "We have been in touch with them on more serious subjects and more persistently than perhaps any government that has diplomatic relations with Peking except perhaps the Soviet Union."

Is collaboration in ideological and strategic confrontation with the Soviet Union the price that Rusk is seeking to exact from Peking for altering U.S. imperialism's aggressive thrust toward a military confrontation with China?

Do some Chinese government figures entertain such a Machiavellian design for diverting the aggressive will of U.S. imperialism away from China and toward her Soviet brother? If so, they are subscribing to a suicide pact with their worst enemy against their best friend. Some Chinese leaders have gone to absurd lengths to describe the Soviet Union as abandoning socialism and embracing capitalism under the guidance of their modern "revisionist" leaders and party.

Lin Piao, who shares with Mao Tse-tung the leading responsibility for the rampaging reaction let loose against the position held by Marxism in the councils of the Chinese Communist Party, the government, the trade unions and Young Communist League, has declared that the Chinese Communist Party can no longer have united action with "revisionists" as represented by the leaders of the Communist Party and the Soviet Union.

Such a pattern of moral deterioration, of the abandonment of sacred principles of workingclass internationalism, is petty-bourgeois panic in the face of the provocative escalation of the Vietnam war by the United States close to the borders of China.

Clearly, China cannot secure an honorable relief from the grave menace of military confrontation with massive U.S. armed forces, already in position through the Vietnam war, by double-dealing with the enemy at the expense of the Soviet Union.

On the contrary, the sole route to salvation for China, facing the threatening prospects of military confrontation with U.S. imperialism, lies in an immediate restoration and solidification of its all-sided fraternal alliance with the Soviet Union. For its national salvation against the new dangers of U.S. aggressive design, as well as to safeguard its revolution from the wasting of its heroic fruits, to save it from the "Thermidor" of disintegration that brought down the French Revolution of the radical bourgeoisie, the Communists of China must recover command of their Party from the careerists and adventurers who make use of the so-called "Red Guards."

The prime source of the pressures heaped upon the people and leaders of China lies in the politics pursued by Washington for the past 17 years. U.S. imperialist policy has been dedicated to the proposition of defeating the revolution in China and recovering that vast country of over 700 million people for a "new field," in which imperialism can recoup its losses and into which it can expand. Not confrontation, but new initiatives to end the state of tension and antagonism between the United States and the Peoples' Republic of China are urgently called for at this time.

The starting point is to stop the bombing and all military action against Vietnam and withdraw U.S. armed forces from this territory so near China. Washington must recognize China diplomatically, support the restoration of the United Nations seat, and negotiate settlement of all disputed questions in the interest of world peace.

The Worker, New York. February 5, 1967

9   Maoism

Lenin once wrote: *"Workers of the whole world, and all oppressed peoples, unite! There is a world to win."* But the logic of Mao Tse-Tung's position is: "Workers of the world, and all oppressed peoples, divide! You have nothing to lose but your future." The dominant influence of Maoism in respect to the world working class and national liberation movements is that of divisionism.

The challenge of Maoism in theory and in practice is, indeed, the gravest attack on Marxism in the 124 years of its history. Maoism in another time, as the intellectual product of an individual, would not constitute the kind of a menace that it represents today. But Maoism, notwithstanding the poverty of spirit of its philosophical position, the erraticism of its economic program, the reactionary course of its foreign policy, is a major force in the world. If it were limited to theory, it would fall of its own weak legs. But Maoism stands literally on the backs of some 800 million people, a people who dwell in what has been described as a "barracks society," where the standards of living of the Chinese millions have been sacrificed and reduced to raw-boned survival fare. In lieu of decent standards of living, they are fed and indoctrinated with the thoughts of Mao.

Mao Tse-Tungism has emerged as a continuation of strategic deviation, a diversion within the working class movement of the character of right social-democratism and a variant of the character of Trotskyism in other periods. The phenomenon of Mao Tse-Tungism is the main deviation in the world Marxist movement today. It is the center and ideological fount, a cover, a point of reference for every substantive deviation, deflection from the main force of activity and march and responsibility of the working class and Marxist movements in every country. It crystallizes and synthesizes an amalgam, a nostrum, a bitter draught of bourgeois individualism, of petty-bourgeois revolutionism, of bourgeois nationalism mixed and spiced and tempered, flavored and masked with Marxist phraseology. But essentially it is a notorious, a *strategic* diversion and deviation from the main direction of Marxism-Leninism and its purpose and cause for being.

Certainly, there is need to probe into the source of Mao Tse-Tungism and its impact and influence on the world Marxist movement and its lessons for all parties. Is it an exotic growth? Or is it an international phenomenon comparable to Trotskyism, social-democratism, and which has its impact and reflection also in our movement, in our working class?

In China, the thought of Mao Tse-Tung has replaced moral and material incentives. The thought of Mao Tse-Tung has replaced the march towards the progressive improvement of the conditions of the masses. Maoism is not another variety of Marxism. Maoism is not Marxism-Leninism adjusted and accomodated to eastern experience and historical background. Maoism is the antithesis of Marxism-Leninism. Maoism is anti-Marxism-Leninism. Maoism is contra-communism, anti-communism. Maoism represents the most ruthlessly determined ideological offensive against the world working class. Maoism in practice represents a colossal threat not only to the U.S.S.R., the prime bastion, the main anchor and pivot in the world revolutionary process; it represents a counterforce to the whole world revolutionary movement. It is a determined, programed scheme to fulfill the mystical, ancient dream of the Great Han nation to dominate the rest of the world. *Maoism is a mockery of Marxism,* but wrapped and packaged in the language, in phrases and quotations lifted out of context from Marxism-Leninism.

Lenin once said, "The dialectics of history were such that the theoretical victory of Marxism compelled its enemies to disguise themselves as Marxists." (*The Teachings of Karl Marx,* International Publications, 1972, p. 51.) Maoism fits this description that Lenin had used to characterize certain anarchist tendencies in his time.

Maoism is a special virulent form of petit-bourgeois revolutionism; a petty bourgeois revolutionism parasitically attached to 800 million people, attached to the revival, the resurrection and the activizing of an ancient, mystical dream of Great Han world domination. Therefore, it is petit-bourgeois revolutionism merged with chauvinism, a virulent, aggressive nationalism. Militant Maoist nationalism is an attempted psychological compensation for grave and even massively tragic failures by the Maoists in the construction of socialism in China, in solving the very difficult problems of developing the processes of socialist development within China.

Lenin scoffingly described petty bourgeois revolutionism as: "menacing, haughty and presumptuous in word, but hollow in deed." (Lenin, *Collected Works,* Vol. 33, p. 21.) The main thing then in Maoism is that petit-bourgeois revolutionism is meant to serve war-oriented, bellicose, great-power chauvinism in its striving for the fulfillment of the mythical, ancient dream of the Great Han people.

Therefore, Maoism is not only an ideological and a practical foe of working class goals, of working class requirements for composing the international unity of the working class in a fighting formation with the world's anti-imperialist forces, with the working class forces within the capitalist world, with the national revolutionary forces of the "Third World" –*Maoism is a distinctive contra-Communist ideology.* Its doctrine is an eclectic concoction. It has picked things, lifted concepts, from this ideology and that ideology and woven them into a crazy quilt that has within it features borrowed from anarchism, features borrowed from the petit-bourgeois revolutionary utopians of the nineteenth-century Proudhonists. It has within it concepts borrowed from the ancient Chinese sages like Confucius and Buddha—for example: the "cult of personality," the blind reverence for authority and the concept of asceticism, as also expressed in the writings and theories of Pierre Proudhon, and others, against whom Marx and Engels had polemized.

Mao's program of denial and asceticism scoffs at the whole conception of social and human development. Socialism has come out of the needs of the working masses to live better, not to live worse. You know, Proudhon wrote a book on the theme "how to live happy, though poor"—entitled *The Philosophy of Poverty,* and Marx polemized against it in his classic, *The Poverty of Philosophy.*

The philosophy of Maoism is empoverished in its conception. It has tentacles not only in contemporary confusion in the area of theory, i.e., similar to many of Marcuse's concepts, but also goes into the ancient philosophical lore of primitive "dialectics." For example, Mao speaks much of the dialectics of this and the dialectics of that, but in his own writings—for example, *On Contradiction*—he catalogues a series of opposites, a series of contradictory relationships, and palms it off as dialectical materialism, as an exposition of the Marxist-Leninist concept of the dialectical process. What are some of these propositions?

He says, without night, day is unidentified. Therefore, day is good to welcome the sun, but night cannot be bad either. And, without death, there is no life; without up, there is no down; without in, there is no out. So, you see, everything has its rational place. But this is not abstract theorizing. This is deliberate obfuscation, confusion—masking the service he renders to the imperialist cause by establishing a front of struggle against the world revolutionary process in general, and against the cornerstone of world socialism, the Soviet Union, in particular.

What is the value of such confusion, such catechisms, such riddles and witticisms? The purpose becomes clear when Mao speaks about ways of contemporary historical development.

According to the Maoist dialectics, World War I resulted in the birth of the first socialist country; the working class took power in one country as a result of World War I. World War I was bad, but World War I was also good. It produced the Soviet Union. The Soviet Union is good, is it not? You will agree, then, that World War I could not have been so bad. World War II was bad; 30-40 million people were killed.But World War II was good; it produced a group of socialist countries and the socialist world system emerged. Is, therefore, peace a good thing? But war is also a good thing. And the consequence is, Mao says, (this is Maoist tautological logic) that wars produce socialism. Therefore, Mao theorizes, and Lin Piao puts it in precise, in popular formulas (he will not be saying them much any more), "Socialism comes out of the barrel of the gun," and is the exclusive, the one-way tactic to effect revolutionary change.

Therefore, Mao theorizes that a military confrontation between the world of socialism and the world of capitalism is inevitable and, historically, war is useful and necessary, because, as a result of it, the whole world will emerge socialist. But, you say, how much of it will be left? The thermonuclear weapons have world-destroying capability. At the Moscow Meeting of Representatives of the Communist Parties in 1957, Mao speculated: "Who can predict how large a toll of human lives the future war will take? Maybe it will be two-thirds of the 2,700,000,000 population of our planet. I say, that is not much, if atom bombs are really dropped."

Mao then went on to say that he was willing, for China's part, to contribute 300 million Chinese to "the quota" for the sake of the victory of the world socialist revolution. Then, expanding his thought, he said: "If half of mankind is destroyed, half of it will be left. Imperialism will be completely destroyed, and socialism, then, will assert itself throughout the world, and, in 50 to 100 years time, the world's population will grow again, even by more than the 50 per cent [that was lost]."

Maoism is a special challenge necessitating new vigilence and new ideological preparation, and the reinforcing of the solidity of our world movement. The strength of our world movement will be viable and meaningful in proportion to the extent that each party, starting with ourselves, fully utilizes the great historic opportunities that are present in *this stage* of the deepening crisis of U.S. imperialism.

Currently Mao's China is experiencing a serious crisis. It is a crisis in the economic sphere. It is a crisis in government, and it is also a crisis in confidence in the leadership. Mao's doctrine in practice is more related to the survival arts for heads of state as elaborated by Machiavelli in *The Prince* than it is to Marx or Lenin. It is concerned with how to maneuver, how to conspire, how to manipulate with one section whom you consider your foes in order to gain advantage of weaker peoples, in order to achieve disunity, and an isolation of the components of the former united position of your "other rival."

There are a few propositions I would like to just touch on briefly in terms of Mao's practice. One, the Maoists came forward early last year with a new conception of the main contradiction in the world. They state that the main contradiction is not between imperialism and socialism, not between capitalists and workers. They present a new equation. They divide the world into "two super powers," the United States and the Soviet Union aligned against the small and poor states, and they therefore call for forming a united front of the small and poor states to struggle against the "two super powers."

China's entrance into the United Nations was a significant anti-imperialist victory, thanks primarily to the unity and allegiance to principle on the part of the socialist countries. An extraordinary alliance against U.S. imperialism in the diplomatic arena was accomplished in the UN, which contributed the major thrust for the seating of China. However, on the eve of taking their seat, the Maoists modified their slogan. They said it is necessary to unite all peoples—not just the small and poor, but all peoples—against the "one-two-super powers." In Chinese cultural tradition numbers play a certain mystical and symbolic role.

"One-two super powers": so it's like "two birds sitting on the bough, one flew away and there remained one now." This was to take into account that Nixon was already committed through his agent, Henry Kissinger, to a new China policy of partnership and alliance. The feast had been set. The terms, the agenda, the reason for its being were prepared and, therefore, in anticipation, it was necessary to break up the "two super powers" into the "one-two super powers."

The "two super powers" are now "one super power." And who is that "super power?" The Soviet Union! But what kind of power is the Soviet Union? The Soviet Union is the power base of the working class in possession of the state. It is the most powerful state power base of the *world working class*. Therefore, to make the Soviet Union the enemy under the mask of "super power" is really to point the arrow at the whole of the working class. The Soviet Union is the finest achievement of the world's working class, whose might and influence have made possible a progressive change in the whole world relationship of forces.

Maoism has set itself the task of winning over the "third world"—to seek to induce and to involve these new nations in its schemes for establishing its hegemony over one of the three basic components of the world revolutionary forces. Maoism approaches this task of winning over the "third world" with a wide spectrum of demagogy. Maoism in practice is two-faced. It walks in one direction on one side of the street, and it backtracks on the other side of the street in the opposite direction. Therefore it is very difficult to pin down in "one, two, three" order just what elements characterize Maoism. If you pin down "one, two, three" descriptive elements of Maoism, then, "four, five, six" will be the negation of the "one, two, three." This is a characteristic part of Maoist "theory." Theory to the Maoist is a device employed not to explain reality but to obscure and obfuscate it, to bury the truth and to blind the masses to reality.

This Maoist method in theory is illustrated in the way Maoism handles the question of nationalism. Within China there are 50 million people who compose the national minorities of China, but they hold no significant posts anywhere. They are generally disfranchised. They have no national status nor prospects of achieving national fulfillment other than forced assimilation into the Great Han people. But on an international scale Maoism has come forward to supply the ideologists, the think-tank experts who operate on the ways and means of continuing the survival of world imperialism, and U.S. imperialism, in particular, with a "theory" on the national question.

Lenin said that if you exaggerate one aspect of reality you can turn it into unreality. If you take a useful slogan for advancing the world revolutionary process in a given time, place and circumstance and generalize it into a governing law for all time, use it unhistorically without regard to the interests of the world revolutionary process, then you turn it into its opposite, and the rope that was to pull the revolution forward a pace turns into a noose to hang up the revolutionary process.

On the world scale Maoism has now come out as the super champion of "self-determination of peoples." But it uses it for the purpose of polarizing, dividing and divorcing the process of unification of the new countries in the socialist world, and divisionism in the anti-monopolist front in the old and established countries, by introducing splits into the program and activities of the working class. At the same time, and in a different situation, Maoism, again with demogogic nationalist slogans, comes out to identify itself with one of the most fearsome assassins of human beings and organizer of genocide known to recent history—the Yahya Khan.

In the Bangladesh civil war we saw these two odd-fellows, Nixon and Mao, lined up passing the amunition to the Yahya Khan, the slaughterer of the Bangladesh peoples who rose against the Yahya's tyranny. The Maoists rationalized that there is a greater principle and a lesser principle, and greater national independence of all of the Moslem peoples should have precedence over self-determination of peoples. This slick, nimble way of shifting grounds without regard to what one said yesterday and come forth with a new bromide, new catechism, a new motto for today, is also characteristic of Maoism in theory and practice.

Maoism brings together all of the living confusion in various ideological systems. It is an amalgam of Trotskyism and of bourgeois nationalism. It is a mixture of petty-bourgeois ultra-revolutionaryism and crude opportunism. The outcome of the struggle against Maoism is assured because of the new world relationship of forces that exists, because Maoism is in contradiction to historical development, and because of the awareness, the vigilance, the Leninist-trained consciousness of the Communist on a world scale. These factors will certainly combine to eliminate Maoism as a serious source of ideological confusion and checkmate Maoism on every level of the practical struggle.

Excerpts from a report to the 20th Convention
of the Communist Party, U.S.A. New York, 1972.

10   Socialist Working Class Democracy

The crises situation in Czechoslovakia's political life grew out of tardiness in adoption of necessary reforms in socialist practice in economic matters and in the further development of the democracy of the socialist society.

When the leadership dramatized its intent to implement necessary reforms by an unqualified removal of all restrictions on "First Amendment" privileges, i.e., of free speech, press, assembly and organization, it was the foes of the Party and the conciliators with imperialism who leaped forward to dominate the "free discussion" and give it an anti-socialist, anti-Communist Party, and Soviet-baiting character.

The basic class force of the new society—the workers—were not participants in the "new dialogue." They hung back while the stage of the "new freedom of unbridled criticism" was dominated by neo-intellectuals and dissident personalities among the career politicians.

The principal direction of the blows of the critics was at the Communist Party per se and at the solidarity ties which Czechoslovakia maintains with its socialist neighbors and fraternal countries of the community of socialist states.

Literally and spiritually they flew into Prague and perched around like buzzards impatiently awaiting their opportunity to tear into the corpse of Czechoslovakia's socialism.

But the great expectations of the enemies of Czechoslovakia and of communism failed to be realized thanks to the common sense and the regenerative powers of the Czechoslovakian working class and its Communist Party vanguard, and thanks to the unequivocal power and viability of the international solidarity of the community of socialist states and the strength of the fraternal bonds of the worldwide Marxist-Leninist movement.

The Czechoslovakian socialist society, this hearty youth of the Czech and Slovak working classes, the offspring of the revolutionary process of the world working class movement, has weathered the worst phase of its modernization crisis and will soon begin to stride toward new socialist achievements in material abundance, political democracy, and spiritual enrichment.

No one expected the hired men of the imperialist press to do other than exploit the opportunity of the Czech crisis for mischief in the service of their masters. But what must give us pause, what constitutes a challenge and calls for better, more timely and more persuasive ideological work on the part of all genuine Marxists, was the presence in the outer fringes of the bourgeois-lovers, the "down-with-the-Communist Party!"'' nihilists of a number of erstwhile friends of socialism and "radicals" of sorts.

True, the noises they made were not bloodcurdling but more like the bleatings of lost sheep, or the regurgitating sounds of sea-sick, fair weather sailors on the waters of revolution, waters which from time to time become storm-tossed.

Still, the effect of their interventions was *not* to strengthen the hand of the revolution or that of the revolutionary party—the Communist Party of Czechoslovakia—but to put challenges to the viability of the party's leadership and to the merit of socialism itself in Czechoslovakia. They put their "challenges" oftimes in highly decorous queries and in tones of wide-eyed innocence. But invariably these delicately worded queries pointed to a sternly indelicate conclusion. That is, they were put forth to "put down" the Communist Party of Czechoslovakia on the one hand, and as a whip for lashing the Soviet Union on the other.

The paramount question of theoretical interest in the Czechoslovakian situation is the question of the state, the nature and operation of its structure and the problems of its reconstruction and renovation. Related to this question are (1) the role of the Party, and (2) proletarian and socialist state internationalism.

"The building of a socialist democratic structure is a continuing struggle," Gus Hall observed in a most perceptive commentary on developments in Czechoslovakia, in an article printed in *The Worker* of April 2, 1968, "It is a struggle against bureaucratic methods . . . that are left-overs of the past. But it is also a struggle against ideas of no structure, of anarchism put forth under slogans of 'total freedom.' "

Lenin considered this kind of question—the question of the state—to be "a most complex and difficult one, perhaps one that more than any other has been confused by bourgeois scholars, writers and philosophers." (V. I. Lenin, *Collected Works* [English language edition], Moscow: Progress Publishers, 1965, Vol. 29, p. 470). "In the question of the state, in the doctrine of the state, in the theory of the state," Lenin taught, ". . . *you will always discern the struggle between different classes,* a struggle which is reflected or expressed in a conflict of views on the state, in the estimate of the role and significance of the state." (Lenin, *Ibid,* Vol. 29, pp. 472-473.)

Leninism teaches that "only by firmly holding, as to a guiding thread, to this division of society into classes" (Lenin, *Ibid,* Vol. 29, p. 477) as the standpoint from which to examine all social questions, will it be possible to correctly appraise the extreme diversity and immense variety of changes that occur, or are theorized about, in *the forms of rule of a given class.* Lenin said:

"If we are not to mock at common sense and history, it is obvious that we cannot speak of 'pure democracy' as long as different *classes* exist; we can only speak of *class* democracy," (Lenin, *Ibid,* Vol. 28, p. 242).

"Pure democracy," he wrote, "is the mendacious phrase of a liberal who wants to fool the workers. History knows of bourgeois democracy which takes the place of feudalism, and of *proletarian democracy which takes the place of bourgeois democracy."* (Lenin, *Ibid,* Vol. 28, p. 242.)

The question of democratizing the structure of socialist society is the subject of a continuing process of development which extends throughout the whole lower phase of Communist society—that is, *for the life span of socialism.* Only on the road from the initial to the higher phase of Communism is really complete democracy possible of attainment. But "Democracy is *a form of the State,* one of its varieties," as Lenin has pointed out, therefore the more "complete" it becomes "the sooner it will become unnecessary and wither away." (Lenin, *Ibid,* Vol. 25, p. 472.)

The working class under conditions of socialism grows numerically and matures politically, ideologically, and culturally at a rapid pace. This makes necessary timely changes in the forms of socialist democracy during the transition from capitalism. Nevertheless, *in its essence, the democracy of socialist society–for the entire lifetime of the socialist state*–retains its *partisan working class character.* It is *proletarian democracy:* democracy of, by, and for the working class and the vast majority of the working people. But this is not complete, pure democracy. In this whole first phase of Communism, the democratic structure and practice will still reflect" . . . *remnants of the old surviving in the new . . ."* (Lenin, *Ibid,* Vol. 25, p. 471).

This will be an aspect of the reality of development under socialism for several decades. Lenin anticipated the drag of tradition and other negative aspects as "economically and politically inevitable in a society emerging out of the womb of capitalism." and subjected continuously to the impact of the pressures generated by a still powerful world imperialist adversary.

Therefore, "the organization of the vanguard of the oppressed as the ruling class," Lenin showed, "cannot result merely in an expansion of democracy, which *for the first time* becomes democracy for the poor, democracy for the people . . .", there must also be *state control* and suppression of counter-revolutionary attempts at restoration or arrest of progress. In this connection Lenin has written that:

"During the transition from capitalism to communism suppression is *still* necessary, but it is now the suppression of the exploiting minority by the exploited majority. A special apparatus, a special machine for suppression, the 'State,' is *still* necessary, but this is now a transitional State . . . and it is compatible with the extension of democracy to such an overwhelming majority of the population that the need for a special machine of suppression will begin to disappear." (*Ibid,* Vol. 25, p. 463.)

The solution of the problem of maximum involvement of the greatest numbers of the working people in decision-making and administrative control in the major matters concerning the political, economic and social affairs of socialist society is an ever unfinished problem. Pravda's commentator, on May 19th, stated it well when he wrote:

"The development of Socialist democracy is an objective and uninterrupted process. Our Socialist democracy is not a congealed scheme; it is not a political mechanism designed once and for all. It needs constant renovation, with some forms and methods being replaced by others, more closely corresponding to the requirements of social development." (Moscow: *International Affairs,* No. 6, p. 11).

But what "forms and methods" are to be changed, and what others are to replace them in the interest of furthering the development of socialist democracy is determined by *the working class approach* which is brought to the evaluation of the given situation. A working class approach to the solution of the problems of the advancement of the democratic aspect of the functions of the state during the socialist phase of communism is of different character and purpose from bourgeois-democratic or from anarchistic conceptions of democratic reforms.

A working-class view of reforms calls for enhancing *the role and the ability of the masses* to genuinely participate "in the administration of government, economic and social affairs." But, as Lenin said, "for the minds of tens of millions of creative men and women" to produce "something immeasurably higher," they must subject themselves to a conscious discipline. "A disorganized society cannot be democratic." (*Ibid,* Vol. 25, p. 461.)

The rapid and rational development of socialist democracy presupposes highly organized, conscious, disciplined action of a maximum of the able-bodied members of society—of the working class, in the first place. Therefore, working-class reforms of the socialist democratic state do not lead in the direction of granting privileges to petty-bourgeois spirits to "drop out" from fulfillment of any social obligations to society, or, of the encouragement of a permissive attitude toward individualistic self-indulgence and anti-social personal behavior. It does not mean the abandonment of a vigilant awareness of the historical period in the world which witnesses the still strong and aggressive presence of a worldwide front of imperialism, notwithstanding the favorable fact of its relatively weakening position.

Foremost in the reforms required to enhance further the development of the democratic life of the socialist state are those related to an expansion of the productive excellence of the socialist economy. Democratic reforms in the superstructure of socialist society are conditioned by the requirements of the solution of the problems of developing an economic base of material abundance. The fullest flowering of individual and community freedom, and the extension of democracy to the point where highly structured state apparatuses for the administration and control of the social functions of the society can be progressively done away with as victories are won in the battle for an economic base of material abundance.

Already, in the socialist countries, the solicitude of the state of the working people's power for the well-being of the individual is materially reflected in the extensive social security assistance and benefits which he receives from the cradle to the grave, with the right to work, to an education, to health protection, provision for old age, etc., being assured by the state. Through the collective ownership of the means of production, wherein the socialist relations of production have freed all working people from exploitation and made real property a public possession, all the benefits of life created by the people go to the people. It is evident that with the solution of the basic question of material abundance, the conditions will have been realized for the elimination of all restraints related to "rationing" short supplies as well as the fact that there would no longer be strong psychological motivation for personal selfish acts of "appropriating" the personal property or social share due other working people.

Political Affairs, New York. September, 1968

11   Three Philosophers: Frederick Engels, Herbert Marcuse and Angela Davis

Quoting from a poem by Nekrasov, Lenin's memorial tribute to Frederick Engels referred to him as a "torch of reason . . .After his friend, Karl Marx . . . Engels was the finest scholar and teacher of the modern proletariat . . .," (V I. Lenin, *Collected Works,* Moscow: Progress Publishers, 1965, Vol. 2, p.19).

Inseparable in their friendship from the first encounter as young men in their twenties until Marx's death in 1883, the great duo who introduced to the workers of the world the true path of struggle for a workers' world shared in inseparable measure in each other's creations.

Epitomizing their service to the march of man in history, Lenin wrote that "they taught the working class to know itself and be conscious of itself, and they substituted science for dreams." (Lenin, *Ibid,* Vol. 2, p. 20.)

Karl Marx's son-in-law and Engels' friend, Paul Lafargue, wrote that "Marx always admired the universality of Engels' knowledge, his quickness of mind which enabled him to switch with ease from one subject to another, while Engels on his part was amazed at Marx's remarkable analytic powers and his capacity for generalization." (Quoted in Y. Stepanova, *Frederick Engel,* Moscow, Progress Publishers, 1968.)

It is the good fortune of history, and of the role of the working class in its making, that these moral and intellectual giants met and merged the great talents of their genius in a lifetime of working collaboration and common purpose. The working relationship between Engels and Marx is history's most creative partnership, and the story of their friendship will always remain a model of inspiration for fostering those selfless relations of true brotherhood which ought to obtain between comrades.

"His (Engels') love for the living Marx and his reverence for the memory of the dead Marx were boundless," Lenin wrote (*Ibid,* Vol. 2, p. 26). His devotion to Marx was a measure of his boundless love for and devotion to the cause of the working class. It was the workers, the primary revolutionary class, whom Marx and Engels disclosed to be that social force which, in the revolutionary action of emancipating itself, was destined to liberate the human race "from the jungle of necessity" and set it upon the ever-ascending high ground of genuine freedom.

In these days when there is much talk of "model building," I think it germane to our needs as Communists, as members of the great leadership vanguard of the changers and remolders of the earth and the age, to pause and take note of that special distinguishing feature of Engels' personality—his working class modesty, his complete absence of self-centeredness and vainglory. Though his close friends sometimes referred to him as "The General" (in admiration of his gallant military role in the uprising of 1848 and his continuous study and expertise in military science), Engels never held nor sought a title or a rank. He never brooded over the fact that his name was often absent from the identification or designation of the science which they—Marx and Engels—had jointly brought forth and elaborated. It was never a problem to Engels to play "second fiddle" to the towering genius of Marx, whom Engels characterized as "the greatest head of our time" and "the strongest heart I have ever known . . ." (Y. Stepanova, *Ibid*).

Engels was always in battle at Marx's side with the enemies of the working class, but he never contended for honor as a rival. Engels abjured flattery and boasting and was merciless in deflating the puffed-up postures assumed by such big ego figures of the workers' and toilers' movement as Lasalle, Proudhon and others, who went about basking in the adulation of cults of admirers and hero worshippers. He was ever the scourge of fanaticism and blind loyalty.

Engels had absolute conviction and faith in the capacity of the working class to think and reason in accord with the dialectical process and to act out their judgments and conclusions in accord with historical science and the compulsions of social necessity.

Engels sublimated any personal ambition he might have had to the great cause of the revolution. His unselfishness, the absence of ostentation and pomp in his public deportment, and the generosity of his contributions to the totality of the work of the collective, was designed to aid and encourage and maximize the contribution of all the colleagues around Marx. In so doing, he did not lessen but enhanced the personal satisfaction which he derived from his services to the revolutionary struggle.

History shows that the esteem for and appreciation for Frederick Engels' great revolutionary works grow with the rise of every new generation of fighters in the workers' cause. There is something Engels tells us about developing the art and method of collective work as a means of multiplying the leadership cadre in keeping with the ever-growing requirements of the rising forces of revolution. He stands forth as one of the most popular and esteemed leaders in the whole of workingclass history and it could never be said of him that he ever once traded principle for popularity.

Engels, like Marx and later Lenin, counted it his responsibility to rally the advanced forces of the party of the working class to confront every attack or maneuver by the enemy or its dupes against the ideological foundations of the party, its program and the practical daily survival struggles of the class.

"It seems," Engels noted, "that every workers party of a big country can develop only through internal struggle, which accords with the laws of dialectical materialism." (*Selected Correspondence of Karl Marx and Frederick Engels*. Moscow: Progress Publishers, 1968, p. 425.) In any event, "contradictions can never be glossed over for long, they are resolved in struggle." (Y. Stepanova, *Ibid*) (From this idea of Engels and his own considerable organizational experience, Lenin evolved the concept of *criticism and self-criticism* as a law of development of Communist Parties which he elaborated alongside that of the structured practice of democratic centralism.)

Engels, whose writing style reflected the spirit of revolutionary passion and arduous involvement as an activist and partisan publicist in all the tempestuous events of his time, wherever people rose against misery or tyrants added some new outrage to the infinite catalog of crimes against humanity, was at the same time one of the most knowledgeable thinkers and theorists in philosophy and natural sciences of modern times. Yet this man, whose erudition matched that of the brightest stars of the Renaissance, had to end his formal schooling before completing the high school level. His acquisition of such vast areas of knowledge is evidence of the extraordinary levels of self-discipline and personal organization which he attained. Still, Engels was no stuffed shirt or intellectual effete. There was no air of the snob about him. He had a great sensitivity for humanity's pains and a profound love of the people. He would indeed say with Marx: "Nothing human is alien to me."

We live at a particular time in history when the general crisis of capitalism descends to its final stage, and, accompanying this fact, there arise on a global scale new opportunities for accelerating the world revolutionary process and for registering vital new democratic and socialist victories by the working class, the national liberation movement and associated progressive social forces. Yet at the same time the forces of reaction, aware of their diminishing strength, desperately seek to stay the verdict of history. They seek to acquire new resources to arrest the growth of strength favoring the side of the world working class and the anti-imperialist movements. It is at just such a time as the present that the revolutionary parties need to rear cadres purposefully, cadres who will strive to acquire and emulate the qualities of character, the appetite for learning, the revolutionary ador, the political courage and personal commitment that are our heritage from the sterling leadership model constructed in the life and works of a Frederick Engels, a Karl Marx, a Vladimir Ilyich Lenin.

*   *   *

World imperialism, particularly U.S. ruling circles, is presently embarked upon a massive, extensive and multi-tiered ideological campaign to divert the minds of rebellious masses from the revolutionary alternative to the deepening misery and threatening catastrophe of capitalism's worsening general crisis.

This ideological campaign of the U.S. imperialists is reflected in the sophistication of its neo-colonialist programs. That is, it stands prepared to seek partial advantages, to chip off bits and pieces of the leadership of the newly radicalized forces of the peace, Black people's liberation, and trade union rank-and-file movements. It patiently persists in identifying and encouraging deviant tendencies wherever they occur——whether in the Communist Party, or the militant youth, radical student or other organizations of the people. While not letting up on its use of police terror, brutal midnight raids, and police-courtroom frame-up conspiracies against revolutionary forces, the ruling-class strategists are now going in heavily for "mixing up the minds" of the left-ward leaning masses.

The most prestigious, influential and skillful producer and circulator of counterfeit "revolutionary" doctrine is Professor Herbert Marcuse who lauds the "heroes" of the black flag of anarchism while heaping scorn on the bearers of the red flag of communism. His name has even appeared on signs carried in demonstrations by guileless youth proclaiming fidelity to "Marx, Marcuse, Mao."

Like a big city hustler at a country fair, Marcuse sustains an almost hypnotic pattern of words that sound softly sibilant and satisfying to the ears, while he works to pick the pockets of the minds of his youthful audiences of any Marxist, scientific revolutionary concepts which may be lying loose there. As a revolutionary philosopher, Marcuse is a mountebank and faker. In truth, he is planting counter-revolutionary attitudes, including scorn for the Soviet Union and all Communist Parties which proclaim their loyalty to Marxism-Leninism and international proletarian solidarity.

Thousands of the most thoughtful and daring of the anti-establishment youth are probing their own path toward the Communist Party and the victorious ideology of Marxism-Leninism. Marcuse is a detour sign on their route of march. He is involved in exhuming and reincarnating the "thought" of the father of American anarchists, Johann Most, and the Russian anarchists, Bakunin and Kropotkin.

"The slogan of the 'Three M's' (Marx, Marcuse, Mao) is a false banner, an impossible amalgam. One cannot reconcile the ideas of Marx with the Marcusean conception of the industrial society," write the Chilean scholars, Carlos Maldonado and Sergio Vuskovic in their recent book entitled *Lenin or Marcuse*. This excellent polemical critique of *One-Dimensional Man* and other Marcuse "standards" itemizes the list of Marcuse's pretentious inventions in revolutionary theory and strategic concepts, and lays bare their counter-revolutionary soul and service to the strategists of imperialist survival.

In his small book entitled *An Essay on Liberation* (Boston: Beacon Press, 1969), Marcuse squeezes together his main thoughts into his own "Little Red Book." This *Essay* is a vertible catalog of sophisticated slander of Marxism-Leninism, the world working class, the world-wide revolutionary process and its greatest achievements—the Communist Parties, the Soviet Union and the community of socialist states.

Marcuse declares that the working class is no longer a revolutionary social force. He sees "the integration of the organized (and not only the organized) laboring class into the system of advanced capitalism." Therefore, he argues, "the search for specific historical agents of revolutionary change in the advanced capitalist countries is indeed meaningless." (Marcuse, *Ibid.,* p. 78.)

With the working class integrated into the establishment and no "historical agents of social change" present, how will Marcuse's "world of human freedom" be delivered out of the revolution or, as he terms it, "The Great Refusal?" He tells us:

"The new radicalism militates against the centralized bureaucratic Communist as well as against the semi-democratic liberal organization. There is a strong element of spontaneity, even anarchism, in this rebellion. Therefore, the aversion against pre-established leaders, apparatchiks of all sorts, politicians no matter how leftist. The initiative shifts to small groups widely diffused, with a high degree of autonomy, mobility, flexibility." (Marcuse *Ibid.,* p. 89.)

Marcuse is here attempting to foster factional disintegration in the advanced organizations of the "Communist as well as against the semi-democratic liberal organization" of the masses.

It must be noted that now Herbert Marcuse has a rival coming up fast for the anti-working class, anti-revolutionary ideological leadership in the United States. He is Charles Reich, the author of *The Greening of America.* (New York: Random House, 1970)

Charles Reich is being sold to the young generation by the media as the truly "in" and "with it" revolutionary teacher. If Marcuse's "thing" is to exploit the militant mood of the youth, to breathe new life into the dry bones of anarchism and, like the Pied Piper of Hamlin, to lead the boldest youth of the New Left into the sea, to waste their revolutionary energy and their precious lives, Charles Reich's mission is to foster an anticipated non-social activist backlash. The advertisement heralding this new Messiah for the "youth rebellion" describes his message as follows:

"There is a revolution coming. It will not be like revolutions of the past. It will originate with the individual and with culture, and it will change the political structure only as its final act. It will not require violence to succeed, and it cannot be successfully resisted by violence. This is the revolution of the new generation."

This is an admixture of the Paulist Christian doctrine of fishing for the individual souls of men and the pseudo-psychiatric mumbo-jumbo of "Scientology." It is a total abnegation of social action because the revolution becomes an act of personal, individual conversion. That is, change the world by first changing the hearts of men. Amen!

Whatever danger to the clarity of the youth Reich may come to represent, at the present it is the petty-bourgeois revolutionariness of Marcuse and his like which are the main ideological agents of confusion on the left.

The Guyana People's Progressive Party journal, *Thunder,* carries in its June, 1966 issue an article entitled "The Police and the Anarchists," written by Engels' friend Paul Lafargue near the turn of the century. But in it Lafargue speaks to and illuminates an aspect of the political reality in the United States today. He writes;

"The capitalist class . . . is the first class of the propertied which has made of the police the most solid pillar of its State and society. Without haggling or counting the cost it spends money for that purpose; it covers all the blind and unlawful brutalities of the police with the mantle of Christian charity.

"The police, treated like a pampered, spoiled child, imagines that it is permitted to do almost anything.

"A former prefect of police, M. Andrieux, in his memoirs garulously revealed that the police furnished the money needed for the foundation of the first anarchist paper published in France, which for the information of all and sundry published recipes for the manufacture of explosives and bombs. . . .

"But in the eyes of the capitalists the police is *so* sublime and sacrosanct an institution that whatever it may do can never be bad. . . .

"Eagerly they spread among the public the falsehood that between anarchism and Socialism there was no essential difference. Anarchism, they said, is the logical sequence of Socialism, the anarchists are courageous people who have the consistency to translate their theories into practice; the Socialists, however, are hypocritical anarchists."

The social, class roots of anarchistic theories and deeds are dealt with by Lenin in *"Left-Wing" Communism: An Infantile Disorder* in 1920. There he wrote:

". . . Bolshevism grew, took shape, and became steeled in long years of struggle against *petty bourgeois revolutionaryism,* which smacks of, or borrows something from anarchism. . . . The petty bourgeois, *'furious'* over the horrors of capitalism, is a social phenomenon which, like anarchism, is characteristic of all capitalist countries. The instability of such revolutionism, its barrenness, its ability to become swiftly transformed into submission, apathy, fantasy, and even into a 'mad' infatuation with one or another bourgeois 'fad'—all this is a matter of common knowledge. But a theoretical, abstract recognition of these truths does not at all free revolutionary parties from old mistakes, which always crop up at unexpected moments, in a somewhat new form, in entirely new vestments or surroundings, in peculiar—more or less peculiar—circumstances." (*Ibid,* Vol. 31, p. 32)

Writing on "Revolutionary Adventurism" in 1902 in old Russia, Lenin said:

"The Social-Democrats (Communists) will always warn against adventurism and ruthlessly expose illusions which inevitably end in complete disappointment. We must bear in mind that any popular movement assumes an infinite variety of forms, is constantly developing new forms and discarding the old, and effecting modifications or new combinations of old and new forms. It is our duty to participate actively in this process of working out means and methods of struggle." (*Ibid,* Vol. 6, pp 194-195)

We must take note, Lenin taught, that "anarchism was often a sort of punishment for the opportunist sins of the working class movement." (*Ibid,* Vol. 31, p. 32)

Notwithstanding this truth, "the attitude of Marxism to anarchism in general stands out most definitely and unmistakably," Lenin emphasized. (*Ibid,* Vol. 31, p. 34)

He further referred to "acts of terror and attempts at assassination" as "tactics we Marxists emphatically rejected." (*Ibid,* Vol. 31, p. 33)

Furthermore, in his work "Revolutionary Adventurism," Lenin wrote:

"We shall always expose people who in word war against hackneyed dogmas and in practice hold exclusively to such moth-eaten and harmful commonplaces as the theory of the transference of strength, the difference between big work and petty work and, of course, *the theory of single combat.*"

And again:

". . . shots fired by the 'elusive individuals' who are losing faith in the possibility of marching in formation and working hand in hand with the masses also end in smoke." (*Ibid*, Vol. 6, p. 195-196)

Contemplating the consequences of ultra-revolutionism, Lenin wrote in 1921 in "The Importance of Gold Now and After the Complete Victory of Socialism" as follows:

"The greatest, perhaps the only danger to the genuine revolutionary is that of extreme revolutionism, ignoring the limits and conditions in which revolutionary methods are appropriate and can be successfully employed. . . . True revolutionaries will perish . . . only if they abandon their sober outlook and take it into their heads that the 'great, victorious work of revolution' can and must solve all problems in a revolutionary manner under all circumstances and in all spheres of action.

". . . we must estimate as soberly as possible which problems can be solved by revolutionary methods at any given time and which cannot." (*Ibid,* Vol. 33, pp. 110-111)

* * *

News comes today that the judicial co-conspirators with the police and their political masters of the monopolist ruling circles have placed their stamp of approval upon the extradiction to California of Angela Davis. There she could be quartered in the death row of the California prison while awaiting the trial in which the state may demand her life.

Angela Davis is the innocent victim of a monstrous frame-up crime by police and government agencies to execute her in order to strike terror into the breasts of rebellious youth and the Black liberation movement. They want to paralyze these movements through invoking mass fear by continuing revengeful lynchings.

Angela Davis is a young Black woman of wide cultural attainments. Already a celebrated veteran of struggle in behalf of inhumanly abused and unjustly incarcerated prisoners of the infamous Soledad prison of California, Angela Davis is well known for her work in support of prison reform. Two years ago she came to the attention of the nation and world as the principal in an effort of the reactionary California Governor Ronald Reagan and the neo-fascist former member of the University Regents, Max Rafferty, to violate canons of academic freedom and ban this young professor of philosophy from her classroom at the University of California. Responding to the latest blow against her freedom Agnela Davis has said: "Reagan and reaction tried to take away my job, now they want to take my life. I do not believe the people will permit them to succeed."

It is the conviction of our Party that the confidence in the triumph of justice in this case, born out of the militant strength, activity and solidarity of the anti-imperialist people, will be sustained, and that the demands of world public opinion will force open the prison gates and free Angela Davis.

There is a bond of connection between Angela Davis and the meaning and message of the life and heritage of the great Frederick Engels.

Frederick Engels and Angela Davis both began their social awakening to the necessity for helping change the world in the interest of the advancement of humanity as young students of philosophy. Both Engels and Angela Davis were precocious students of the most prominent philosophers of their day. Engels along with Marx thoroughly mastered all the works of Hegel—a discipline which uniquely equipped them to subject Hegel's philosophical system to profound critical appraisal and to abstract from it its rational kernel. They rescued its dialectical method from Hegel's idealist philosophical system for the service of the working class—the truly dynamic and historic social force for the forward march of man. Both Engels and Angela studied in Germany. Engels broke through the restricting bourgeois idealist boundary of Hegel; indeed, he joined with Marx in elaborating dialectical and historical materialism as the scientifically verified philosophical negation of Hegelanism and all bourgeois philosophical systems. The young student of Hegel, Frederick Engels, went beyond his master to arrive at Marxism.

The lovely young woman philosophy scholar, Angela Davis, unhappily did not have the good fortune to discover a professorial master of the caliber of Hegel. She became the aptest pupil of the most publicized and romanticized "radical" philosopher in the West—the German-born Herbert Marcuse, of whose role we have already spoken.

Like Engels, who went beyond the idealism of Hegel to dialectical materialism, Angela Davis likewise goes beyond her teacher along a path away from Marcuse and to Lenin.

From Hegel to Marx was not an easy journey even for the co-founder of Marxism to make. Certainly there is much that is personal testament in the brilliantly lucid and compassionately appreciative analysis that Engels made of Ludwig Feuerbach. Ludwig Feuerbach was a philosopher *in transition* from Hegel to Marx. I don't know how far Feuerbach went on the scale that separates these two positions, but how passionately Engels wished that he would make it!

Angela Davis is a young philosopher. She is an honest scholar and dedicated partisan of the freedom aspirations of her people—the segregated, racially persecuted, super-exploited, discriminated-against Black folk of Alabama, the South and our nation. She is a philosopher in transition from Marcuse to Marx and Lenin. She heralded her commitment to traverse that distance when she refused to deny that she had joined the Communist Party, despite all blandishments and despite all threats by the authorities.

Angela Davis has extended her hand toward the working class, the only true social lever for the elevation of all oppressed humanity, and the class base and focus for all human progress in our epoch. I believe it is certain that the workers of the whole world will grasp her hand in a mighty grip of international solidarity and will make the cause of her freedom from prison and the shadow of the executioners' chamber their very own cause.

After the events of 1849, the youthful Engels was compelled to leave his homeland and build a new life among strangers. But he found compassion, fraternity, understanding and honor in those distant places where he journeyed, for Engels was always one of the family, the great family of the international working class which he never left and which never abandoned him.

Neither police agents-provocateurs nor the old peddler of philosophical "revolutionary" junk will succeed in putting Angela Davis in the "trick bag" of the anarchists. Angela Davis is a *Communist* and the demand of the masses will set her free. As a Communist, the commitment of Angela Davis is to the reasoned revolutionary science of Marxism, not to the nihilist tactics of anarchy.

Lenin quotes Engels as saying that "the historical theory of Marx is the fundamental condition of all *reasoned* and *consistent* revolutionary tactics." (Marx and Engels, *Selected Correspondence,* Moscow: Progress Publishers, 1965, p. 353). It is because of her identification with the cause of Marx, Engels and Lenin that the bourgeoisie hates Angela Davis. And that is why the world's toilers love her and will demand her freedom.

In closing I wish to address this proposal to our dear Comrade Walter Ulbricht. Here, in this capital city of the German nation, here on the freedman's soil of the workers, where each man shows concern for the other and no man exploits his brother, can there not be raised from an international fund subscribed to from delegations in this hall, a worthy statue to that modest man Frederick Engels, fighting son of Germany and a brother and founding father to us all!

Speech at the International Scientific Conference, Berlin,
German Democratic Republic. November 12-13, 1970

12   The Triumph of Angela Davis

Angela Davis, is back in the struggle for a better life for the workers of our country, for lasting world peace. and for an end to racism and injustice. The name of this intrepid Communist is known across the length and breadth of the world.

Angela Davis, scholar of philosophical systems and student of Marxism-Leninism, university lecturer and publicist. Angela Davis, courageous woman Communist, who in the face of the nearly two-year ordeal of imprisonment and official persecution, conducted herself in the lofty tradition set by Georgi Dimitrov at Leipzig, Germany, by U.S. Communist Party leaders at Foley Square, New York. She has won the hearts and admiration of millions. Angela Davis has triumphed over the political plot of the ultra-reactionary clique in the ruling class to make a sacrifice of her freedom and even her life as an act of legal terrorism and intimidation against the sweeping progressive, peace and revolutionary currents which have been arising in the United States.

Many factors entered into the making of the victory won in the freedom of Angela Davis.

First of all, Angela's innocence of the diabolical accusations made against her was apparent from the beginning. Basing herself upon this truth, Angela came forward confidently to turn the tables on her accusers, to show that the motive of the prosecution was really to perpetrate a legal lynching in order to throw fear into the hearts of the masses in struggle for an end to the aggressive war which the United States wages in Vietnam, Laos and Cambodia, to divert the movement and discredit the leaders of struggles for democratic reforms in behalf of the rights and equality of the Black Americans, and to inflame a new wave of hysteria against and persecution of the Communist Party of the United States.

Furthermore, Angela conducted a political defense from the day the government declared her a "wanted" person and the FBI launched its frenzied and theatrical hunt for her—utilizing posters which labeled her "Public Enemy No. 1"—and the State of California charged her with conspiracy to commit murder, kidnapping and jail-breaking. When she was put under arrest and rushed to prison in chains, where she was held for 16 months without bail under the most stringent and cruel physical circumstances, the President of the United States Richard Nixon-—congratulated the then head of the FBI, J. Edgar Hoover, in the course of a national television speech upon his success in "capturing" her and characterized her as a dangerous terrorist and "Communist conspirator." Through the work of her defense committee and through her own energetic work in sending out statements and giving interviews from prison, Angela repudiated the charges and calumnies placed against her. In this work throughout the trial the Communist Party was at her side and played a leading role in her defense.

Angela's defense from the outset was predicated upon the fact that she was a member of the Communist Party of the United States who always aspired to fulfill the obligations of that relationship, observing the party's policies and tactics and earnestly striving to master the treasure trove of its ideology, Marxism-Leninism. It was made clear long before the courtroom trial commenced that Angela Davis, the American Communist, could no more be guilty of complicity in the desperate prisoner release attempt executed by the daring 17-year-old youth Jonathan Jackson at the San Rafael courtroom than could the great Bulgarian revolutionary Georgi Dimitrov have been guilty of complicity in setting fire to the Reichstag in 1933. Communists are not practioners of individual actions of violence carried out behind the backs of the masses by "heroes" or elite circles of conspirators. Communists put their reliance in the aroused consciousness of masses. Their tactics in the struggle for seeking the righting of particular cases of injustice, as well as for realizing democratic reforms and fundamental social changes, dictate policies of mass struggle, of enlightened action by the working people and popular masses.

Within the arena of the courtroom, Angela shared in the legal burdens of her own defense. She made the opening presentation which left its enduring impact upon the minds and hearts of the jury. At the same time she had the services of distinguished legal defense counsel. When at the end of the three-months trial the defense attorney completed his summary in Angela Davis' behalf, the jury in its majority was moved to tears.

Though the monstrous dimensions of the frame-up hoax against Angela Davis were laid bare in the courtroom through the activity of the defense committee, it nevertheless came as a surprise to many, if not most, that a jury of all white people in the "middle class" community town of San José could side with the victim in defiance of the propaganda broadside of leading newspapers and the arm-twisting pressures of Governor Ronald Reagan's forces and those of President Richard Nixon. What was truly revealed by the action of the jury in handing down a speedy and unanimous verdict of innocence on all counts was the sense of disbelief in the establishment's integrity. The jury's verdict in the Angela Davis case not only affirms the purity of her innocence of the frame-up charges but discloses the crisis of confidence existing in the United States between the people—even of "Middle America"—and the policies of the class establishment.

The valor of Angela, the excellent work of her legal staff, the enormous activity carried out by the Communist Party of the United States in her support were all vital factors in gaining her freedom. But decisive to this victory over a monstrous political frame-up whose first victim was to be Angela Davis, but whose real objective was to set up the Communist Party for outlawing and to conduct a widespread witch-hunt against the fighters for democratic advances and an end to the war, was the role played by world public opinion.

The Communists throughout the world saw at the start that this case against Angela was a maneuver of the ruling class to rationalize and initiate a wave of suppression against the popular movement for peace, democracy and the Communist Party in the United States. The initiative taken in the socialist countries, the Soviet Union, the German Democratic Republic, others, the consistency and imagination displayed in the massive campaigns of solidarity with Angela which were developed in France, Italy, India, Chile, Venezuela, Uruguay, Canada and countries throughout the world where Communist Parties and organized fighters for peace and human rights are found, registered that kind of universal mandate of the peoples of the world upon Washington as well as the ordinary citizens of San José County which simply could not be ignored.

The victory of Angela Davis is in a real sense a product of and a testament to the new correlation of world forces as between progress and reaction. The peoples' forces standing for justice, peace and progress, are mightier *when organized* than the will of the most powerful and arrogant and cynical of the world's imperialist ruling circles. These forces attest to the new position of strength held by the mighty trinity of streams which compose the surging river of the world revolutionary process. Its might will generate ever more victories in the days ahead.

World Marxist Review, Prague, Czechoslavakia. August 1972

13   Petty Bourgeois Radicals and Real Revolutionaries

The world today is distinguished by the fact that yesterday's bondaged millions are everywhere engaged in the politics of revolutionary struggle to reconstruct the order of things—political, economic and social. In all countries the best of the human race is deeply engaged in the struggle to secure the end of tyranny, exploitation, and racism; in the struggle to open the way to a peaceful, prosperous and happy life for all mankind. As never before in the history of the world, there is a spirit of solidarity which links working people and fighters for freedom of all lands and climes in ever stronger bonds of mutual aid and fraternity.

On a world scale the demonstrable main tendency is the rising development of the revolutionary process. The revolutionary process had its genesis, of course, in the contradictions inherent in the class-stratified, exploitative character of capitalist society. Over fifty years ago, with the capitalist world in the throes of a general fraticidal war between its two rival camps for the plunder of the human race, wracked and ruined by the economic consequences of the mass killing game, the working class of Russia, led by the party of the Communists with Lenin at its head, broke the world dominance of capitalist imperialism, and took the power and commenced the building of socialism on one-fifth of the earth's surface. In so doing, it forced world capitalism into the first stage of its *general crisis*. Although capitalism was still the social system whose influence was decisive on a world scale, it no longer was so exclusively. It no longer existed on a sizeable part of the earth and it confronted the challenge of a yet weak, but growing rival.

In spite of the courageous endeavors of the advanced forces of the world working class, and of that solitary establishment of world working class power—the Soviet Union—the jungle laws of imperialism prevailed and led to the bloodiest war known to man. However, thanks to the role of the socialist Soviet Union in determining the outcome of this war, which imperialism prepared and its most ruthless fascist practitioners initiated, capitalism was weakened on a world scale and the working class in a number of countries was able to throw off its discredited yoke, and in league with broad combinations of popular forces, to take the power.

Consequently, from the lusty infant of October 1917, socialism emerged from World War II as a world system of states covering more than a fourth of the globe, and counting in its population almost a third of humanity. The growth of socialism into a *second world social system* powerfully increased the state power base of the revolutionary process of the world working class, and gave added leverage to the struggle of the revolutionary forces throughout the world. The advent of socialism onto the stage of history as a world system distinguishes the *second stage* of the general crisis of capitalism.

On the basis of this alteration in the relation of forces between capitalism and socialism, the all-round general crisis of capitalism now undergoes a further deepening. Socialism and the influence of the working class grows in power; capitalism declines in influence and suffers the loss of one area after another of its former colonial reserves, and its internal contradictions are aggravated all down the line. Attesting to capitalism's general crisis, and contributing to it, is the growth of the anti-imperialist movements, the revolutionary movements for democratic, working class and socialist goals.

We who have had the joyful experience of being in the Soviet Union during these festival days of celebration of the 50th Jubilee of the October Revolution, bear witness to the enormity of socialism's accomplishments. The attainments of the Soviet Union, the senior in the powerful world partnership of socialist states, stands as an immense source of strength and inspiration to the revolutionary movement throughout the world. The triumphant advances being constantly made by the system of socialist countries in competition with capitalism in all spheres is further shifting the balance of forces on the international scale in favor of socialism. This qualitative strengthening, and the great successes made by the family of socialist states, have created an international situation most favorable to the rapid development of the world working class movement for peace, democracy, national freedom and socialism.

Thanks to the successes registered in all spheres by the socialist countries in their competition with capitalism, socialism is becoming ever more attractive to all the peoples of the world. The power of attraction of the ideas of Communism and the exhibit of its works in socialist countries and in their world relationships grow stronger from year to year and appeal to broad stratas of the population of the capitalist world. Not only from the working class, but in increasing numbers, new recruits are entering the field of struggle against imperialism and in the name of socialism from the masses of the toiling farmers, the urban petty-bourgeoisie, the peoples subjected to racial persecution and super-exploitation by the monopolists and from the student youth and the intellectuals.

The enlistment in the working class cause of the struggle against imperialism by new waves of the victims and opponents of the capitalist monopolists is both an evidence of, and contribution to, the further deepening of world capitalism's general crisis.

The mass crimes, the depredations against humanity, which the apotheosis of world imperialism—the government of the United States of America—is committing against the peoples of Vietnam causes many, of a broad-class spectrum, who fear war to look with revulsion upon the system of society in whose cause such a barbaric war is being waged. Out of their experience in the struggle to stop the aggressive war which the U.S. imperialists are waging in Vietnam, large numbers are coming to conclude that the system of capitalist imperialism itself must be abolished.

With the grip of imperialism weakened on the chains of those in bondage within their colonial holdings, with the aid of powerful moral, diplomatic and material solidarity of the socialist world and the world working class movement, the unfree peoples have emancipated themselves, or, are rising to destroy the last vestiges of world capitalism's colonial system.

The cause of the freedom and the emancipation of the unfree peoples has produced a great phalanx of national liberation movements which independently enter into the world-wide revolutionary process in support of, and alongisde of, the world working class movement. Large numbers of fighters for national equal rights and freedom from colonial bondage follow the logic of their experience with imperialism into the ranks of the conscious revolutionaries for a socialist alternative.

The main thing of course is that the radicalization of the working class in the capitalist countries becomes progressively more visible and politically manifest in this phase of the general crisis of capitalism.

The successes of the national liberation movements in freeing the peoples from colonial bondage also sever such ties as may bind segments of the working class in the imperialist countries to the coattails of "their own" monopolist exploiter class, and thereby free the class struggle in these imperialist countries for sharpened and intensive development, For this and several other reasons related to the intensification of the rate of exploitation of the workers and their increasingly unfavorable comparative status with that of workers in socialist countries, the present stage favors the growth of the world Marxist movement among the basic working class strata of the population.

To anticipate and cultivate the new opportunities for growth of the Communist and workers parties among the working class strata now, is basic, indeed is determinative for fulfilling the historic task of the coming third stage of the general crisis of capitalism, the stage of the transition from capitalism to socialism. For it is the working class component of the revolutionary movement that provides the *natural strategic stability* and concentrates its focus on the vital field of class struggle.

Recently compiled data attest to the enormous growth in the numerical strength of the world Communist movement. Some 50 million members are enrolled in Communist Parties in 90 countries on all continents. In the five-year period from 1961-66, this largest organized political movement in the world increased its numbers by 14 million. And, since the end of World War II, the Communist Parties of the world increased their membership two and two-and-a-half times. The major areas of membership increase are first of all those areas which have been blossoming with revolutionary anti-imperialist vitality under the warming sun of the favorable new world relation of forces. In Asia, Communists increased 15-fold, in Africa 10-fold and in Latin America the Communist Parties increased their number seven times over.

This is itself a telling commentary as to the depth of capitalism's general crisis. Those areas and peoples of the world, which only yesterday were the reserves for imperialism, are today centers of mass recruitment of Communists.

The mass enrollment of these new revolutionary forces has posed before the Communist Parties certain serious ideological and organizational challenges due to the fact that these forces have come largely from non-proletarian classes. They have come to the party out of their experience in the mass struggles for Vietnam, for national liberation, against discrimination and racism, for agrarian reform and livelihood. They are from the poor workers in agriculture and of the urban petty bourgeoisie—the students, the intellectuals, the professionals. The assimilation of the non-proletarian revolutionary forces into the Communist Parties without adulterating the theoretical purity or diminishing the Leninist norms of organizational standards is a present and exacting task urgently confronting our parties in many countries, and generally speaking, on a world scale.

It is a welcome sign of the times, of the stage we are upon that the petty bourgeois militants—from the cities and the countryside—enroll in movements of mass actions, and the best among them come to our Party. At the same time, they generate the main pressure and constitute the primary source for the current attacks upon vital features of the Communist Party's policies in the spheres of ideology, organization and tactics.

In the United States at the present time the main attacks from the left upon our Party and efforts to negatively influence its course now come from those who stand upon positions of petty bourgeois radicalism.

Let me offer in evidence a case history of the depredations against revolutionary realism currently exercized by a principle exponent of the reckless radicalism of the petty bourgeois deviation. Representatives of, and major publicists for, the most pretentious non-party and ex-party petty bourgeois vagrants of the political left-bank, are the editors of the magazine *Monthly Review,* Paul M. Sweezy and Leo Huberman.

With some reputation as liberals—even Marxists—in academic circles, they have set themselves up as the senior counselors to, and theoretical innovators of "up dates" of Marxist (really) r-r-revolutionary doctrines for the young wave of radicals of the "New Left."

The pattern of the anti-working class, anti-party, demogogic and diversionary work of these theoreticians of petty bourgeois radicalism is clearly revealed in an editorial article entitled "The Black and the Red," which appears in the September 1967 issue of their magazine.

Commencing with a correctly sympathetic appraisal of the rebellions of the poor which flared forth from the Black ghettoes of Newark, New Jersey and Detroit, Michigan last July, the authors proceed to the elaboration of a "new theory" for the Black people to conduct their struggle for equality and freedom. Their theory calls for the fight against Black discrimination and oppression to be waged through . . . *"the development of sniper warfare which is a form of urban guerrilla warfare."*

To our Party the main new feature of Detroit's uprising was the absence of white vs. Black racial violence, and the fact that the white workers were participating in the resistance to the police and joining with the Blacks in expropriating foodstuffs and household goods from the stores. But to the gentlemen radicals of the *Monthly Review*, the main thing was snipers on the scene. In the course of several pages of playing "sniper" or "soldier," and advising on the ways of urban guerrilla warfare, they set forth the following directives for the Black movement in the United States: "The 'ghetto jungles of America's large cities' can accommodate numerous Black guerrilla bands. No matter how anxious many of the people concerned . . . may be to remain out of it . . . it is not the wishes of the majority but the determination to fight of a militant minority plus the dialectic of the unfolding struggle itself which will decide who is and who is not to be drawn into the maelstrom."

Now that "the Blacks of the ghetto jungles of America" have guns and are grouped into guerrilla bands, who are they to shoot? This is the *Monthly Review's* reply:

"The ghetto lacks the means to project its power outside its own narrow confines. . . . This is most obvious in a military sense. If a Black guerrilla band ventures out of the ghetto, it must operate in an entirely hostile environment from which it can expect no help whatever."

But whom do the Black guerrillas shoot?

Editor Sweezy and Co. is getting to that. He explains: "All struggles against oppression are therefore by their very nature wars on two fronts—against the 'external' oppressor and against his 'internal' allies and collaborators." Since, as the editor observed before, "the ghetto vis-a-vis the outside world is relatively powerless", the Black guerrilla fighters can't get through to the real seats of the power, so they must wage their guerrilla warfare within the ghetto (!); that is, writes Sweezy, they must wage "the struggle against the enemy's fifth column of collaborators, infiltrators, provocateurs, and informers."

But this task of shooting out of the way those other Blacks who show less than enthusiasm for the operations of the Black guerrilla bands can get messy and difficult to confine to the proven enemies of the resistance movement; the time has then arrived, we are told, for a genuinely *Revolutionary* political organization to be born out of the guerrilla's gun. "What is needed," we are told, "is a clandestine organization, disciplined, security-conscious, with a highly developed intelligence system enabling it to differentiate friend from foe, and above all possessed of the will and the moral authority in the community to mete out justice to those who betray the cause." Then, "without for a moment relaxing their necessarily clandestine anti-fifth-column activities, they will tend to form something like above-ground 'liberation fronts' which will for the first time bring real political organization and representation to the ghetto masses . . . they will also take on economic and social functions which are normally the responsibility of Constituted Governments."

But the Black ghettos suffer from the lack of everything now——houses, employment opportunities, schools, hospitals—how can they benefit as a barricaded isolated outpost when still within the confines of the center city?

"Blacks in the U.S.," says Sweezy, "are without illusions about the possibility of accomplishing anything by the methods of bourgeois

democracy; and don't believe in the worth of reforms inside the ghetto.
. . . This world must be revolutionized; there is no other hope."

Blacks will just have to wait for that great day a'coming, Sweezy
gloomily opines, because "if the military power which the ghetto can
bring to bear on its environment is small, this is no less true of its
political power in the traditional sense. Here the chief weapon of the
ghetto dweller is the vote . . . as a means of putting pressure on city,
state and federal governments it is practically valueless. If the ghetto
sends its own representatives to outside governmental bodies, they are
in a hopeless minority. And if it uses its votes to support one or other of
the establishment political machines, it simply helps to decide the particular identity of its oppressors."

Furthermore, says Sweezy, "the capitalist-imperialist system created
its black ghettos, exploits them in various ways to its own profit and
advantage, and means to hold on to them. . . ." (Besides) "to allow
Blacks to escape, to simply walk out of the center of the empire, all
those in the super-exploited periphery will be greatly encouraged to
follow their example."

Nothing can help you now concludes our author, save the psychological values you will accumulate through your guerrilla war games in the
ghetto. However, "those of us who are outside these areas . . . will be
laying the groundwork for the day when a common struggle for common aims will be possible."

The gentlemen revolutionary theorists who prescribed the above for
the Black freedom movement in the U.S. are working against the development of the real revolutionary process. Such policies (as it is said)
belong not to revolutionary politics but the field of criminology.

These pretenders to Marxism—editors of the *Monthly Review* who
also count themselves valued counsellors on the problems of the Latin
American revolution—if heeded would bring tragedy and defeat to the
Black freedom movement.

It would be well for us to inquire more profoundly into the purposes
and consequences of the theoretical interests of these two continental
adventurers in the affairs of the revolutionary developments in the
Americas. Marxist-Leninists will recognize familiar features in the advice which Sweezy and his associates give to the Black people in the
United States.

Here is, indeed, a sorry display of the diversionary, the essentially counter-revolutionary character of the tactics and strategy of petty bourgeois radicalism.

It is well known that a singularly important feature of the 22 million oppressed Black people in the United States is their predominant working class composition, and that the 70 per cent of the Black people who are urban and working class are not a separate but an integral part of the American working class, notwithstanding the fact that they suffer all manner of racial discrimination. In Sweezy's "thesis for the Blacks," there is no single mention of this workingclass composition of the Black people. But this factor of the working class composition insures objective bonds between working class white masses which prove more powerful than the subjective imposition and cultivation by the monopolists of racism and anti-Black prejudices. It indicates the main way for the development of the struggle to secure Black freedom; that is, the strategy of Black-white working class unity, of Black people's working class alliance in the struggle against the common foe of the monopolist class oppressor and exploiter.

It is characteristic of the theoreticians of petty bourgeois radicalism to represent the national liberation movements as divorced from the working class movement. Indeed, they represent it as being in contradiction to, and opposed by, the working class.

While questioning the leading role of the working class in the further development of the world revolutionary process, such mock Marxists as Sweezy exaggerate and extend the task of the national liberation movement far beyond its historic role and capability. They sneer at the working classes of the capitalist countries, dub them aristocrats who have become a part of the establishment of the monopolists. They assign to the national liberation movement the task of the revolutionary overthrow of imperialism, a task to be performed, of course, under the directional baton of such disenchanted drop-outs from the bourgeoisie as Sweezy and Co.

Regis Debray in his *Revolution in the Revolution* (New York: Monthly Review Press, 1967) even boasts that ". . . in a group of revolutionaries of bourgeois extraction . . ." are really found the "connecting link in the worker-peasant alliance."

Having rejected the leading role of the working class, the petty bourgeois radicals scorn the Communist Parties as conservative and old fashioned.

They are hostile critics of the Soviet Union and scoff at the force of its influence, and of its socialist successes in favoring and accelerating the world revolutionary process.

In the single example, which we have cited, of the harmfulness of the petty bourgeois theoreticians upon the practical daily work of the movement, other points are self-evident. These theoreticians make obvious identity with the position advanced by kindred petty bourgeois souls in Peking and elsewhere who have been busy inventing new dogmas to govern tactics and strategy, unscientific dogmas and methods which could misdirect the revolutionary movement and impose unnecessary detours and setbacks.

Our two editors are not untypical of a new breed of anti-Leninist ideological tinkerers and adventurers who have been born of, and in turn seek to insinuate their viewpoints among, the non-working class forces of the world revolutionary movement.

They exert an extravagant expenditure of energy striving to tailor the theory and alter the structure of the movement to correspond to the diktat of their petty bourgeois prejudices, romanticism and vanities.

They are busily refurbishing old and long discredited theories of revolutionary action as first set forth by various brands of anarchists, terrorists and rebellious student romantics.

They seek a way to make social revolution against capitalism without winning the working class.

They seek a passage to socialism without, and in opposition to, the Party of the Communists.

In our country, the influence of the petty bourgeoisie departure from Marxism-Leninism as reflected in the writings of and or upon—Mao Tse-tung; Regis Debray (*Revolution in the Revolution?*); Paul N. Sweezy (*The Monthly Review* magazine); James Boggs (*The American Revolution*); and Franz Fanon (*The Wretched of the Earth*)—have a serious and disorienting effect within the broad left and sometimes upon some of our own cadre.

It is timely to join issue with all those of our friends and foes who act to exert pressure against the activism of our Party in upholding the integrity of its policies and defending the Leninist standards of its organization.

Lenin always sought out the class roots and causes of the particular contrary tendency and deviation in the developing revolutionary process.

"There are . . . moments," wrote Lenin in his well-known article, *The Revolutionary Phrase* "when a question must be raised sharply and things given their proper names, the danger being that otherwise irreparable harm may be done to the Party and the revolution.

"Revolutionary phrase-making, more often than not, is a disease from which revolutionary parties suffer at times when they constitute, directly or indirectly, a combination, alliance or intermingling of proletarian and *petty bourgeois elements,* and when the course of revolutionary events is marked by big, rapid zigzags. By revolutionary phrase-making we mean the repetition of revolutionary slogans *irrespective of objective circumstances* at a given turn in events, in the given state of affairs obtaining at the time. The slogans are superb, alluring, intoxicating, but there are no grounds for them; such is the nature of the revolutionary phrase . . ." (V.I. Lenin, *Collected Works* (English language edition), Moscow: Progress Publishers, 1965. Vol 27, p. 19)

Profiling the nature of the petty-bourgeois radical, Marx wrote in reference to Proudhon, that he "glorifies contradiction because contradiction is the basis of his existence. He is himself nothing but social contradiction in action." (K. Marx, *The Poverty of Philosophy,* New York: International Publishers, 1973. p. 193)

Still, the whole point of our concern is not that we fear contact and alliance with the militants from the petty-bourgeois masses; on the contrary, we must welcome this harvest of recruits to the revolutionary movement and count it a further evidence of the winter of capitalism's general crisis and the wide and deep penetration of the revolution's appeal. The challenge is to ideologically win over these non-proletarians to the standpoint of the Marxist-Leninist party of the working class. What Lenin taught in reference to our attitude toward work in the right-led "reactionary" trade unions, applies in equal measure to our task in connection with the "new wave" of radicals from the ranks of the non-proletarian masses. Lenin wrote that.

"A certain amount of 'reactionariness' . . . is inevitable. Failure to understand this signifies complete failure to understand the fundamental conditions of the transition from capitalism to socialism. To fear this 'reactionariness," to try to avoid it, would be the greatest folly, for it would be fearing that function of the proletarian vanguard which consists in training, educating enlightening and drawing into the new life the most backward strata and masses of the working class and the peasantry." (Lenin, *Ibid,* Vol. 31, p. 51)

In our epoch the banner of Marxism-Leninism flies at the head of all the struggles in which peoples join for the advancement of humanity toward the satisfaction of the material needs and spiritual happiness for a world of peace, brotherhood, freedom and abundance—for Communism!

Speech at the International Conference on Problems
of the World Working Class. Moscow, U.S.S.R., 1970

14   When The Age of Man Began

Historians are wont to arrange the history of civilization into several "ages" for ease in recounting it. They refer to the Age of Enlightenment, the Age of Science, the Age of Reason, etc.

We are now living in an "age" of an altogether different quality from any that has previously been known to history. The age in which we live was ushered in on November 7, 1917 by the social action of ordinary working people of factory and farm of Russia, under the direction of the Party of the Communists which was headed by V.I. Lenin.

The Communist-led revolution of November 7, 1917 introduced a new age to history—The Age of Man.

The titanic talents for leadership of Lenin, like the collective genius of the Party which he led, were all directed toward serving the cause of the liberation of man from political oppression, economic misery, cultural darkness, and debasement of his dignity.

The success of the Great Russian Revolution foretold the coming triumph of mankind over war and want, and the ultimate emergence in all countries of societies dedicated to the satisfaction of the true material and spiritual needs of its citizens, to unity within the national families, and to peace and friendship among the nations of the earth.

This Age of Man which the Russian Revolution initiated is being, and will be ever more, characterized by man's mastery over the elemental forces of nature as well as of the social relationships within human society itself.

For the first time in human history, there in the Soviet Union and to varying degrees in the other socialist countries, man is establishing rational relations within his society so as to insure that the bounty of nature and science will serve the requirements of man himself. The concept of "everything to ennoble the life of man" is now the prime purpose and unfolding reality in the affairs of society and the workings of science and art in the Soviet Union and the socialist countries.

There man has emancipated himself from penury under the blind forces of nature and from the injustice of the political rule of exploiting classes. There he is not only a conscious participant in, but also verily a maker of his own history.

On this day in the distant rice paddies of Vietnam, the lifeblood of all humanity is figuratively flowing out from a gaping wound which the guns of the U.S. government's aggressive forces have inflicted upon the innocent body of a young and beautiful nation fighting for its freedom.

The shameful war which the mighty imperialist ruling class of the United States is waging against the small nation of Vietnamese people mocks but does not negate the Age of Man which November 7, 1917 heralded.

On the contrary, thanks to the victories over imperialism and colonialism already achieved in so many countries, U.S. imperialism is now left to fight its unjust war alone, while the overwhelming majority of the world's people associate themselves in sympathy and material aid with the victim of imperialism's aggression—Vietnam.

This horror-war which the United States armed forces are waging against Vietnam is adding to all the contradictions by which the U.S. imperialist class is riven, and will result in foreshortening the term of its reign as the dominant class in U.S. society. No class is so powerful that it can withstand the tides of history. The tides of history rise inexorably against the aggressors and colonial overlords everywhere in the world today.

The presence of the U.S. imperialists on the backs of the Vietnamese people contradicts the laws of history and cannot long abide. This is a prophecy that can but be true, thanks to the process of the change in the relation of class forces on a world scale in the history of our time which the Revolution of November 7, 1917 began.

The Worker, New York. October 20, 1965

15 Peaceful Coexistence! There Is No Other Way!

In our epoch, the relationship of world forces is such that war has ceased to be a fatal inevitability. The noble goal and historic need of a "world without arms and without war" can be achieved, we are convinced, given the ideological unity, the unity of will and action of the Communist and Workers' Parties everywhere working resolutely and energetically among the broadest masses of the peoples, thereby rousing the vast majority of mankind to effective, militant struggle for peace.

We believe, comrades, that in supporting the main line and substance of the Draft Declaration we are taking a position which fully corresponds with the burning needs of the working class of our country, with the self-interest of the overwhelming majority of the people of the United States.

In recent months, an increasing number of Americans have come to realize their need for peace, the urgency of their self-interest in a world without war. Moreover, they have begun to register their realization in action for peace. And we cannot evaluate too highly the contribution to this development within our country made by Soviet diplomats at the United Nations and statesmen guests. Their reasonable, principled and humane approach to the problems of disarmament and peace has had a profound impact on the American people.

Never has the internal front of struggle against the reactionary foreign policies of United States imperialism been more important than it is today. This ruling class is armed with thermonuclear weapons and certain circles within it are disposed to use them in an attempt to hold on to, or extend, their shrinking sphere of domination in the world. Hence, the success of popular battles to wrest the power of decision and action from the hands of the most bellicose sector of the monopolists, in the course of which the strength and unity of the basic anti-monopoly forces around the core of the working class will be built up in mass struggles and electoral contests, so as to be able to oust the monopolies from governmental power and bridle them economically. The success of such a struggle, we believe, can well determine the fate of a large section of mankind as well as that of our own country.

The General Secretary of our Party, Gus Hall, wrote:

> U.S. imperialism has suffered a number of serious setbacks. These flow from and are the products of a new relationship of world forces. However, *in the final analysis,* it is *the people of the United States* who must take the aggressive policies of the imperialists of their own country into the historical woodshed.
>
> The gateway to progress, to peace for the United States, is blocked by the policies of a group of greedy monopoly forces, entrenched in the economy, in the political life, in the military and in the government. These policies are in ever sharper contradiction to the interests of the people. As has happened on a world scale—the balance of weight between these forces will tip to the side of the people and against the forces of imperialism and war.
>
> Those who steer America's foreign policy cannot but reckon with the reverberations that their activities produce both on a world scale and in our country. And in this sense the masses of people in our country will, increasingly, influence the foreign policies of the United States . . ." (From: "The Heartland of Imperialism Facing the

Future," by Gus Hall; *World Marxist Review,* Prague, September 1960).

This struggle of the anti-monopoly forces in the United States pivots upon the fight to compel a redirection of foreign policy from a "cold war" position to a genuinely peaceful co-existence policy on the part of the present and incoming government and for a program of radical disarmament. In the forefront of our struggle is the fight to compel a retreat from and abandonment of all occupied positions and military dispositions—in Taiwan, in Guantanamo, Cuba; in Berlin, German Democratic Republic; in the South of Korea and 200 other places around the world. The struggle to defend and advance the domestic social conditions of our people—the struggle for economic welfare, for civil liberties, democratic renovations, equality of the Black people and the advancement of the political status of the workingclass—is related to, serves, and is rendered possible by the struggle for the realization of a policy of peaceful coexistence and disarmament. This is why the struggle for a governmental policy of peaceful coexistence and disarmament becomes the focus of all other domestic struggles.

A capitalist-endowed foundation, The Fund for the Republic, recently brought out in the United States a quite remarkable study on the nature of the arms race and the consequences of its continuation for the people of the United States. The authors of this research and inquiry entitled their study, *Community of Fear.* It is a graphic and scientifically substantiated revelation of an aspect of contemporary world reality. Without declaiming their conclusion, the authors nonetheless establish the case with irrefutable fact and figure that mankind confronts no more urgent necessity than to impose an end to the arms race, than to work for general and universal disarmament.

It is absolutely impermissible for any Communist in the world to adopt a light-minded or belittling attitude toward the terrifying possibilities of destruction in the present arsenals of thermonuclear weapons. There must be *one common estimate* of the enormity of the tragedy to humanity that would result from a world-wide nuclear war.

What were some of the revelations of these research specialists to whom I referred?

During the greater part of World War II, strategic bombing planes carried block-busters of TNT which weighed a little over 20 tons.

Today a modern strategic bomber can carry an H-Bomb which has the destructive force of 20 million tons of TNT. *One thermonuclear bomb releases more destructive energy than that released by all the bombs dropped on Germany and Japan during World War II.*

Concurrently with the revolution in the destructive power of explosives, there has been a revolution in the speed of delivery. Today, the ballistic missile can transport thermonuclear explosives at speeds greater than 10,000 miles an hour. For instance, Washington D.C. is 30 minutes ballistic missile time from Moscow.

At this hour, there is stockpiled in the thermonuclear bomb arsenals of the nuclear powers explosive material corresponding to about 10 tons of TNT for every inhabitant of the world!

The researchers and authors of this study gave the answer as to what happens when one of these thermonuclear war-heads on an intercontinental ballistic missile explodes. On a clear day, a ten-megaton burst in the atmosphere 30 miles above the earth could set fire to combustibles over an area of 5,000 square miles!

According to these authors, in the continental United States with about 130 Air Force and other military installations, any thermonuclear blow that would make sense from a military point of view would involve a minimum of 100 delivered bombs with an explosive power of 1,500 megatons. Such a blow would result in the death or injury of no less than one-third of the population—60 million casualties.

Is it correct to bring forward such a grisly picture of the consequences that would befall people if a nuclear war should be unleashed? It is. These bourgeois authors render a genuine service to the cause of the struggle for peace. The effect of their revelations is to shatter complacency and rouse in the people a consciousness of the dimensions of the danger of the arms race and the necessity to join the struggle for peace.

Such revelations help the American people to realize that in modern times the United States itself would become a major battle field should imperialism launch another war. In two previous world wars the country was immune to direct attack and wrongly enriched itself at the expense of other peoples. But in a nuclear war the American people would immediately be subject to devastation so great as to bring into question their very existence as a nation. This danger in itself becomes an important factor in convincing the people that they must force upon the ruling monopoly group a change in course from the cold war policy to a sincere policy of peaceful coexistence. There is no third way. Our party holds that the paramount task before the American people—before all mankind—is the securing of world peace.

This conviction was forcefully expressed by our 17th National Convention whose main political resolution (*On the Fight for Peace and the Struggle Against the Monopolies,* December 15, 1959) states:

> Peace is the urgent objective, the common need and common hope of people everywhere. Heretofore this has been a dream deferred, an elusive aspiration, passed down from generation to generation. Now the conditions have matured for transforming this dream into reality, into a way of life for all nations of the world. For peace has become a necessary condition for the very existence and further development of human society, just as war with modern methods of annihilation has beomce unthinkable. The peaceful coexistence of nations with differing economic and social systems, and competition between them for peaceful pursuits, is the sole alternative to an atomic catastrophe.

The resolution also avers:

> . . .For the first time in human history the possibility now exists for the elimination of the scourges of war and the release of the full potential of the human race for the solution of the age-old problems of poverty, disease and ignorance. These new possibilities have been created by profound and irreversible changes in favor of the camp of peace, freedom and social progress.

The soundness of these views has been amply borne out by events. "Nor are they in the least negated by the rise in world tensions growing out of the Summit failure. Moreover, our experience and views are in harmony with those of other Communist Parties." (From a resolution adopted by the National Committee, CPUSA, August 8, 1960).

In our country the slogan of general and complete disarmament, raised so dramatically and effectively by Soviet spokesmen at the United Nations, evoked widespread favorable response. Perhaps some comrades in the socialist world do not grasp fully the impact of this slogan in a country like the United States, where from one-quarter to one-third of the economy is based, directly, or indirectly, on the arms race. It is true that monopoly tries to make it appear that any cut in arms would bring an economic catastrophe. But the fact is that since the beginning of the year, the economy has stagnated, and in the last few months has begun to decline, despite the increase in arms spending. Permanent unemployment has been growing as a constant tendency since the beginning of the arms race more than ten years ago. Wide sectors of the people have been adversely affected by the inflation and taxes induced by the arms economy and by other negative effects of war spending. It is becoming clear to millions of our people that defense of living standards and necessary social legislation cannot be assured while the arms race goes on and the call for utilizing the military funds for peaceful social purposes evokes increasing popular support.

For anyone to minimize the awesome meaning and consequence for humanity of a thermonuclear war would be to violate the dictates of elementary commonsense. Historical materialism, the dialectics of Marxism-Leninism has nothing in common with the neo-dialectics of some kind of disaster theory of history for social progression. It would be contemptuous of all of mankind's humanist heritage to speculate or theorize on such a theme. Theory should be an extension of commonsense, not a violation of it.

Now certain people [Mao Tse Tung and his supporters] assert that peace may be possible. They would concede that the proposition of the non-inevitability of war has some merit. But then they hasten to make soaring statements and to declaim about the character of the social order which would prevail, all over the that portion (or particle?) of the world which would survive a thermonuclear war. They seem to be absolutely certain that the shape of things to come in a post-nuclear war would be a world Communist order. In the book, *Long Live Leninism,* (Peking, 1960) our Chinese comrades have charged that:

The modern revisionists are panic-stricken by the imperialist policy of nuclear blackmail. They develop from fear of war to fear of revolution, and proceed to not wanting revolution themselves to opposing other people's carrying out revolution," (see p. 105, par. 2)

and have proclaimed that:

On the debris of a dead imperialism, the victorious people would create very swiftly a civilization thousands of times higher than the capitalist system and a truly beautiful future for themselves. (p.22)

But what comfort can be wrung from this prophecy?

A thermonuclear war *must be prevented.* If those who advanced such ideas are so pessimistic about the timely organization of the favorable relationship of forces *capable of stopping a war,* a relationship which already exists, how is it that they are so optimistic about the outcome of such war? Indeed, such a war would make a radioactive wasteland of such vast areas of the earth's surface, would lay such waste to the constructions of modern civilization, that it would pose such problems *for the social organization of the survival victims that we could offer no assurances of its character. Such a social order erected on the wreckage left from a world-wide thermonuclear war would be a mutation in the history of social development. Such a disaster as a thermonuclear war would cause a qualitative interruption in the historical tempo of human development. It would not be even a grotesque representation of the Communism of enlightened man's goal and mankind's objective need.* In my opinion, the editorial committee should take pains to see that there will be no sentence in the Declaration that would comfort those who minimize the all-out struggle to prevent the unleasing of thermonuclear war in the name of confidence of victory for "our" side.

As with the rest of the world, Communists and progressives in the United States are greatly inspired by the successes of the Chinese Revolution. There is a long traditional feeling of closeness to China among our people and over many years the Communist Party of the United States has had warm, fraternal relations with the Communist Party of China.

Much of what we have read in recent months from the Communist Party of China and the restatement of the view of its Central Committee yesterday contradicts all we have learned from many Chinese comrades in the past about dialectical thinking, the relation between theory and practice, the necessity of unity in principle and flexibility in practice, the richness of the variety of forms and possibilities in the tactics of the united front in domestic and world politics. May we ask the Chinese comrades: How would we in the United States fare if we were to accept, for example, the proposition that there is only one road to socialism for us—to prepare for the violent road of civil war? Would China not suffer also if we were to do this? In respect to the attack of the Central Committee of the Communist Party of China on the thesis of the possibility of peaceful transition to socialism—let us be reminded of this simple truth: *that the purity of revolution is not reckoned in the volume of blood that is shed but in the degree that the oppressed class displaces the ruling class in power.*

One thing further, in regard to the tiger image of U.S. imperialism. We have also used the image of the beast in popular presentations because it is a familiar image in our country. But we put it quite differently from our Chinese comrades. For example, recently in greetings to the Popular Socialist Party of Cuba, we said:

"The aggressive, interventionist circle of the U.S. imperialists is roaring like a tiger and baring its fangs at Cuba. It wishes to make her its victim.

"Yankee imperialism is an old tiger, and blind to the new world reality; nevertheless, it is dangerous, very dangerous. With each new wave of the rising tide of the anti-imperialist movement, the area in which the tiger of imperialism can have his way grows smaller and smaller. Nevertheless, a tiger remains a tiger—to the end a deadly and dangerous beast of prey. Even when increasingly isolated and marooned, it retains its essential character."

In any event a popular expression cannot be elevated to the level of theory. One should not canonize a fable or endow it with the authority of a political law as some apparently want to do with Mao Tse-Tung's "paper tiger" expression.

I must tell you, comrades of the Central Committee of the Chinese Communist Party, in our country *the enemies of China and of all the socialist world have recently decked out their propaganda with choice tidbits from the articles of "Long Live Leninism." True, they slander and attack us Communists no matter what we say, but why help them and at the same time confuse and alienate our friends?* When Wadsworth, the mouthpiece of imperialism in the United Nations, tried to frighten neutral nations from supporting the Chinese Peoples' Republic's right to its lawful seat in that body, he read lengthy quotations from the articles published in *Peking Review*. At that, many friends of China's just rights exhibited embarrassment. But Soviet comrades conceded nothing to the sly enemy, rather they riddled his allegations and delivered smashing blows at him. They led the fight for the seating of China. *Remember and value this international solidarity, my dear brothers and comrades, for it is of the essence of communist internationalism.*

Not only has the enemy used these bad writings and certain incorrect actions to prejudice public opinion, but the enemy and its trotskyite agents—from the left and the right—have sought to use them to try to revive a phase of factionalism and disunity in our Party. I may tell you, however, that their hopes are doomed to disappointment because we have passed through a painful experience with factional methods and groupism and we shall not tolerate their revival.

Comrades, we wish that our meeting will result in firm agreements to end once and for all the negative phenomena which threaten the unity of our powerful and glorious world Communist movement. Dear comrades of the Central Committee of the Chinese Communist Party, you have gotten yourselves into a blind alley on some questions. It is lonely and dangerous to us all for you to be there. Don't stand on ceremony. Turn around and come back to the main road on those basic questions that threaten alienation. Your comrades wait to embrace you! It is easier that way. And besides, *it's necessary*.

I think the mistaken view of the CC, CPC has its objective source in the one-sided experience of the Chinese Revolution which developed through a 22-year civil war. A *Red Flag* article on "Experience of Chinese Peoples' Revolution," reported in Hsinhua News Bulletin of November 3, 1960, states that Comrade Mao Tse-tung in his article, "On Peoples' Democratic Dictatorship," pointed out that in a semi-colonial and semi-fuedal country like China there was no parliament to be utilized nor did there exist the legal right to organize the workers to conduct strikes. *"In China the main form of struggle is war and the main form of organization is the army,"* Comrade Mao Tse-tung wrote.

In my opinion Comrade Mao here points to both a part of the glory and part of the *objective basis for the present errors* in the thought of the Chinese Party leaders on a number of questions of estimate, strategy and tactics of the present epoch. Comrade Mao has revealed the one-sidedness of the experience of the Chinese Revolution, and consequently, of its leading personalities. Possibly this tends to influence theoretical generalizations. But of course it is the Chinese comrades themselves who must determine the source of their errors, of their mistaken views and correct them. It is the responsibility of all the fraternal parties of the world to help them correct themselves in good time before serious damage is done to our cause, our unity and our prospects for world peace and socialism's triumph in the whole world.

In the name of the Communist Party of the United States, our delegation expresses its full support of the main line and basic substance of the Draft Declaration of the Communist and Workers' Parties.

Speech at the World Conference of Communist Parties.
Moscow, U.S.S.R. 1960

16   The Power of Fraternal Unity

"**O**ne for all and all for one" is a cherished motto, commonplace in the memory of all. The great French writer, Alexander Dumas, made it the slogan of the swashbuckling heroes of his well-known novel, *The Three Musketeers*. But in the land of the Soviets it is no longer a mere ideal but a succinct description of an ever-developing reality in the character of relations between the nations and nationalities which make up the great family of peoples that is the *Union of Soviet Socialist Republics*.

More than 100 distinctive nations and nationalities, with representation of practically every racial type, and expressing themselves in some 70 languages, compose the 247 million people who inhabit the expansive territory of the USSR.

The conscious and voluntary cooperation of the members of this great family of nationalities, encompassing some one-twelfth of all the people of the earth, forged a union for the attainment of their common goals and to safeguard and attain the fulfillment of their individual aspirations.

The union of the multinational population of the Soviet Union is realized on the basis of the combination of two constituent organizational aspects: *class interests and national interests*.

ON A SOLID BASIS OF CLASS UNITY

The primary foundation of the unity bonds of the Soviet people rest upon the all-nationality common fraternal workingclass material interests and commitment to the building of socialism and the realization of communism. It is, above all else, the international (and interracial and intercultural) organizational ties of the working class of all the nationalities which constitute the unseverable links at the foundational level of the unity of the mighty USSR, a "nation of nations." And in the leadership of the system of international workingclass organizations of Soviet peoples of all nationalities, stands forth the highest organized formation of the Union-wide vanguard of the class and of all working people, the Communist Party of the Soviet Union; this, guided by Lenin's science of Marxism, was the first party of socialist revolution, the pioneer party of the construction of socialism over one-fifth of the earth's surface, the leader in the march of the nations toward the communist future of mankind.

Secondly, the peoples of the Soviet Union are organized as a complex of free and equal national communities, autonomous national regions and sovereign national state formations.

The USSR is a state union, a federation of 15 national republics wherein "the sovereignty of the whole is oranically combined with the sovereignty of its components—the Union Republics." (S. Rashidov, "Triumph of National Policy," *Sovietskaya Moldavia,* September 1, 1972.)

In addition to the sovereign republic status of the 15 nations which compose the Union, all nationality communities of people enjoy the right to territorial autonomy in which to exercise their culture and national language, and provide the determining leadership of their own national development. There are in the USSR 53 Union republics, autonomous republics, autonomous regions, and national areas. Every nationality, large or small, with new languages (some 45 nationalities acquired a written alphabet only since the October Socialist Revolution) or old languages, enjoys the full equality, respect and dignity of all others.

The October Revolution, led by the Russian Communist Party headed by the great Lenin, not only resulted in the emancipation of the working class from capitalist exploitation through the overthrow and abolition of capitalism, but it also liberated imperialist Russia's "prisonhouse" of its captive nations and oppressed nationalities.

On December 30, 1922, at the First All-Union Congress of Soviets, meeting in Moscow, delegations representing all the formerly oppressed peoples and nationalities of the Soviet Union joined with their revolutionary workingclass liberators (first among whom was the Russian proletariat) in the formation of a multinational state of free and equal nationalities, a state of a type new to history—the Union of Soviet Socialist Republics.

This USSR, this voluntary union of friendly working peoples of many tongues and national features, in the course of the last half century has inscribed epoch-changing achievements in the history of the world. It has done so in terms of the vast socio-economic advances made by the Soviet peoples in such an historically short span of time, and in terms of the unprecedented heroic and selfless service rendered to the peoples of the world on the fields of battle for mankind's salvation from fascist slavery, in solidarity with the peoples fighting free from imperialist bondage. It has done so in upholding the cause of peace, equality and friendship of peoples, and in advancing world science and culture.

One of the greatest achievements of the USSR, and probably its most important contribution to the world's peoples, is its own creation. The USSR has been developing and modeling a prototype structure and living example of a state wherein peoples of different nationalities, races, with unequal material and cultural beginnings, can attain freedom and growth in relationships of mutual aid and interchange of values, as brothers and sisters in a happy family governing themselves on a rational, just and equal basis.

What are some of the material indices of the historically unequalled strides forward registered by the peoples of the USSR—which attest to the superiority of the USSR as a state system, as a humane, rational and fraternal peoples' community?

FRUIT OF COOPERATION AND SOCIALISM

Life expectancy of Soviet people has more than doubled since the last decade of the tsar's empire. It is now one of the highest in the world—70 years. But it is not only the number of years of life that has increased; the quality of living has been enormously enriched and at a pace unequalled in the history of any people.

As compared to 1922, the year the USSR took its present state form, the national income has increased 112 times. Between 1950 and 1971, it increased 5.6 times, while the national income of the United States merely doubled. The gross national wealth of the USSR is estimated to be over 1,200 billion dollars! (All Soviet statistical data cited are from the publication *Soviet National Economy: 1922-1972* by the USSR Central Statistical Board, Moscow, 1972.)

And there is not one capitalist on the scene to rake off a cut for himself from this wealth, which belongs to the whole people. Indeed, three-fourths of the annual wealth accumulation in the USSR goes directly to the satisfaction of the material and cultural needs of the people.

Since the Revolution, the average income of industrial workers has increased 8.3 times, while that of farmers is now 12 times what it was in 1922.

This is in startling contrast to the well-known fact that the lion's share of the wealth of the United States is in exclusive command of a mere handful of billionaires and that the whole production process is geared to the satisfaction of the profit greed of the capitalist-monopolist clique of robber barons.

Currently, the USSR's share in world industrial production is one-fifth; in 1922 it amounted to a mere one per cent!

In 1922 the Soviet Union's steel production was barely one percent of that of the United States, whereas today, at 120.7 million tons, it surpasses the U.S. output and that of every other country in the world.

In general, mechanization has replaced the former woefully burdensome toil of man and mules in the agricultural production process in the USSR. The 15,500 state farms and the 32,000 collective farms which produce foodstuffs and industrial raw materials are scientifically operated, electrified, up-to-date establishments. And the technical and cultural levels and resultant sociological changes in the life-styles of the 40 percent of Soviet people who still work in the countryside, grow closer to and in many areas already approximate, those of the 58 percent who are urban dwellers. By 1972 the gross output of agricultural produce has increased to five times what it was in 1922.

THE PEOPLES PROSPER

In the Soviet Union, "the wealth of the nations" *is* the riches of the people. Income from wages and salaries is but a smaller part of the whole picture of the steadily rising living standards of the people. The larger part is the collective, social "wages" received by all Soviet citizens without any discrimination or favor. Public funds insure free medical aid, free tuition, pensions, vouchers for sanatoria and holiday homes, and other social benefits.

There are 28 doctors and 111 hospital beds for every 10,000 persons in the whole Soviet Union, as contrasted with only 1.8 doctors and but 13 beds per 10,000 in 1922.

Each year for the past five years, some 10 million people have acquired new housing in the USSR. New housing is increasing at a present annual rate of 92 units per 10,000 of the population. This ratio will increase during the course of realizing the current 5-year plan.

The rapid rise in production and dramatic gains in the material means for satisfaction of the ever-expanding "creature comforts" requirements of Soviet men, women and youth are accompanied by an ongoing revolutionary advance in providing for the cultural needs of the people. The characteristic feature of Soviet culture is its internationalist, workingclass, socialist content, manifested in and through a wide diversity of national forms. Soviet culture is a harmonious ensemble of interrelated distinctive national components, progressively undergoing mutual enrichment, as each part strives for excellence in making its contribution to the whole.

Before the Revolution, some 45 of the 100 nationalities who spoke different tongues had no written languages. And three-fourth of the whole propulation—including those with the most advanced cultures, like the Russians and Ukrainians—could neither read nor write. In the areas between the largest cities, where the overwhelming majority of the peoples lived as peasants and poor workmen, illiteracy held sway.

Today, the 50th anniversary jubilee year of the USSR's establishment, finds the Soviet people ranking first among nations of the world in mass educational attainment. Some 80.2 million people attended educational establishments. At any given time, one of every three Soviet citizens is engaged at some level in academic, scientific or technical studies. Of all the scientific workers in the world, one-fourth (1,002,900) are in the USSR.

The Soviet Union leads the world in book publishing. It prints every fourth book published in the world. Since 1922 some 38.3 billion books have been printed in the USSR, not only in Russian, but in all of the 89 languages spoken in this unique family of fraternal nationaliies, as well as in 56 foreign languages. The Soviet writers continue the rich literary traditions of the past in Soviet times. The concert hall and theater stage of the USSR enjoy world renown for their magnitude and artistry.

It would take many pages simply to catalog the most remarkable socio-economic and cultural attainments of the USSR as a whole over the past 50 years. But the most vivid picture of the USSR's meaning for mankind is seen in the advantages which accrued under this model socialist state system to the formerly most oppressed peoples.

FROM LAST PLACE TO FRONT RUNNER

The spectacular advances registered in the life of some of these peoples are summarized in the following passage from an article by the Soviet historian, E. V. Tadevosyan:

To overcome the backwardness of many peoples inherited from the past, the Soviet state, in the process of socialist construction, took measures to insure that the economy and culture of the national regions develop faster than those of more advanced regions. Thus, while the industrial output of the USSR as a whole increased 92 times on the average between 1913 and 1970, the increase in Kazakhstan and Moldavia was 146 times, in Armenia 184 times, in Kirghizia 188 times. In the standard of education the population of these republics have either closely approached or even exceeded the average for the country. According to the 1970 all-Union census the number of employed people with higher or secondary (complete or incomplete) education per 1,000 in 1970 was 653 in Uzbekistan, 682 in Turkmenia. While the number of college students of Russian, Ukrainian and Byelorussian nationality increased 26-28 times between the 1927-28 and 1968-69 academic years, the number of Turkmen students increased diring the same period 212 times, of Kirghizian students, 220 times, of Tajik students, more than 250 times, of Uzbek students, more than 280 times, of Kazakh students, more than 310 times.

The accelerated development of the national regions made it possible for nations, which only a few decades ago had lagged behind for several historical epochs, to catch up and to enter socialism simultaneously with the other peoples of our country and share in the building of a developed socialist society. ("Soviet People—A New Historical Community," *Voprosi Istorii KPSS,* Number 5,1972.)

PEOPLE OF COLOR IN THE TWO WORLDS

It is particularly instructive to contemplate the comparison in status between such formerly oppressed people of the USSR and the Black American people of the United States. The Kazakhs would be classified as "Black" or "colored" or "Negro" if they lived in the USA, as distinguished from the "white"-skinned Americans.

The number of Black American people in the United States is approximately twice the size of the Kazakh population in the USSR. (Blacks are about one tenth of the total United States population, while the population of Kazakhstan is about one-twentieth of the population of the USSR.)

The people of Kazakhstan (being a full-fledged nation) exercise their right of political self-determination as an independent state, a free and equal member of the 15 Union republics which comprise the Union of Soviet Socialist Republics. It has its own legislative, judiciary and executive branches of government, as well as its own economic, social and political institutions and administrative structures. It has a flourishing culture and its own language. While the 12-million-plus Kazakh people exercise the commanding political power in their national territory and enjoy unchallengeable equality and access to everything everywhere in the entire USSR, such political democracy and total enjoyment of civil rights is not the condition of the 25 million Blacks of the United States of America.

As for a just participating share in government, not to speak of self-government in the areas where they are a majority in the population, Blacks in the United States—despite two centuries of bitter struggles—are far from securing this democratic objective.

There is only one Black man in the United States Senate of 100 members. In the House of Representatives, where 435 are seated, sit only 11 Black congressmen and one Black congresswoman. One of them, Congressman Louis Stokes, pointed to the fact, during a speech on the floor, that, "Of the more than 500,000 elected officials nationwide, less than one percent are Black although Blacks are 11 percent of the total population." And in the southern states, where fully half of the 25 million Blacks still live, they hold only 40 of the 1,085 state legislative seats.

In the administration of the courts, only a token number of Blacks wear the robes of judges. (But how different it is when the *prisoner* totals are compiled!) Of the 459 federal judges there are 21 Black men and one Black woman. Yet of the prisoners given sentences of death and executed between the years 1930-1967, Blacks accounted for 53 per cent of the total. In the jails of the largest cities, Blacks account for 70 or 80 percent of the total number of prisoners. "Not that we are more criminal than others," as Dr. W. E. B. DuBois stated, "but we are poorer and Black folk and therefore more often arrested."

Though just 11 percent of the population, Blacks are 20 percent of the unemployed. Those finding work are customarily limited to the least desirable, hottest, heaviest and hardest toil at the lowest wages. (In

1970, of the low-earning household workers, 42 percent were Black.)

According to figures of the Department of Commerce, one of every three Blacks live in poverty, and in 1970 lived at an average level of $1,300 below the poverty line. One-half of the total number of Black teenagers are jobless and out of school.

Of the 300,000 physicians in the United States, only 6,000 are Black. Where the majority of Blacks live in New York City—in the ghetto areas of Harlem, Bedford-Stuyvesant, etc.,—there are only 10 doctors available per 100,000 people. The overall ratio for the city is 278 doctors per 100,000 people.

In New York City, where 55 percent of the school population is Black, only 10 percent of the teachers and five percent of the principles are Black.

Kazakhstan, where 98 percent of the people were illiterate only some 50 years ago, now has over 150,000 of its own teachers. It has a splendid university and a system of 10 colleges. Under the direction of the Kazakh Academy of Sciences are some 165 research institutions enganging the creative labor of thousands of scientists and scholars, among whom are 300 Kazakhs who have earned Doctor of Science degrees. In the Kazakh language alone, there have been published 12,700,000 copies of books of 898 different titles by the Kazakh literary and scientific workers.

Blacks in the United States, though they are twice as numerous as Kazakhs in the USSR, and have been a component people of a multinational state four times longer than the lifetime of the USSR, know no such status as the Kazakhs have attained. And the reason lies not in the stars. The reason for the difference in achievements is in the fundamental opposite nature of the social systems within which these respective peoples live and work.

The deprivation of Blacks in the United States is a result of the operations of the class exploitative system of capitalism. The swift rise of the Kazakh people in the USSR from agonizing backwardness to a people standing shoulder to shoulder with the world's foremost achievers, in the front ranks of socio-economic progress and at the highest cultural levels, is a consequence of the socialist transformation of the political and economic system following from the destruction of the chains of capitalist-imperialist bondage.

Whereas laws and constitutions of capitalist countries such as the

United States proclaim "equality of rights," which is given certain formal legal recognition, the reality of that *equality* under capitalism is deprived of any real substance for the masses because they are denied the *material means* to exercise the "equal rights." Frederick Engels stated it long ago:

". . . capitalist production takes care to insure that the great majority of those with equal rights shall get only what is essential for bare existence. Capitalist production has, therefore, little more respect, if indeed any more, for the equal right to the urge towards happiness of the majority than had slavery or serfdom. (F. Engels, *Ludwig Feuerbach*, New York: International Publishers, 1974, p. 39.)

Behind such a record of great material accomplishments of the peoples of the USSR in the economic and socio-cultural fields is the unfolding of the politics of social revolution. It speaks to the leadership role of the Communist Party of the Soviet Union, skillfully and determinedly guiding socio-political development in accord with the ideological heritage of Marxist-Leninist science, and in correct application of the Leninist principles and concepts to the solution of the national question in general, and to the correlation between the national interest and workingclass internationalism in particular.

THE LIGHT OF LENIN'S TEACHINGS

What are some of the principle Leninist concepts which guide the practice of the USSR in respect to harmonizing and developing in their interdependence the national and class aspects of this new community of Soviet peoples, the citizenry of the USSR?

The first concept, that contributed most to the realization of the first genuine multinational state of free and equal peoples in history, the USSR, has to do with Lenin's theory of the organizational international composition characteristic of the Communist Party.

The operations of imperialism itself objectively enlisted the national liberation movements into the world revolutionary process. The struggles of oppressed peoples to throw off the yoke of imperialist domination were allied to the struggle of the working class against the ruling class of monopolists, of capitalist exploiters. The struggle for national emancipation became a specialized form of the international class struggle against the exploitative reign of captial. Lenin enlarged upon Marx's great slogan, "Workers of the world, Unite . . .," to encompass this new objective relationship. Lenin's call was—"Workers of the world and *all oppressed nationalities,* unite; you have nothing to lose but your chains!"

"The socialist revolution," Lenin wrote in 1919: "will not be solely, or chiefly, the struggle of the revolutionary proletarians in each country against their bourgeoisie—no, it will be a struggle of all the imperialist-oppressed colonies and countries, of all the dependent countries, against international imperialism." (V. I. Lenin, *Collected Works,* Moscow: Progress Publishers, 1965, Vol. 30, p. 159.)

Lenin perceived that the struggle for socialism is inseparably connected with the struggle of the oppressed peoples for liberation from the imperialist chains of national oppression. He saw that the victory of the working class over capitalism required from its vanguard party consistent work to forge a conscious common revolutionary front of the two component aspects—class and national—of the freedom-seeking masses enslaved by imperialism.

To provide the leadership to this historically prescribed combined operation against capitalist-imperialism required a workingclass party of a special type in terms of its own composition. *For a leadership party of the working class to carry out historic international tasks, it had itself to be international, not only in concept and principles but in its physical composition.*

The party of the Communists of Russia, before and after the revolution, was ever a model of an association of men and women without exclusion or distinction as to nationality, racial or cultural origin. The fraternal international and interracial composition of the Party added to its prestige and authority in waging the ideological struggle and performing massive educational work to overcome the bourgeois heritage of chauvinist and nationalist prejudices in the minds and practice of the masses of toilers.

By the precept of its own example and by ardent political-educational work in the course of leadership of the workers' struggle, Lenin's Communists won the main forces of the organized working class of Russia to the principle of internationalism as the obligatory form for the trade unions and all the class organizations of the proletariat. Lenin insisted on the international brotherhood of the workers, on class unity across all national lines, as *the organizational form as a matter of principle* and an indispensable requirement for waging an effective struggle against capitalism with all of its international aspects. Internationalism of the working class of Russia was promoted internally and externally as the key ingredient in Lenin's prescription for readying the working class and ensuring it the leading role in the social revolution.

At the very beginning of his life's work, Lenin had formulated this guiding concept. "It is necessary to strengthen, despite the bourgeois and petty-bourgeois nationalists of any nation—the unity of the workers of all nationalities in Russia." (Lenin, *Ibid,* Vol. 5, p. 18.)

Lenin reared the Communists and—through them, the Russian proletariat, in the spirit of a common brotherhood with the working people of all nations and nationalities. He established in their consciousness not only the humanity of the demand for equality of all peoples of whatever nationality and for their inherent right to be free, but also the revolutionary need for the closest alliance with them in the common struggle. Such an alliance could be realized only on the basis of the proletariat of the oppressor nation advocating freedom and "equality in all things," including, for oppressed *nations,* political self-determination—the equal right to form their own states and for secession if they so chose.

WORKING CLASS SOLIDARITY KEY TO UNITY

Lenin taught, and the history of the rise and success of the USSR has proved, that the firmest bonds of an enduring unity can be welded between the proletariat of the *oppressor* people and the movement of the oppressed nationalities *providing* the Communists, in the first place, work at it. Lenin wrote that "socialists must explain to the masses in the *oppressor* nations that they cannot hope for their liberation, as long as they help oppress other nations. . . ." He said: "This was the point of view adopted by Marx when he taught the proletariat that 'no nation can be free if it oppresses other nations.' " And further: "Only this point of view can lead to a consistent application of the principle of combatting any form of the oppression of nations; it removes mistrust among the proletarians of the oppressor and oppressed nations, makes for a united international struggle for the socialist revolution (*i.e.,* for the only accomplishable regime of complete national equality), as distinct from the philistine Utopia of freedom for small states in general, under capitalism." (Lenin, *Ibid,* Vol. 21, pp. 293-294.)

Lenin also called for struggle to eradicate practices and attitudes of racism, the ideological poison and "practice of barbarism" that is inspired by the imperialist ruling class to "justify" its enslavement of the oppressed nationalities and to foster division among the toiling masses.

The objective opportunity for realizing in life the coming together into a single allied front of the working class and of the national liberation aspects of revolutionary struggle is not an automatic or easy thing to accomplish. It requires that the Party pursue a firm, principled course in respect to building international relations between the working class and the oppressed peoples based upon the teachings and principles set forth by Lenin and wholly verified in the more than half a century's experience of the Communist Party of the Soviet Union.

In the national question (as in all other aspects of the revolutionary process), Lenin's point of departure was always from the perspective of the international workingclass interests as against those of the bourgeoisie (national and international). He said:

> If the proletariat of any one nation gives the slightest support to the privileges of its 'own' national bourgeoisie, that will inevitable raise distrust among the proletariat of another nation. It will weaken the international class solidarity of the workers and divide them to the delight of the bourgeoisie. (Lenin, *Ibid,* Vol. 20, pp. 424-425.)

Lenin taught that the workers of the oppressing nation must be won to recognition of the fact that:

> The policy of oppressing nationalities is one of *dividing* nations. At the same time it is a policy of systematic *corruption* of the peoples' minds . . .

> But the working class needs *unity, not division.* It has no more bitter enemy than the savage prejudices and superstitions which its enemies sow among the ignorant masses. The oppression of "subject peoples" is a double-edged weapon. It cuts both ways—against the subject peoples and against the Russian people. That is why the working class must protest most strongly against national oppression in any shape and form. It must counter the agitation of the Black Hundreds, who try to divert its attention to the baiting of non-Russians, by asserting its conviction as to the need for complete equality, for the complete and final rejection of all privileges for any one nation. (Lenin, *Ibid,* Vol. 20, pp. 237-238)

Without ending national division between the workers of the two largest national components of the class, victory over tsarism was impossible, Lenin argued. He said:

> "The Great-Russian and Ukrainian workers must work together, and, as long as they live in a single state, act in the closest organizational unity and concert . . . This is the imperative demand of Marxism. All advocacy of the segregation of the workers of one nation from those of another, all attacks upon Marxist 'assimilation,' or attempts, where the proletariat is concerned, to counterpose one national culture as a whole to another allegedly integral national culture, etc., is *bourgeois* nationalism, against which it is essential to wage a ruthless struggle. (*Ibid,* Vol. 20, p.33.)

In general, in respect to the multinational capitalist states, Leninism holds that: "There is only one solution to the national problem (insofar as it can, in general, be solved in the capitalist world, the world of profit, squabbling and exploitation), and that solution is consistent democracy." (*Ibid,* Vol. 20, p.22.)

Here Lenin, showing the relationship between the struggle for democracy in general and the fight for the special democratic rights of the oppressed nationalities in particular, also takes off from the point of common *class* interests of the toilers of both the oppressed and the oppressor nationalities. Lenin said:

> "Working class democracy, the demand for the unconditional unity and complete amalgamation of workers of *all* nationalities in *all* workingclass organizations—trade union, cooperative, consumers', educational and all others—in contradistinction to any kind of bourgeois nationalism. Only this type of unity and amalgamation can uphold democracy and defend the interests of the workers against capital—which is already international and is becoming more so——and promote the development of mankind towards a new way of life that is alien to all privileges and all exploitation." (*Ibid,* Vol. 20, p.22.)

With the leverage given by a strengthening of the international, common class-bonds between the workers of the oppressed and oppressing peoples, Lenin saw that freedom for the oppressed nationalities would manifest itself in one or another form of territorial political structure. Those oppressed nationalities who were constituted as nations could demand to exercise their right to independent state sovereignty and determine voluntarily their respective relationship to other states.

THE FORMS OF NATIONAL POLITICAL FREEDOM

Lenin's policy on the solution of the national question calls for support to the *right of nations* to self-determination up to secession. At the same time, he pointed out that within such a new state, "the class-conscious workers do not advocate *secession*. They know the advantages of large states and the amalgamation of large masses of workers." (*Ibid,* Vol. 20, p. 110.)

The national question, however, is much more extensive than that of the subjugated nation-state; it is also a matter of the oppression and suppression of communities of people in different stages of social development and making up different types and configurations of national formations.

To provide oppressed nationalities, who were not in the category of nations, with an appropriate form of territorial autonomy in which to exercise the power and direction over their own lives and development, Lenin considered to be a necessary part of a correct program for the solution of the national question. In this connection he saw raising the demand to replace "obsolete divisions [such as gerrymandered political-administrative units—wards, districts, counties . . . J.J.] by others that will conform as far as possible with the national composition of the population." (*Ibid,* Vol. 20, p.50.)

As we have seen, the USSR today is composed of not merely the 15 equal national republics, but within the member republics of the Union there exist Autonomous National Republics, Autonomous National Regions and National Areas—all of which have representation in the Supreme Soviet as well as in the Soviet of the respective republic.

While championing *the right* of self-determination of nations, Lenin strongly opposed any "consecration" of nationalism on the part of the proletariat. Always, he asked: "Which should be put first, the right of nations to self-determination or socialism?" And always he answered: "Socialism should." (*Ibid,* Vol. 27, p. 27.)

Furthermore, he said: "It is the Marxist's *bounden* duty to stand for the most resolute and consistent democratism on all aspects of the national question. The task is largely a negative one. "That is, to . . . combat all national oppression? Yes, of course!" But this position does not admit of support to national exclusiveness, or of national egotism, which "converts bourgeois nationalism into an absolute category" and "Exalts it as the acme of perfection." (*Ibid,* Vol. 20, pp. 34,35.)

". . . the Marxist fully recognized the historical legitimacy of national movements," Lenin has written. "But to prevent this recognition from becoming an apologia of nationalism, it must be strictly limited to what is progressive in such movement, in order that this recognition may *not lead to bourgeois ideology obscuring proletarian consciousness."* (*Ibid,* Vol. 20, p. 34. Emphasis added.)

The class-conscious workers never came out for separatism or nationalist divorcement from other peoples. Lenin stresses:

> "The proletariat cannot support any consecration of nationalism; on the contrary, it supports everything that helps to obliterate national distinctions and remove national barriers: it supports everything that makes the ties between nationalities closer and closer, or tends to merge nations." (*Ibid,* Vol. 20, p. 35.)

For the working class to command the requisite forces for ousting the exploiter and oppressor class from power, establish the rule of the proletariat, organize the economy on the basis of the socialist ownership of the resources and means of production along with abolition of private exploitation of social labor, in short, for the working class to gain the socialist revolution, it must win to its side the oppressed nationalities in battle for their freedom by championing their national liberation cause.

Correspondingly, for the oppressed people to win their national freedom from the imperialist, they need to ally their cause to that of the workingclass struggle for socialism.

By helping the Russian proletariat to overthrow the common oppressive ruling class, the prisoner-nations of Russian imperialism participated in creating the socialist socio-economic and political conditions for securing their own national freedom and abolishing all manner of national, racial and cultural inequality, discrimination and humiliation.

To further the process of construction of socialism and to bind closer the ties of unity and fraternity of the many peoples whose cooperation and revolutionary action made possible the victory of the proletariat and the establishment of the Soviet Union, the Communist Party carried out Lenin's principle of rendering to the formerly oppressed peoples every possible material aid so that they could liquidate the evil heritage of under-development in the shortest period of time. By allotting resources in a disproportionately greater share to those nationalities which had been held back and most victimized by imperialist exploitation and oppression, these peoples were able to leap from their former unequal status and take their place alongside the more developed nations in a relatively short span of years.

THE SOVIET EXAMPLE SPEAKS TO MULTI-MILLIONS

When one considers that there are some 2,000 distinctive peoples in the world—nations, nationalities, tribes—and something less than 150 states, it is apparent that the problem of the solution of the national question and its relationship to social revolution is one of the most important social tasks of the contemporary period.

The experience and spectacular accomplishments of the Soviet Union in solving the problem of realizing the aspirations of formerly oppressed national communities to equality, freedom and unfettered material and spiritual development, affirm the power of Marxist-Leninist theory and Party guidance for the solution of this most complex of revolutionary problems.

The great flourishing community of free and equal peoples—the USSR—stands forth as a model and witness to the creative power of the Leninist way to freedom, happiness and kinship of the nationalities.

For there in the USSR, all-round socialist development has taken place, under the leadership of its Leninist Communist Party, wherein racial tensions, national antagonisms and inequalities between nationalities have become things of the past. In the USSR, which was born only 50 years ago "new, harmonious relations, relations of friendship and cooperation" have formed "between the classes and social groups, nations and nationalities," and out of the common victorious struggle for constructing and defending socialism, "a new historical community of people, the Soviet people, took shape," to the glory and inspiration of mankind. (L. I. Brezhnev, *Report of the CPSU Central Committee to the 24th Congress of the CPSU,* Novosti Press Agency Publishing House, Moscow, 1971.)

Political Affairs, New York. December, 1972

17   The Power of Communist Unity

The history of the Communist International was that of a great school of leadership; it was a daring affirmation and herald of the historic coming of world revolutionary working class unity. The affirmation of proletarian internationalism—which is the theme of these sessions—has an urgent timeliness about it.

The Communist International (CI) taught the workers of the world *the power* of their unity and *the use* of that power to free themselves and all mankind from tyranny and exploitation. Unity is the heavy armour in the arsenal of the working class in waging its struggle against capitalism in every country and against imperialism globally.

"Disunited," wrote Lenin, "the workers are nothing. United, they are everything." When Lenin wrote these words he was expressing a conclusion in reference to the workers in general. But what of the class conscious, the most farsighted, the most militant, the most advanced workers and the matter of unity?

Unity is even more important for the units and national detachments of the leading class if they are to win victories in the struggle for mankind's liberation from all the chains that bind peoples in dungeons of economic, political and social want.

"The class conscious workers," wrote Lenin, "regard as a crime the fragmentation of the forces of the genuine Marxists."

It was to begin the process of putting an end to the "crime of fragmentation of the forces of the genuine Marxists" that Lenin took the initiative in the founding of the Communist International. Here in the former Tzarist empire where the indomitable Russian working class had taken power, in the name of and in behalf of the "workers of the whole world" whom Marx had enjoined to *Unite* as the condition for losing their chains, the Communist International was organized and set upon its work.

But unity never has and never will come of itself; it has to be worked for by those who understand its necessity, and fought for against those who seek to thwart its development. And furthermore, there are no others to do it save those who grasp its necessity.

Notwithstanding all the inspired speculation and efforts at insinuating their viewpoints into the internal affairs of the world wide fraternity of the Workers and Communist parties, the scribblers for the imperialists cannot conceal the alarm and fear of their bourgioise masters at the progress registered at the recently-concluded Preparatory meeting for the now-scheduled International Conference of World Communist and Workers Parties. The forthcoming world conference which will be held in Moscow on June 5, 1969 will assuredly mark a historic step toward strengthening the bonds of unity which obtains between the "genuine Marxists" of all the countries and nations of the world.

Fully aware of the determined efforts of the most class conscious workers to *work* at bringing about such a new quality of cohesion between the national detachments of the revolutionary forces, the strategists of imperialism are going all out to abort all efforts toward unity in an extraordinary ideological campaign and by means of less cerebral subversion such as bribery, provocative diversions, and all sorts of blandishments.

Before the October Revolution, international solidarity consisted of rendering support to the class struggle of the workers against the capitalists in various countries, and to the struggles of the prisoners of colonialism to gain their national freedom.When, however, the world working class achieved a state power base in first one country—the Soviet Union—and then, following World War II, in a number of countries, solidarity with the working class cause of world social re-volution, *proletarian internationalism, came to mean support to the workers not only as victims of capitalist exploitation and colonialist slavery, but most importantly, the support of the working class as ruling class in states where the proletariat has already taken power*.

At this stage in the development of the world revolutionary process, to advocate for proletarian internationalism and, at the same time, to deny support to the working class in power to retain its position as the ruling class in the face of difficulties flowing from the international class struggle is to indulge in demagogy and act the Philistine.

Today, it is not enough to be for the victims of capitalism; to be a real proletarian internationalist, one must stand no less firm in support of the victorious working classes who have taken power—and taken it in the name of the world working class, holding the fort, as it were, often against great difficulties, for those of us who still have a distance to go to close the gap with the *in-power* group of glorious achievers of socialist revolution in their respective countries. Every capitalist nation is but an uneasy and temporary unity of class forces with diametrically opposed national interests. It is not enough for a Communist to simply identify as a national patriot. The *Communist must be a national patriot in the service of the working class, the international proletariat.* Every genuine Communist is *a true national patriot but not every erstwhile patriot is a fighter for the real national interests, the interest of the working class.*

The gravest challenge to proletarian internationalism and consolidation of the true potential and real strength of the world revolutionary and working class forces are the problems which the Mao ruling group in China impose upon the revolutionary movement of the world working class forces. Now, in the wake of the madness of the frenzied "cultural revolution" comes an armed incursion into the territory of its best friend, its socialist neighbor, who has been its greatest benefactor in all manner of material assistance and technical aid. Even a fascist Spain does not lay claim by military means on the territory of a fascist Portugal. It abides by the elementary rule for peaceful relations between states, that of not violating the borders of the other's territory. Is this not to be expected from socialist China in her relations with her Soviet neighbor, the pioneer and senior in the entire community of socialist countries?

In an apparent bid for favor from China's worst enemies—U.S. imperialism (and its client-countries-in-crime)—the Mao ruling circle seems determined to forfeit the friendship of its staunchest supporter in the world community of nations—the Soviet Union.

It is necessary to speak of this development when we consider the theme of internationalism from this high platform graced by the heroic bust of the great Lenin and under the banner of Marx's call for the brotherhood of the proletarians! The blood of the soldier-workers who stand guard over the achievement of the toilers of the whole world—the USSR and the family of socialist states—has been shed opposing a bourgeois property grab which even reactionary bourgiois nations renounce in these days. It will not brush under a rug, and we denounce the

Maoist clique for the shame of it and the foul blow it delivers to the hard-fought unity of the world proletariat and anti-imperialist movement.

Our Party gained much experience as a result of the work of the Communist International. The names of a number of the comrades from the history of our Party, and some who are still at work among us, are personalities in the life and works of the CI. From John Reed, who exchanged notes with Lenin at the first meeting of the CI to the late former General Secretary of our Party—Eugene Dennis, our Party supplied a number of cadres to the work of the CI. Our Party was part of such mass campaigns as Russian famine relief, and aid to Spain, including the famous Abraham Lincoln Brigade. Even today, comrades who learned the art and science of the united front, to set into motion the effective action of the masses, are playing vital roles in the greatest international task before our people: that of forcing the Nixon government to end the war against the people of Vietnam and withdraw the troops.

From work in the CI, a number of comrades—notably the late James W. Ford—grasped the dynamics of the Leninist approach to the solution of the national question and understood how Black liberation in its correlation to and combination with the class struggle, was all-important for social progress in the United States. The late William Z. Foster, for years the Chairman of our Party, contributed a piece of pioneer work in his *History of the Three Internationals* (New York: International Publishers, 1955). In it he pointed to the vital importance of international solidarity with the Soviet Union.

Friendship with, and learning from, the experience of the trail-blazing Soviet Union remains the keystone of all meaningful strategies for socialist revolutionary victories in our time. Any revolutionary party that claims to be communist and yet insists upon an anti-Soviet Union or anti-CPSU position can be likened to a square wheel. It will not carry anything very far and that short journey will be too bumpy to benefit the passenger. The working class, history tells us, will not for long ride in such vehicles equipped with square wheels when all the while there is a Leninist model alternative.

May the great new thrust of international proletarian solidarity bring about the earliest victory to the peoples of Vietnam in battle to eliminate the U.S. imperialist aggressors from their native soil!

Long live the unity and international solidarity of the real Marxists!

Long live the Soviet Union, the first in the parade of the nations who have taken and will take the road of revolution for the downfall of capitalism, and for the stride forward from socialism to communism!

Speech at the Scientific Conference on the 50th
Anniversary of the Communist International (CI).
Moscow, U.S.S.R. March 26, 1969

18   What U.S. Communists Are About

The theory and practical activity of the Communists helps the working class and popular masses "to take a conscious part in the historical process of the transformation of society that is going on under our eyes."

The goal of the Communists is not some abstract ideal to which reality must conform. Rather it is the scientific projection of that which will result from the resolution of the contradictions already existing in the present reality. "Marxism," said Lenin, "is not a dogma, but a guide to action." (V. I. Lenin, *Collected Works,* Moscow: Progress Publishers 1965, Vol. 17, p. 29)

For the purposes of study and exposition, Marxian theory, or Marxism-Leninism, may be presented in three component parts —philosophy, economics, and socialism—but they are three parts of a single whole, of one unitary system of social science that requires the combination of its theory with practice. For the laws of materialist dialectics—which is the essence, the fundamental theoretical tap root,"the living soul of Marxism"—are drawn from "the real world, both of nature and of history," to cite Frederick Engels' words.

Albert Einstein, the great physicist, once said: "When I study philosophical works I feel that I am swallowing something which I don't have in my mouth." The young Karl Marx must have shared this feeling while at work on his doctoral thesis on the "Philosophy of Jurisprudence." He later concluded that "the philosophers have only interpreted the world, in various ways; the point is to change it." And Marx himself subsequently worked out a new rational scientific philosophical system which both explained and indicated the direction and methodology to change the world.

DIALECTICAL MATERIALISM

Dialectical materialism is the philosophy and method of Marxism-Leninism for studying and divining the laws of motion and actual force which transform everything that exists. It is a dynamic materialist conception of the world and a method of scientific knowledge of the laws of its motion.

The word "dialectic" derives from the ancient Greek term for "debate." Subsequently Hegel popularized the use of the term to mean all motion by means of contradiction. Hegel perceived that development in thought was a product of the negation of the old and the creation of new ideas and concepts. Indeed, motion and development are universally produced in this way.

Marx extended the Hegelian dialectic beyond the area of thoughts and ideas and employed it in the study of motion and development in the material world both in nature and in society.

Dialectical materialism, i.e., the philosophy of Marxism-Leninism, has been fashioned by men out of the necessity of humanity to have an instrument for its consious guidance in the development of history.

Already in the sphere of the natural or physical sciences, man has advanced over nature in a significant number of particulars. Some of our laboratory machines and tools "are more sensitive than the senses which Nature gave man," Peter Kapitza, the noted Soviet physicist, reminds us in his article in the April, 1962 issue of the *Bulletin of the Atomic Scientists*. And he goes on to illustrate that "the microphone hears better than the ear; photo cells see better and over a wider part of the spectrum than the eye; our feeling of balance is much less perfect than that of the scale. Only one sense—smell—is better than our devices." But in the sphere of our relations in production and in political society in our country we still grovel on the primitive level of "laissez faire."

LAWS OF SOCIAL DEVELOPMENT

As physicists must learn the laws of nature, so Communists, as scientists of society, strive to learn—and would have the working people learn—the laws of social development, of the historical motion of society. Marxism-Leninism is the system of the views and teachings of Marx, Engels and Lenin. In their totality they constitute that body of thought and generalized experience from which the guide lines of the ideology and theory of the modern Communist movement are drawn.

The philosophy of Marxism-Leninism rests on the fundamental concept of the primacy of matter, that is, of the prior existence of objective, material reality that is only subsequently revealed to man's consciousness through his sensations. Marxism is a materialist philosophy as distinguished from a spiritualist, metaphysical or idealist philosophy. "The great basic question of all philosophy," wrote Frederick Engels, "is which is primary, spirit or nature? And the answers which philosophers gave to this question split them into two great camps: those who asserted the primacy of spirit to nature and, therefore, in the last instance, assumed world creation in some form or other, comprise the camp of idealism. The others, who regarded nature as primary, belong to the various schools of materialism." (F. Engels, *Ludwig Feuerbach,* New York: International Publishers, 1972, p. 68)

"The ideal," wrote Marx, "is nothing else than the material world reflected by the human mind, and translated into forms of thought." That is to say, that mind, consciousness, thought, ideas, spirit, ideals are the products and functioning of the human brain, of matter, even as "man himself is a product of nature, which has been developed in and along with its environment." (K. Marx, *Capital,* International Publishers, Vol 1, p. 19)

MATTER IN MOTION

The materialist base of Marxist philosophy is to be distinguished from the old, mechanistic materialist concepts. To Marxists, there is nothing static in the material world, in matter. The very mode of existence of matter is motion. "Never, anywhere, has there been matter without motion, or motion without matter, nor can there be," wrote Engels. (F. Engels, *Anti-Duhring,* New York: International Publishers, 1973. p. 68)

The materiality of the real world is ever in motion, of coming into being, developing, and passing away. Our conceptions of structure and characteristics of matter evolve with the progress of science. Matter itself undergoes infinite changes—that is, of passage from one state to another: for example, the transformation of the positron and of the electon into photons and vice versa, or of the conversion of light into corpuscles. Yet, the materiality of the world remains, matter does not disappear; though it undergoes many transformations (such as between mass and energy and space and time—i.e., matter in motion), it can neither be created nor destroyed.

To this materialist conception of nature, Marx and Engels applied dialectics. "The great basic thought being," in Engels' words, "that the world is not to be comprehended as a complex of ready-made things, but as a complex of processes, in which the things apparently stable . . . go through an uninterrupted change of coming into being and passing away." (Engels, *Ludwig Feuerbach,* p. 44)

Marx and Engels defined dialectics as "the science of the general laws of motion, both of the external world and of human thought." "For dialectical philosophy nothing is final, absolute, sacred. It reveals the transitory character of everything and in everything; nothing can endure before it except the uninterrupted process of becoming and of passing away, of endless ascendency from the lower to the higher. And dialectical philosophy is nothing more than the mere reflection of this process in the thinking brain." (Engels, *Ibid,* p. 12)

"The dialectical outlook," writes Waldeck-Rochet, outstanding French Marxist, "considers the world of which man is a part as a unified and coherent whole, where objects and phenomena are organically linked, react one upon the other and condition each other reciprocally; a world in a state of motion and perpetual change . . . the motor of this movement and incessant change which thus asserts itself in nature, in society, and in thought, is the struggle of opposites, or the contradiction which is inherent in things themselves and constitutes the fundamental law of dialectics." As the "struggle of opposites" and its corollary, "the unity of opposites," can be represented as the first law of the dialectical process of development, so it is possible to identify other phenomena which fuel the motor of the movement within things—the second law of development being "negation of negation," and the third law the "transformation of quantity into quality" and vice versa.

These "three laws of dialectics," however, as Lenin noted in his book, *Materialism and Empirio-Criticism,* do not exhaust the representation of the many-sided character of the dialectical process of development.

HISTORICAL MATERIALISM

Dialectical materialism, then, is the philosophical foundation of Marxism-Leninism. Marx applied it to the study of society. This work of Marx and Engels, this "extension of dialectical materialism into the domain of social phenomena," was their creation of historical materialism, the materialist conception of history, or the essence of society.

Its essence is that just as materialism in general explains man's awareness as the consequence of man's existence, and not conversely, so materialism applied to the social life of mankind has to explain social consciousness as the outcome of social being.

The historical materialism of Marx pointed the way to an all-embracing and comprehensive study of the process of the rise, development, and decline of socio-economic formations. Marx showed that "the history of all hitherto existing society is the history of class struggles," that the class struggle is "the mainspring of events" in the social history of man, that it will find its resolution finally in a classless society following the ascension to power of the working class, and that the very processes of modern capitalist society operate to prepare and equip the working class to fulfill its historic destiny to resolve the basic contradictions of capitalist society—the alienation of the producers from the means of production and the returns on the products of their labor. As Marx prophesied:

"The monopoly of capital becomes a fetter upon the mode of production which has sprung up and flourished along with, and under it. Centralization of the means of production and socialization of labor at last reach a point where they become incompatible with their capitalist integument. This integument is burst asunder. The knell of capitalist private property sounds. The expropriators are expropriated." (K. Marx, *Capital,* New York: International Publishers, 1933 Vol. 1, p. 763)

THE COMMUNIST PARTY'S PROGRAM

Such are some mere fragments of the universal philosophical and theoretical values of Marxism-Leninism which is the heritage, the acquisition, of the working people of hand and brain in all countries.

The Communists strive to master the use of this science of society —to bring this science into play, to fathom the way to solution of the most urgent problems and longer-term aspirations of the people of our nation in conformity with the best interests of all mankind.

Toward this end, the Marxists have constituted themselves into an organization—the Communist Party of the U.S.A. The Communist Party has a program that is responsive to all the major questions of our times which bear upon the interests of the working people and the nation.

What are the most urgent problems which our people confront, and what does the Communist Party of the United States advocate for their solution?

PEACE OR NUCLEAR WAR

The problem of problems of our nation and of our times is to prevent the outbreak of thermonuclear war. To secure the peace of the world is the primary task of all mankind, the indispensable enabling measure for the solution of all other questions on the agenda of history.

Last September, President John F. Kennedy stated that the goal of disarmament is "no longer a dream—it is a practical matter of life or death. The risks inherent in disarmament pale in comparison to the risk inherent in an unlimited arms race."

Yet, in the teeth of this awareness that continuation of the arms race can only add to the risk of thermonuclear war, the President added further stimulus to this mad race to the brink of world disaster by resuming the atmospheric testing of nuclear weapons at the very time that negotiation toward disarmament was in progress in Geneva. He has not decreased the military budget; on the contrary he has upped the share of the military in the national budget.

In spite of such nobly expressed peace statements by the President, the present Administration presses doggedly along the path of the cold war laid out by Winston Churchill and John Foster Dulles. The essence of this cold war policy in foreign affairs is to strive for a military position of strength sufficient to cow the Soviet Union and the community of socialist states into accepting U.S. terms for the solution of all disputed questions in world affairs. It is a continuation of the reliance upon war or the threat of war as an instrument of national policy.

This policy has been a total failure and has no prospects for success in the future. Fortunately for our country, millions of our citizens have become aware of this truth and are increasingly taking practical measures to articulate their criticism of the present bankrupt course in foreign policy. Professors and scientists have placed full-page ads in leading newspapers; students have maintained steady peace vigils around the White House; hundreds of thousands of women and youth are marching and demonstrating with banners calling for the stopping of the bomb tests, for disarmament negotiations, for peaceful settlement of the Berlin question and a turn toward peace in our foreign policy. *The movement of U.S. planes and troops in division strength into South Vietnam is a new flash point of danger on the cold war fronts.* The danger of this civil war situation being escalated into another Korea is clear and ominous.

In the real world of today, the keystone for a peaceful foreign policy is an acceptance of the necessity for relations of peaceful coexistence with that other mighty nuclear power—the Soviet Union. It is in the most advanced self-interest of our nation to establish peaceful coexistence with the Soviet Union as the bedrock of our foreign policy. On such a foundation it will be relatively easy to arrive at negotiated settlements and agreements on all questions of dispute in the world arena, including the lifting of the armament burden from the shoulders of mankind, thereby releasing massive resources for satisfying the material and cultural needs of the peoples of all nations.

LIBERATION OF PEOPLES YET UNFREE

Related to the first task of all mankind—the struggle for world peace—is the struggle of the colonial and unfree peoples for national sovereignty, freedom from alien domination and racial discrimination, for the right of peoples and nations to equal human dignity, unfettered economic and cultural development, and political self-determination.

From Angola on the West to Capetown in the South, there still remain in Africa, in conditions of near slavery, some 70 million human beings. These super-exploited drones of imperialism must have their freedom and sovereign national rights.

As Lincoln said, "A people who denies freedom to others deserve it not for themselves." So it is that the people must prevent the narrow exploitative interests of U.S. monopolists from dictating government policy in our relations with the newly-formed nations and still unfree peoples struggling for their emancipation from the bonds of imperialism. In this regard, it is in our national interests to rectify our relations with the Republic of Cuba and accept the fact that her people have chosen another social system in the exercise of their sovereign right of self-determination. Our government's relations with all countries—small and large—should be on the basis of mutual non-interference in each other's internal affairs, on the basis of full equality and mutual respect.

In respect to peoples yet unfree, in this 100th year since the Emancipation Proclamation, the 20 million Black citizens of our country still are compelled to wage unending struggle for their Constitutionally-proclaimed, yet generally withheld, equal rights. All decent minded Americans must join in the fight of the valiant Black people to secure their freedom from segregation, discrimination, and racial ostracism. The whole world measures the depths of the "free world's" hollow pretensions by the perfidy of the Senators' filibuster and the President's ineffectiveness in failing to secure the passage of even a tepid right-to-vote bill in the face of the general disfranchisement of more than 12 million Blacks in the southern states.

THE PEOPLE'S LIVING STANDARDS

There is the whole area of problems relating to securing the livelihood and advancing the living standards of the masses of the people.

Our big country with its bountiful natural resources and vast industrial plant ought by right to be, but verily is not, an "affluent society." The statistical averages of the living standards of our people are impressive when compared to those of all other nations. But these "averages" mask the stark reality of the extreme polarization of the national wealth. On the one hand, there are the affluent few who project their opulence before the world as the well-advertised image of the "American way of life." On the other hand, there are many millions of Americans living in poverty and in conditions of extreme deprivation in this, our land of plenty.

In the recent study by Leon H. Keyserling, produced by the Conference on Economic Progress, entitled *Poverty and Deprivation in the United States,* the true dimension of the economic plight of millions of our countrymen is graphically documented. This study records the fact that 20 percent of the total personal income went to the highest five percent of the nation's families, while the lower 40 percent of all families shared only 15½ percent of the national personal income total.

Two-fifths of the population, more than 77 million Americans, live in a state of poverty or extreme deprivation. And the authors of this study correctly observe that "the new technology makes persistent poverty intolerable by making it avoidable."

Yet "we tolerate large and chronically rising unemployment, consequently freezing millions in poverty or deprivation when we have the technology to prevent it."

Indeed, the percentage of unemployed to the total work force still hovers around the 5.5 percent mark.

ECONOMIC MEASURES

It is apparent that the nation cannot long tolerate this state of affairs. A number of immediate economic measures are called for to relieve the acute want of the deprived millions of our citizens. Among those measures that urgently need to be taken, we would list the following:

1. Curb the export of capital and encourage the export of capital-goods. This will require an end to the embargo on trade with the potentially vast markets of the socialist third of the world's population. The export of capital liquidates jobs at home and produces a deficit in the balance of payments situation, but the export of capital goods would increase employment opportunities for our workers.

2. Vastly increase the investment of social construction—low-income housing, hospitals, schools, etc. But this requires a reduction of the military budget and rerouting of the taxpayers' capital into constructive channels.

3. Reduce the work week to 30 hours without reduction of pay. Enact a government-financed retraining program with "G.I. benefits" or the equivalent for workers displaced by automation.

4. Establish public ownership with democratic administration and control over the chronically sick corporate industries, such as big steel, the railroads and coal mines.

5. Establish effective controls against the price-gouging practices of the monopoly corporations.

6. Reform the tax structure. Abolish all taxation of the two-fifths of our citizens who dwell in poverty and want, substantially decrease the tax burden on the middle income brackets, and increase the taxes of the wealthy and the big monopolists.

SOCIALIST TRANSFORMATION

Over a hundred years ago Karl Marx defined the objective, the goal of man in the economic sphere. Man strives to attain a relationship to the total economy in which "each will produce according to his ability and receive in accordance with his need." (K. Marx, *Critique of the Gotha Programme,* New York: International Publishers, 1973. p. 10)

But before such a lofty economic height can be realized, the working people of our country, in alliance with other anti-monopoly sections of the people, must attain political power, displace the representatives of capital from the halls of Congress and the seats of government, and establish the base of a new social formation—socialism.

Already, in the Soviet Union and other countries embracing a third of the earth's population, the working people have established socialist society. The Soviet Union, having completed in the main, the building of socialism, is now launched on a vast construction program for the building of the material base of communism. Surely, our own working class and nation will derive much inspiration from the successes being attained by the Soviet people, and in due time, and after our own fashion, will also take the necessary steps to change our old-fashioned and hurtful capitalist system for a new, up-to-date, scientific and rational model—Socialism.

DEFENSE OF DEMOCRACY

Communists are not nihilists. We treasure the riches of our democratic heritage and alert the people to maintain vigilance against those who would destroy the democratic achievements of our people. Such a danger exists. Pro-fascist forces have arisen from the arch-reactionary and right-wing political grouping in our national life.

From the Dixiecrat demagogues and the Goldwater conservatives, to the General Edwin Walkers, the John Birchers, the Minute Men conspirators and the avowed Nazi emulators of the Lincoln Rockwell stripe who comprise the spectrum of the ultra-right, all have a common hatred for the democratic processes and are united in their attack upon civil liberties and the Bill of Rights heritage of our people. Likewise, they have a common cause in their general advocacy of policies of war in international disputes.

The rise of this ultra-right on the political scene is a product of the continuing cold-war policies of the government. In its turn, the ultra-right seeks to pressure the Administration toward a reactionary course on both foreign and domestic issues.

The actions initiated by Attorney General Robert Kennedy to enforce the patently unconstitutional McCarran Act against the Communist Party is the most glaring example of a cowardly capitulation to the pressures of the pro-fascist ultras on the part of the Kennedy Administration in this most sensitive area of civil liberties. Already, Gus Hall, the Party's foremost spokesman, and Benajamin Davis, formerly a New York City Councilman, have been arrested under this monstrous law. Morever, proceedings have been initiated which could result in the suppression of the newspaper, *The Worker*. I have been arrested and sentenced to six months in prison and am now on bail pending appeal of sentence for daring to uphold the freedom-of-the-press privilege of the First Amendment.

The McCarran Act is a fascist-type law which parallels the draconian terms of certain of Hitler's Nuremberg laws, including the provision of several concentration camps for its expected victims. For example, Gus Hall, or any Communist, could be subjected to five years in jail and a fine of $10,000 for each day that he refuses to register as a member of a so-called "Communist-action organization," which is defined in the law as a criminal conspiracy in the service of a foreign power.

Of course, neither Gus Hall, nor any Communist, will ever be witness to such a lie. The requirements for the preservation of the basic elements of Constitutional government and those democratic safeguards represented in the Bill of Rights, command the citizens of our country to demand that Attorney General Robert Kennedy take the necessary measures to nullify it.

THE PEOPLE WILL DECIDE

The Communists believe that the people are the great makers of history; that the masses of the people undertake and accomplish great deeds. Social necessity defines these tasks: the necessity to be free from poverty and ignorance, from material deprivation and cultural darkness. The necessity to strive toward a social relationship making for maximum happiness wherein the family of man would dwell together as brothers, freed from the oppression of man by man.

The Communists believe that in the course of the daily struggle to secure their urgent needs, the masses of the people will acquire a vista of the morrow's horizons as illuminated by the theory of scientific socialism, of Marxism-Leninism and the program of the Communist Party.

The adoption by masses of the socialist goal will be born out of the necessity and lessons of the struggle for their daily needs. And in due time, our countrymen, like the peoples of all nations, will act out of that necessity, do away with the old and dilapidated capitalist system, and replace it with that historically-determined modern social formation —socialism, the first stage toward Communist society.

Debate with Senator Edmund Muskie at
Colby College, Maine. May, 1962

19   The Communist Party

The working class of the United States is charged by history with fulfillment of the role of final emancipator of the peoples and liberator of the toilers of our nation from all manner of economic exploitation, political oppression, social deprivation and racial and national discrimination. It is destined by the laws of social development to displace the reigning class of the exploiters and violators of the liberties of the peoples—the class of the capitalist monopolists—which now dominates the economy and rules the state. When the real producers of the nation's wealth take political command of the country's affairs it will, in the process, sever all the imperialist chains which the monopolists have imposed upon other peoples and countries.

But long before that point in political development is reached in our country, long before our working class and its allies come to power and replace capitalism by the rational, scientific and humanist system of socialism, our working class is called upon to accomplish great immediate tasks, whose fulfillment is a vital and indispensable step in the transition to revolutionary social change.

First and foremos. among these urgent undertakings is the imposition upon the existing Administration and Congress of a consistent course in foreign policy which will make irreversible the agreements entered into with the Soviet Union, and each of the steps taken toward compliance with the conditions for peaceful coexistence and toward the repudiation of war as an instrument of national policy.

Together with this overall issue of world peace, with the struggle for establishing safeguards against the outbreak of war and toward progressive disarmament, the working class faces other important tasks. It has to be the initiator of massive popular struggles against the monopolists on the economic and political fronts, where the capitalists are imposing skyrocketing consumer prices, inflation, onerous tax loads, cutbacks in social services, mounting joblessness and other burdens on the backs of the working people.

There is also the urgent task of raising the level of the struggle to eliminate racial discrimination and national oppression of Black Americans, Chicanos, Puerto Ricans, Indians and Asians. And in the course of these struggles, the working class must strive to continue strengthening the class outlook and democratic control of the mass organizations of the working people—of the trade unions, the organizations of the Black liberation movement, of the youth, the women, of the fighters for peace, of the students and cultural workers, etc. In sum, the working class is charged with the responsibility of leading the struggle to unite all sections of the people in a powerful anti-monopoly alliance.

In the sphere of organizational tasks before the working class, the number one point on the agenda remains the systematic preparation for a mighty new mass political role for labor and its allies in the national political arena. To respond adequately to the Watergate disclosures of the monopolist conspiracy to trample civil liberties and introduce neofascist structures in the top strata of government requires that the working class enter the political-electoral aren on a really broad front and under the independent banner of an anti-monopoly party in which it is the leading force. It requires a struggle to replace the corporation spokesmen in Congress and government at every level with genuine representatives of labor, Black Americans and other sections of the people.

For the working class to wage a winning fight for its immediate needs and to fulfill in good time the epoch-making role which has been mandated it by history, the class itself must have a special instrument of guidance and leadership. It must have a vanguard party which attracts to itself the best, most far-sighted and broad-visioned, thoughtful and hard-fighting sons and daughters of all nationalities from within the ranks of the masses. It has need of a vanguard party skilled and experienced in the art and science of leadership of class battles, in the tactics and strategy of struggles on a broad front. It has need of a science of society and social development capable of accurately assessing moving reality and pointing the way for the formulation of programs for advancing the struggle of the masses toward particular immediate goals and toward the coming historic victory over the exploiter-class adversary.

There is such a party. It is the Communist Party of the United States of America.

"The Communist Party is a working-class party. The Communist Party is a party of Marxism-Leninism. There are no other Marxist-Leninist parties in our land." These statements affirming our Party's essence appeared in an article by Gus Hall, General Secretary, on the occasion of the 50th anniversary of the Party's birth. Contrary to what some may say, our Party, wrote Gus Hall, "has given the class struggle a direction—a revolutionary direction. It has helped to instill in the workers a consciousness of the class nature and class solution of the problems of the individual workers. This has influenced the character of the class struggle. The Communist Party has nurtured and planted the seeds of socialism among American workers. The significance of this contribution will grow as the struggles of the working class move toward the historic point of a revolutionary transition from capitalism to socialism." ("The Party of Marxism-Leninism," *Political Affairs,* September 1969.)

What Gus Hall said at that time is attested to by ever wider circles now. The most earnest fighters in defense of the living standards and the liberties of the people, the most militant battlers against racism and discrimination, the crusaders for world peace and disarmament—all who want a future for themselves with a higher quality of life—have reason to note with satisfaction this affirmation by Gus Hall that the Communist Party of the USA is no mere wish, hope or aspiration but an important and ever-growing dynamic presence on the U.S. political scene. It is the vanguard of our class and a leadership force for the future progressive development of our nation.

During this month of September, when we mark the 54th anniversary of the founding of our Party, every Communist has reason to feel a special pride in being a Communist. To Communists, these days are aglow with a sense of historic accomplishments for the cause of peace and progress on a global scale. The strength of the people's concern and their concerted action to give expression to their spirit of international solidarity with the victims of oppression and aggression, combined with the great growth in the prestige of the socialist community of nations and its ability to act for peace and against aggression and oppression, has brought forth a great victory for peace in Indochina and put all who still advocate war as an instrument of national policy on the defense. The peoples of the world are more and more coming to see that the ever-growing strength of socialism, as represented particularly by the Soviet Union, is a power for the promotion of peaceful relations between countries of different social systems, and constitutes a mighty bastion of support to all who stand forth in the struggle for peace, freedom and social progress.

The struggles of the peoples of Africa to consolidate their victories over colonialism by developing their national life in progressive social directions goes forward, while aid to the ongoing, unfinished national liberation battlefront increases. In Cuba the torch of socialism glows brighter from year to year. Despite reaction's fierce resistance, whatever the outcome, the chosen course of Chile's masses is irreversable.

In the Middle East, the boots of the Israeli aggressors still tramp the occupied territories of Israel's Arab neighbors and there is no peace there. The best people in Paraguay are held in the jails of the dictator Stroessner. Our heroic sister parties fight valiantly in Brazil and Guatemala against savage reactionary regimes which count on Washington's aid. But the dawn of a new democratic phase in the struggle breaks over Argentina after years of repression. Notwithstanding the surge of reaction and the imposition of the Bordaberry dictatorship, Uruguay's working class remains undaunted. The struggle continues.

We Communists, who feel a special kinship with the workers and toilers of the whole world, experience the sense of optimism that flows from the achievements registered by our brothers in the socialist countries, and the unrelenting and often victorious battles of our brothers struggling against imperialism and its reactionary appendages abroad. The present is overflowing with opportunity to join in great struggles of the masses, and the future is bright with promise for ever new victories.

Our Party comes to its tasks at this critical juncture in our national history well equipped to become a signal factor in providing leadership to our class and peoples struggling to find a way out for the nation from the deepening crisis. At the age of 54 it has experienced much, struggled long on a wide front of confrontation with the class enemy. In theory and practice it has gained a maturity that fits it for an ever greater responsibility of leadership of the working class and the unfolding mass struggles. The history of our Party embodies the richest experiences and many of the most significant personalities in the history of the modern labor, Black liberation and other social movements of the past 54 years.

Our Party was born in the period of the first major struggle to organize the mass-production industries on the part of the more far-sighted trade union leaders. William Z. Foster, the outstanding leader of the great steel strike of 1919 and already a well-known political personality at that time, joined our Party and played a leading role in its history until his death in 1961. Our Party's role in the growth of the modern trade union movement is acknowledged to be of major importance by friend and foe. The initiative our Party displayed in the great depression of the thirties in organizing the unemployed and leading great struggles for relief and welfare paved the way for compelling the enactment of social welfare programs.

Our Party was the first political party to elevate the question of the struggle for securing full, equal rights to Black Americans to the level of a principle. It did much to win white workers to the concept of building class unity through organizing struggle against the color bar. The slogan of "Black and White, Unite and Fight!" rang through the streets of the country during great struggles for jobs, civil rights, the defense of victims of lynch terror, etc.

Our Party was in the vanguard of the struggle to democratize the South and led in organizing the struggles of Black Americans and of white working people for attainment of their economic, political and human rights against the racist reactionaries in the cities and in the countryside. From the thirties on we were in the forefront of the fight against the frameups and legal lynching of Black Americans. And most recently our Party has been instrumental in the outstanding victory won over the forces of racism and reaction in the freeing of Angela Davis.

In the thirties our Party helped to build a powerful youth movement in the United States. And today, in conjunction with the Young Workers

Liberation League, it works actively to build a mass youth movement, particularly among working class and Black and other oppressed youth.

Our Party played a distinguished role in the great world-wide mobilization of all national and democratic forces in a broad phalanx, political and military, which rallied to the call of the Soviet Union to fashion a common front to smash the rampaging armies of Hitler and his Japanese and Italian fascist partners. Many young Communists gave their lives for revolutionary Spain as members of the International Brigade. Communists were outstanding anti-fascist fighters at home and abroad during World War II. In the postwar years the Party maintained its role as a vanguard fighter for peace. It led in the struggle against the U.S. imperialist aggression in Indochina and made a signal contribution toward compelling the withdrawal of U.S. military forces. And today it leads in the struggles against the menace of war in the Middle East and in Africa.

From the time of its founding our Party has been a staunch champion of working class internationalism, an unflagging fighter for world working class unity. In particular, this has found expression in its unwavering defense of the first land of socialism, the Soviet Union, and in its constant struggles against anti-Sovietism in all its forms. These struggles have contributed significantly to the new improvements in U.S.-Soviet relations and the advances toward peaceful coexistence.

Our Party has also fought for the unity of the world Communist movement and against the divisive, splitting activities of the Maoist Chinese leaders, and not least against their rabid anti-Sovietism. We were, in fact, among the very first to challenge Maoism as an abandonment of Marxism-Leninism, as a dangerous "Left" revisionist, nationalist trend.

Our Party was the center of the resistance to McCarthyism in the post-World War II period. For its organized opposition to this neo-fascist thrust and its energetic challenge to the atom-bomb blackmailing policies of the government, and for its denunciation of the Korean invasion, every effort was made to destroy our Party. Under the provisions of the notorious Smith and McCarran Acts, most of the Party's leaders were either jailed or forced to live the hunted and harried existence of outlaws. An anti-Communist hysteria swept the country, thousands lost their means of livelihood and suffered every form of persecution and defamation. McCarthyism was ended but our Party lived. It gradually restored itself on an even more solid foundation of principled policies and a creative program fashioned to meet the needs of our reality in firm accord with the scientific guidance of Marxist-Leninist principles.

Our Party has confronted and defeated every effort of the enemies of the working people and of socialism to destroy it. It has gained great experience in leadership through participation and in initiating big and small struggles in the furthering of the people's immediate and long-range working class interests. In the course of its proud history it has also had to contend with diversionists, deviators, Right and "Left" revisionists, liquidationists, cowards and traitors. But always the efforts and influence of the class enemy were countered by the rallying of the main forces of the membership behind those principles and steadfast comrades who provided the leadership required to restore and retain our Party on the Leninist course.

In the 54-year history of our Party there emerged as fighters, builders, and leaders of our Party and class, Communists who will deserve lasting honor in the pantheon of our nation's history. They are too numerous to name here with acknowledgement of their particular contrubutions. Suffice it to say that we take pride in the outstanding roster of Communists of the Lenin mold that our Party has produced, and who in their turn have helped to ensure a great prospect for the spreading influence and growth of our Party. Henry Winston fills with highest honor the office of National Chairman, the position formerly occupied by the legendary Elizabeth Gurley Flynn, and earlier by William Z. Foster and Eugene Dennis. Gus Hall, the General Secretary of the Party, had worthy predecessors in Eugene Dennis and earlier of Charles E. Ruthenberg.

Speaking before the 19th Convention of our Party, Comrade Winston called for "an accelerated tempo of work" on the part of all Communists of every level of responsibility to do those necessary things for further building the Party, and what he said then remains most applicable now as a challenge for each of our readers: "We live in times," said Henry Winston, "in which class and revolutionary consciousness can mature in days and weeks where it would take months and years in so-called normal times. . . . We live in times in which the Communist Party can and must be built quickly, particularly in the shops, and this is the most important organizational imperative before us. . . .. We can undertake this work because we have justifiable faith in our Party. We have faith in our Party because we have faith in our class, and because we have that faith in our class, we have unbounded faith in the future!''

In the respective countries of the world, it is the Party of the Communists which is at the helm of the modern revolutionary movements for the social emancipation of the working class, of the fighters against national oppression, and of all forces in battle against capitalist exploitation and imperialist bondage.

The workers themselves, Karl Marx foretold over a hundred years ago, "will have to do the most for their final victory by becoming enlightened as to their class interests, by taking up their own independent party position as soon as possible. . . ." His colleague, Frederick Engels, added that, "For the proletariat to be strong enough to conquer on the day of decision . . . it is necessary that it should form its own party . . . a conscious class party." (Marx and Engels, *Selected Correspondence,* Moscow: Progress Publishers, 1965, p. 409.)

Some 30 years after Engels' comment was written in a letter to a colleague, such a party of the working class, headed by Lenin, put an end forever to capitalism's world monopoly with the establishment of the workers' power and the first socialist society in one of the biggest countries—Russia.

The Communist Party is indeed a center from which the most advanced representatives of the working class and its allies, the oppressed Black people first of all, are "becoming enlightened as to their class interests," and the most effective ways to advance them, through their membership and participation in its activities.

The Communist Party is a mass leadership organization of the working class (Black and white as well as Chicano, Puerto Rican and other minority nationalities). It strives to contribute effectively to the cause of the working people and their allies in battle for immediate demands and longer range goals. It draws its membership from among the most thoughtful and dedicated participants in struggles of the people for relief from "the violence and plunder, the blood and mud," the class exploitation and racist injustice that is the common fare of the masses under the reign of the capitalists. The Communist Party is the party of leadership of the working class struggle and of social revolution. It considers reforms gained within the confines of the capitalist system not as the objects of the class struggle of the working class but mere by-products of the revolutionary process, which must be crowned with the ousting from power of the monopolists and their replacement by the working class and its allies; by the replacement of capitalism by socialism.

The Communist Party elaborates general (strategic) policies and specific and limited (tactical) plans to guide its work. Such policies and plans are drawn up on the basis of a profound analysis of the actual developing situation. Such an analysis of reality is the starting point in arriving at sound policy for furthering the interests of the working class and the cause of progress. But to properly perceive and correctly assess the meaning and requirements of a given course of development, one needs the tools of science to assist the process of determining the correct course to take. There is such a social science—Marxism-Leninism. The Communist Party utilizes this science to illuminate problems of relationship and direction, of ways and means most effective for practice. Marxism-Leninism offers a scientific theory of social development. Indeed, it embraces the general theory, the living science of social revolution, with its concrete stages of development and corresponding strategical and tactical requirements.

The structure of the Party, its system of organization, is patterned to most effectively participate and exert maximum influence upon the developing democratic and revolutionary process; to participate within and alongside of the organizations of the anti-monopoly forces, of the working class movement, of the Black people's freedom front. The individual has membership in a given shop club, college club, or neighborhood club. Through their club life members strive to improve their knowledge and effectiveness in the mass struggles of the people. They carry on activity and education for the program of the Party and for socialism. They work to enlarge the influence and membership of the Party. The members elect delegates to regular conventions which in turn elect leading committees for the respective local, state or national organizational level. Conventions also elect leadership.

The Party insures istself of the authority to carry out its program and policies through a system of voluntary discipline based on the principle of the binding obligation of the decision of the majority on any disputed question after debate is concluded.

The Communist Party is a participating partisan of all of the struggles of the masses seeking to scale the heights to gain the highroad of social progress, the road that leads to the true emancipation of labor from exploitation and the oppressed peoples from tyranny, the open road to socialism. At the same time, its vision and understanding, its advanced theory and policies—which are based not merely on a full knowledge of the current reality but on the generalized historical and world-wide experience of the working class, its Marxist-Leninist science of revolution—place it in a forward position in relationship to the best organized columns of the most revolutionary class. The Communist Party also goes ahead of the class as its scouting party, its trail blazer, so to speak. From such advanced posts it is able to provide directional signals to the leading forces and main army of the working class and its allies.

At the same time the Party fulfills positions of responsibility throughout the ranks of the workers organizations, at all levels of the struggle. On the merits of their contributions Communists are advanced to leadership of the working class as the organizational form of the revolutionary process advances.

The strength of the Communists lies in their close ties with the masses of the working people; in the unity of their own ranks; in the maturity and soundness of their leadership based upon their thorough knowledge of the scene as illuminated by the revolutionary arts and science of Marxism-Leninism.

The Communist Party is not only a leadership influence within the mass organizations of the working class and its allies; it is the vital political party of the working class and all those who are oppressed by capitalism. It confidently aspires to formally represent the class as a whole in elective offices of the mass organizations—especially the trade unions, and in local, state and national political offices.

The Communist Party aspires to be the leading party of the working class in the daily struggles and final confrontations with capitalism. It is confident that on its merits it will win the right to leadership of the working class during each stage on the route to power, and after.

Political Affairs, New York, September, 1973

part II

Black Liberation

. . . everyone knows that the position of the Negroes in America in general *is one unworthy of a civilized country–capitalism* cannot *give either* complete *emancipation or even complete equality. . . . Shame on America for the plight of the Negroes!*

V. I. Lenin

20   Adventurism Versus Black Liberation

Like every decent-minded person, the progressive columnist, Mr. I. F. Stone, was angered and shocked by the enormity of the Florida "justice" which prepares the legal lynching of Walter Lee Irvin—an innocent Black youth, already lynch-maimed—just after the lynching murder of Mr. and Mrs. Harry T. Moore, leaders of the National Association for the Advancement of Colored People (NAACP). Under this stimulus, Mr. Stone tells us, he set down his uninhibited thoughts on the Black people. Mr. Stone forewarned his readers that he would express himself "ignorantly, brashly, and presumptuously." This is indeed an unfortunate preparation for so serious a task as the consideration of such a matter as the destiny of the fifteen million Black people in the United States, whose fate is indissolubly linked with that of the entire American population. That his article, "Who Will Free the Negroes?" in the *Compass* of February 17, 1952, evidences in truth a full measure of "ignorance, brashness and presumptuousness," on the author's part does not, however, eliminate its importance.

The significance of Stone's article lies in the fact that he has brought together and expressed in abbreviated form, in the space of a single column—elements of the highest level of consciousness on the Black question thus far obtaining among non-Marxist liberals (Black and white), as well as the main incorrect policies, the chief ideological and tactical errors presently discernable in the movement for Black emancipation from oppression. In addition, Mr. Stone. in the article as a whole, applies a peculiar exceptionalism to Black people in the United States with regard to social action, as though they were merely an undifferentiated, oppressed mass, unstratified by class division, and in some mysterious way capable of moving "Right," "Left," or "Center" at the command of a leader-agency.

No, Mr. Stone, the Black community is not so uncomplicated! Unity has to be forged in struggle (external and internal)! The leaders will secure their authority and win the allegiance of the Black masses in conflict and struggle with false leaders and wrong policies. Moreover, their effectiveness as leaders will depend on the correctness of their program, and the energy and ability they display in organizing the masses to struggle for their aims. Is this not the outlook in regard to the presently split labor movement currently saddled with a corrupt and imperialist-minded leadership? Is this not the outlook in respect to the peaceful and progressive aspirations of the bulk of the American people now so shamelessly betrayed by the jingoism and demagogy of the twin Parties in power?

But, let us start from the beginning and deal with the main content in Mr. Stone's article. We find, first of all, certain things in Mr. Stone's article which are to be welcomed. Mr. Stone has awakened to a certain recognition of the objective fact of the national character and status of the Black people in the United States.

In defining the Black people as a "submerged nation within a nation" he resurrects Otto Bauer's idiocy of a nation being simply a cultural linkage of common ethnic units. The religious obscurantists and the racialists, not only the Bundists in old Poland and Russia, relied on the slogan of "cultural autonomy". (Cheap! It cost the ruling tyranny no land!) Catholicism, Zionism, Moslemism, Hinduism, Aryanism, all utilize "cultural autonomy" for their reactionary ends. Therefore, the formulation of the status of the Black people in the United States as being "a nation within a nation," though indicative of a step forward in the development of Mr. Stone's understanding of the Blacks' status, is neither scientifically accurate nor sufficient as a popular presentation of the question.

Mr. Stone has more than once written admiringly of the development of the Anglo-Saxon juridical system. Now, looking upon the attempted legal lynching of Walter Lee Irvin, and back over the whole 300-year history of the Black people in the United States, he comes to the conclusion that American law is, as far as the Black is concerned, but the codification of an all-pervading white supremacist doctrine and practice, a white chauvinism that is as organic a part of the vaunted Americanism of our national ego as any other of its "living traditions." He despairs of the "sterile" legal process ever grinding out justice to free Black Americans. "In any community," Mr. Stone writes, "the law is fundamentally the law of the dominant race or class. America's law is white man's law." We would add the word "rich" to "white man's law," and then hasten to agree with this thought of Mr. Stone. The law is not only designed to buttress the interest of the oppressor in its domination of the oppressed, but most particularly it is drawn to serve the even narrower interest of the wealthiest class segment of the oppressor people. Indeed the Black people, after Martinsville, Laurel, Ocala, and Cairo, can entertain few illusions about the "sterile legalisms" of the courts and the "law" to protect or secure their rights. But is this to say the Black people should abandon the courts and the "law" as an arena (and at times a weapon) of struggle? We say, of course not! Mr. Stone does not make clear the difference between reliance upon the courts and the law as opposed to seeking advantage, tactically, of utilizing even the jaundiced chambers of mock class-justice for the struggle.

In his article Mr. Stone manifests a shocked awareness of the "brutality, irrationality and savagery" of white chauvinist practices leveled against the Blacks in the United States. He is appalled at the evidence that this rampaging virus of white supremacy cannibalism has infected such widespread strata of the white population who share, more or less, a direct responsibility for its continuation; that all white people to some extent share in the guilt and are a party to the genocidal crime against the Black people; that actively or passively, they are beneficiaries, recipients of material and psychological privileges compounded out of the misery, exploitation and indignities heaped upon the Black masses.

Says Stone, ". . . every white man to some degree benefits from cheap Negro labor, if not in his factory, then in his home." And, again, he declares: " 'The People' as white people are responsible for what happens to the Negro and should be allowed no scapegoats." And Stone states furthermore, that, "Like Armenians living among the Turks in the old days, or Jews in Hitler Germany, Negroes live in America among white people indoctrinated from childhood with hostile and hateful attitudes."

Unlike many liberals who are given to a simple-minded and deliberate minimizing of the gravity and danger of the cancer of anti-Black racism to all sections of the white population, Mr. Stone sees with horror the breadth and scope of the white supremacy corruption that has so deeply imbedded itself in the consciousness and practices of so large a section of the white people in the United States and is warp and woof of the whole legal, governmental, cultural and economic structure. While appreciating the spirit, the "heat reaction" of Mr. Stone's "discovery" of the denseness of the fog of white chauvinism over the minds of millions in this country, we must point to the basic error of his contention that the toiling white masses have an economic stake in the perpetuation of the oppression of the Black people. On the contrary, to paraphrase a famous observation of Karl Marx in reference to the English working class vis-a-vis Irish freedom: the abominations of the U.S. whites have a main source in the segregation, discrimination and oppression of the Black Americans.

That *the economic and political beneficiary of the super-exploitation and national oppression of the Black people is the white capitalist ruling class and not the white toiling masses* should necessitate no documentation. The profits accruing from greater exploitation of the Black masses are utilized to batten down the hatches of the whole working class and popular masses in their striving to expand their living standards and political liberties. As Lenin wrote, "a people which oppresses another cannot itself be free." The super-profit taken from the special robbery of the Black people does not go into the white worker's wage envelope, but into the money bags of the bosses. The bosses in turn use part of this special increment from the Jim Crow exploitation of the Black people to buy congressmen to rivet more Taft-Hartley laws, wage freezes, and other links in the chains which bind all labor—Black and white—to capital's golden chariot. They also use portions of their super-profits to subsidize the Ku Klux Klan and Dixiecrats. Still other portions are "invested" in tinseled crumbs of special privileges—material and psychological—to certain sections of the skilled white workers and to a few Black intellectuals, whose role it is to divert the working masses, Black and white, from the path of unity and solidarity; to prime the pump of the Jim Crow system for generating ever more super-profits for the imperialist. Also, Mr. Stone overlooks the fact of the existence of a not inconsiderable progressive wing within the labor movement which fights consciously for Black-white unity and against the super-exploitation of the Black workers.

However, the conclusion Mr. Stone arrives at from the cited "observations" is the most dangerous kind of defeatist nonsense. He concludes that "all white people" are incurably saturated with anti-Black hatred and it is futile "drivel" for the Blacks to orient their strategy for liberation on the possibility of effecting a fighting alliance with the white working masses. He scorns the possibility that the white masses are capable of understanding the economic and political necessity, in their own real self-interest, to give up the "privileges" of their anti-Black prejudices and to join the struggle for Black freedom. Here Mr.

Stone surrounds the incarcerated Black people of 15 million by an undifferentiated, united, solid, all-class mass of 135 million hate-hardened white people and bids the Black to fight his way free! No, thanks, Mr. Stone, we must reject this "brash" (also provocative, irresponsible and criminal!) invitation to national suicide. (A super-"Leftist" position pushed to the extreme always comes to coincide with its "Right" counterpart; the Dixiecrats demanded that Blacks "submit, retreat to genocide"; our author advises "to hell with allies, advance to genocide!")

Of course, Mr. Stone protests he is ". . . not suggesting that white people are irremediably bad in their dealing with Negroes . . ."—but all his arguments belie this self-serving qualification. This is precisely what he has argued to establish and this cannot be escaped with a debater's trick!

Mr. Stone would hardly deny the role of consciousness and the capacity of the white masses to undertake social action in respect to such vital questions before the people which he has championed, and continues to champion as defense of peace and democratic rights and the advancement of economic security. Is it not strange that Mr. Stone is so defeatist about the ability of the white masses to awaken to a consciousness of where their true self-interest lies in respect to the fight for Black freedom?

In short, Mr. Stone urges Blacks in the United States to develop a national consciousness and give it material expression in a centralized united organization of a particular type. This is excellent advice and in one form or another is a long standing aspiration ever alive in the hopes of masses of thoughtful Blacks. The question however, remains: How is such organizational unity to be materialized? What are the obstacles to its realization that have to be overcome and how? On what programmatic basis is this unity to be fought for and forged? What shall be the limited and long-term strategic goals? What shall be its forms of struggle? What strata of the dominant white population will it look to for support, strategic alliance, tactical agreements, temporary mutual-interest coalitions? How does the movement utilize the contradictions besetting U.S. imperialism in the world arena by virtue of the growth of the camp of socialism, the national revolutions in the colonies, the expanding world-wide peace front, etc.?

Mr. Stone is either obscure, contradictory or silent on these vital questions. Neither national consciousness nor its matured reflection in a single, united all-class Black liberation movement will come to pass spontaneously at the behest of a seer or philosopher (be he ever so wise). It has to be organized and fought for, and will finally emerge as a result of the overcoming of the ideological and tactical differences which have their base in the respective class divisions existing within the community of Black people. It is exceptionalist sophistry to argue otherwise.

We turn now to a particular examination of certain ideas expressed by Mr. Stone which, if not relentlessly combated within and in respect to the Black liberation movement, would constitute most dangerous retarding factors in its development.

What does Mr. Stone offer as a strategy for altering the relation of forces in favor of the Black people's freedom struggle? Nothing! On the contrary, he "alters" the relation of forces permanently in behalf of the despoilers of Black freedom. Stone presents the white people of all classes as a solid phalanx arrayed in determined and eternal opposition to the liberation aspirations of the Blacks.

According to Stone, ". . . to look for any kind of mass white support in the Negro's struggle for full emancipation is a waste of time." Furthermore, he contends, "if anything, in the South itself, the so-called 'common man' is far more brutal, irrational and savage in his attitude toward the Negro than the upper class. 'The people' sit on juries. 'The people' man the police forces. 'The people' make up the lynch mobs. . . ." From this he arrives at the conviction that "The Negro and his white friends [From the above remarks of Mr. Stone, one is a little startled to discover that the Black still has white friends!] need to break away from nonsensical stereotypes which pretend that somehow what happens to the Black in America is not the work 'of the people.' This is democratic mythology and ideological drivel."

Here we have the outlandish proposal that the Black freedom movement should abandon as "a waste of time" any strategy of advancement based on forming a fighting alliance with white workers, poor farmers, or other oppressed strata of the white population. Here we are presented with a playback of the combined chorus of the Faulkners, of the Southern Regionalists and assorted Black bourgeois nationalists from Booker T. Washington to Marcus Garvey to E. Kinkle Jones.

Is white chauvinist doctrine and conduct widespread among the white working masses and within the trade union movement? Of course it is! But the decisive factor that must be grasped is that this white supremacy ideology and shameful conduct stand in open contradiction to, and conflicts with, the economic, political and cultural interests, necessities and aspirations of the white toiling masses. Therefore, in their own self-interest, they are compelled to shed these anti-Black prejudices in one area after another in order to defend and advance their economic and social interests against their capitalist ruling class exploiters. Hence the material basis for alliance between the Black people's movement for freedom and the working class movement for economic, political and cultural progress is an objective reality, not "ideological drivel," as Mr. Stone scornfully asserts. The big task of the enlightened "white friends" and of the Black people's leadership is to bring this consciousness to the labor movement and popular masses in order that the white working people will be enabled to take action on the basis of an understanding of the true situation.

Furthermore, Mr. Stone insists that the white working masses "are more brutal in their attitude toward the Negro than the upper class." In his endeavor to confront the struggling Black people with a solid front of white antagonists, to make his arguments against the struggle for Black-white unity, Mr. Stone does not address himself to the question: Who, today, what class segment of the white population, controls the reins of almost total power and keeps the Black people in subjection? Who, indeed, but the genteel lynchers of Wall Street and Washington who coin $4.5 billion annually from the direct economic robbery of the Black alone! Are not Wall Street's "gentlemen," the Truman-MacArthur-Dulles camp, more guilty of the massacre of Korea's millions than the soldiers who have put the torch to the Korean nation?

Yes, we rightly demand the death penalty for the lynchers, but we never forget or forgive the inspirers and organizers of the mob who are never found at the scene of the crime but observe all the social amenities of polite society in the Big House of the ruling class. Moreover, where Black-white unity was achieved, as in the Abolitionist movement, during Reconstruction, in the Populist effort, in labor struggles, it has been with the white masses.

If the Black people's movement hearkened to Mr. Stone's advice on this score the path would lead to isolation and destruction.

Since Mr. Stone's main poisonous advice to Blacks referred to above, namely, "to cast off all considerations of effecting alliance with the working class movement and go it alone," is throretically indefensible, we are prepared for his next amazing proposal, which amounts in fact to ideological nihilism. Writes Mr. Stone: "Neither 19th century liberalism nor 20th century proletarianism is enough for the Blacks. The conceptions of the brotherhood of man and the solidarity of labor are not adequate for his plight."

All other peoples require social theory to give consciousness and direction to their social action in order to advance their cause of liberation and social progress. But for the Black people Mr. Stone rejects the crystallized experiences and most advanced thinking of the various peoples of the world, the product of over 2,000 years of struggle by the oppressed against their oppressors. The absurdity of Mr. Stone's position becomes more evident. One need only add that the Marxist-Leninist position on the national question has proven its vital and indispensable service to the strivings of enslaved peoples to attain their national liberation in the past and it continues to do so among every unfree people in the world. The Black people, in the solution of their problem of national liberation, precisely because of singular obstacles in their path, needs not less, but more of the enlightening wisdom of the Marxist-Leninist science of liberation. This science provides a tested compass, a guide to correct action, fusing theory with practice.

After isolating the Blacks from their only logical allies, depriving them of the aid of all known theories of progressive social change, Mr. Stone now tells them to march forth against the white multitudes and free themselves. "Who'll free the Negroes?" Mr. Stone asks rhetorically in half the title of his article—and answers in the other half, "They must do it themselves." The great Black leader of the Abolitionist movement, Frederick Douglass, some hundred years ago, formulated the rejoinder to Mr. Stone's query much better in the following way: "He who would be free must himself strike the *first* blow." To strike the first blow doesn't mean the same as "go it alone." The whole concept of Douglass' great and successful leadership of the Abolitionist movement was based on the central strategic importance of building alliances of the Black slaves linking up their interests to those of a majority force of the American people to overpower the slavemasters' oligarchy.

Now, let us see what advice Mr. Stone has to offer his "Light Brigade" on the eve of its fated brave charge, in the way of battle plan and tactics. But without ridicule, seriously now, what suggestion has Mr. Stone offered in the article under examination in the field of tactics to the leaders of the Black liberation movement. They are nothing more than the carrying out of retaliatory terrorist adventures by "hero-bands," individuals whose deeds, it is presumed, would ignite the "doleful" and "slumbering" Black masses into some kind of spontaneous revolutionary upsurge which would carry the day for freedom. Let us quote Mr. Stone's "thought" just the way he "brashly" puts it down:

"The most terrible blow struck against the British in Palestine by the Jews was when the Irgunists whipped British officers in retaliation against the whipping of Irgunists. These blows resounded throughout the Middle East." And he adds: . . . "Why should Negroes permit a Negro to be killed by a sherrif or a cop withour retaliating physically?"

Indeed, there are times and circumstances when physical self-defense is mandatory for individuals as well as entire communities when beset by would-be murderers and pogromists, and the whole history of the Black people in this country is replete with numerous courageous illustrations of this truth. But this has nothing to do with what Mr. Stone is suggesting. He is advocating that the Black liberation movement should adopt terror (or counter-terror) as a tactical policy, a principle, a basic technique of liberation. Mr. Stone, who claims to be "anti-ideology" when it comes to the question of the Black freedom fight, is here revealed as offering up to the Black people the long since buried corpse of noxious anarchist "theory" as a tactical guide for the liberation movement! Here Mr. Stone adopts the pose familiar in the early stages of all revolutionary social movements: whose impetuous young firebrands who envision themselves in heroic messianic postures, rolling back seas with their own two hands for the sheep-like masses, chasing history before them.

It is well to recall that those impatient petty-bourgeois intellectuals; those cultists who go into ecstasies over every formless and directionless elemental explosion from the crowd; those clever inventors of short-cuts, of gimmicks to set the wheels of social change in motion, historically have succeeded only in destroying themselves, wrecking the organizational machinery and throwing back the purposeful, conscious movement of the genuine social action of the masses toward freedom. The doctrine of terror (or counter-terror) is as inevitably a companion piece of bourgeois nationalism as is its opposite number: capitulation and accommodation to the continuation of a modified domination by the imperialist oppressor. Objectively, both tendencies are in the service of the oppressor power. From Bakunin down, the ideologists of terror tactics ended up in the employ of the oppressor power. Just so today, the practitioners of terror tactics and CIA operatives often are in the hire of the Wall Street general staff seeking world domination and plunder. We must be on guard against the siren songsters of terror tactics and anarchistic action, no matter how sweetly their melodies might touch sympathetic chords in some outraged hearts. We must recognize and dare to characterize them for what they are—agents provocateurs! This is something for Mr. Stone to think about.

Mr. Stone's article is interlarded with many more confused and contradictory statements and half truths than we have here subjected to analysis and they will be apparent to the thoughtful reader. We would suggest to Mr. Stone that he do a great deal more serious study and examination, and that he engage in somewhat more practical services in regard to the Black freedom fight before rushing into print with another column full of "advice" to the Black people's leaders.

*   *   *

What do we see as the general course of development of the Black people's freedom fight? Briefly put, it is that the unity of the Black people is being and will continue to be forged and will create ever higher organizational forms; first of all, around the commonly acclaimed demands and aspirations voiced by all classes of the Black people—namely, an end to disfranchisement and discrimination, for equal rights and opportunities. Subsequently, demands may be advanced of a more distinctly anti-monopoly people's and working class character.

The Black liberation movement will strive to develop a stable alliance with the progressive labor movement and all other democratic strata of the white population; it will gain strength from, and in turn rely on, the forces of peace, democracy, anti-colonialism and socialism in the world arena.

Its tactics will be based on those forms of mass struggle that are familiar to, capable of being understood by, and readily entered into, by the masses at any given period. It must resolutely combat and reject all "Left" adventurism and Right capitulationism in its own ranks and constantly strive to introduce higher levels of consciousness into the actions of the masses, bringing clarity and perspective to their struggles.

Political Affairs, March, 1952

21   Universal Suffrage — the Gauge of
The Maturity of the Working Class

The Southern state governments and their block of representatives and senators in the Congress enjoy no shadow of a popular mandate. They derive their authority from a narrowly restricted electorate of moneyed white people, political job holders and ignorant lackeys of iron-fisted Democratic Party machines. They rule in the exclusive interest of this narrowly drawn electorate and of Wall Street and its Southern minions of plantation, mine and factory.

In the whole comity of nations of the world, no other country except South Africa can lay claim to have disfranchised so many people in so many "free elections" for so long a time and still have the gall to proclaim itself a democracy!

From 1877 down to the present day, the systematic exclusion of Blacks from the "democratic process of marking a ballot on voting day" remains for the ten million Black people of the South the barely breached law of the land. Some six Southern states (Alabama, Mississippi, Virginia, Arkansas, South Carolina and Texas), with the largest percentage of Blacks to the population, still retain the poll tax. This poll tax is cumulative in some states like Alabama, for example.

In addition to the poll tax, there are the infamous powers exercised by Boards of Registrars with absolute authority to determine a would-be voter's "educational and character" qualifications required for exercising his constitutional right of suffrage.

A number of other "legal" devices, laws and practices are in force throughout the Southern states, designed to effectively frustrate any local move to sizably increase the electorate beyond that which the "State House" machines can control. (The classic exhibit of machine control of the elections and all public political life in a Southern state, is provided in the instance of Tennessee which has been under the autocratic domination of the Crump machine—with poll tax and now without the poll tax—for some forty years. Or, one can point to the unrelieved control by the Byrd machine in Virginia's political life for the past thirty years.)

However, the primary means of disfranchising the Southern toiling masses in general, and the Black people particularly, used by the ruling oligarchy, is neither of these "legalisms" but *pure and simple police and Klan terror*. This organized terror against would-be Black voters runs the gamut from threats and loss of employment to beatings, house-bombings, cross burnings, police murders and mob lynchings. One need only recall the bomb-assassinations of Mr. and Mrs. Harry Moore in Florida, or the shooting to death of Maceo Snipes in Georgia while they were actively campaigning to get Black citizens the right to register for voting.

The present fight of the Black people in the South to exercise their federally constituted right of franchise is a highly important sector of the front of struggle of the oppressed Black people for equal rights and liberation. And it is furthermore a vital *offensive battle* in the resistance movement of the entire working people and popular masses against the continual encroachments being made by the imperialist ruling circle of the government upon their hard-won general democratic rights and constitutional liberties.

The valorous fight that Southern Blacks are putting up to exercise their suffrage rights must not be viewed by the workers and democratic-minded people in the rest of the country as merely a heroic spectacle of a courageous people, objects of plaudits and inspiration. Rather, *this fight of the Southern Blacks for the ballot must become the fight, the cherished cause, of all fair-minded people everywhere in the country, and of the labor movement in the first instance*.

National developments and world events have infused this simple endeavor of the Southern Blacks to right an ancient wrong done them (their disfranchisement) with a new quality, an added feature of enormous significance. Success or defeat in this fight of Southern Blacks for the ballot will bear directly upon the determination of the major question of our times for our country and the world: the question of war or peace; reaction or progress.

What an enormous vitalizing and democratizing effect it would have upon the voters (and indirectly upon the entire electoral process in the United States) if the five million or more ballots of the presently vote-less, freedom-aspiring, progressive-minded, oppressed Black citizens of the South were counted on the issues and candidates which are to decisively determine the course of the government in the next immediate period ahead! Can anyone doubt that these votes would tip the scales decisively in favor of peace, liberation and social progress and against the cold and hot war machinations of the ruling Wall Street clique; in favor of restoring and deepening the democratic foundations against the reactionaries and all their racist practices and usurpations of the peoples liberties?

Indeed, all of this democratic promise and more is inherent in this struggle for the right of the Black masses of the South to vote. It is the inescapable duty and obligation of the labor movement and all progressive forces to take up this fight (in their own self-interest), support it in every way, and help enlarge it beyond its present guerrilla proportions, to make of it a national crusade, the property of all decent minded, democracy-loving citizens wherever they live and whatever be their political party allegiance.

The post-Civil War history of the principal upsurges in the struggle of the Black people in the United States for full suffrage rights reveals that they never approached the struggle as an isolated fight based on abstract justice. On the contrary, Blacks always related their cardinal democratic demand for "manhood suffrage" to the interests and general progressive welfare of all the people. They related, and sought to align the movement for Black suffrage in particular, and equal democratic rights in general, to the dominant progressive note then being struck in the political life of the country. This, for example, is seen in the following instances of big upsurges in the Black suffrage movement.

In the post-Civil War "Black Codes" (statutes which nullified the Constitutional rights of Black citizens) years the great Frederick Douglass, at the head of the Black liberation movement, boldly aligned that movement with the swelling militant movement for women's suffrage.

In the first two decades of the 20th century, the sagacious and scholarly W.E.B. Du Bois sought allies for Black suffrage from the widespread "populist" and muckraking "trust-busters" movements.

From the latter half of the 1930's to the late 1940's, the right-to-vote movement received its greatest impetus and its principal leadership from the Southern Negro Youth Congress. The Black suffrage movement at this phase of its development was related to labor's strivings toward independent political action. This period marked a high point in the national interest engendered, and participation achieved, in behalf of Black suffrage. A National Committee to Abolish the Poll Tax came into being, and was joined by scores of trade unions, fraternal, social, civic and religious organizations. This movement received financial and moral support from the Congress of Industrial Organizations (C1O) and several big affiliates of the American Federation of Labor (AFL) and Railroad Brotherhoods. The late Congressman Lee Geyer of California and the "New Deal Bloc" of Congressmen introduced and fought for a bill to abolish the poll tax.

The fruits of this edition of the "vote movement" had its most dramatic manifestation in the widespread mass militant fight of Blacks throughout the South to become registered to vote in the 1949 elections, when the Black vote in the South reached its post-Reconstruction peak of over a half-million. It is estimated that the Black vote in the South reached one million in 1952 and one and a half million in 1956.

Therefore, the experiences of previous peaks in the history of the Black right-to-vote movement teaches, and the present situation dictates, that the movement of the Southern Black people for universal suffrage *must also in this period align itself with a broad cardinal, progressive force in our national political life. Such a force is the peace and anti-imperialist movement in our country and the world.*

Peace is the banner under which all decent, all fair minded, all democratic, forward looking and progressive individuals, groupings and classes must inevitably assemble. Inexorably all "good people" will be moved to take up the banner of the struggle for peace to safeguard the future of mankind from the unbridled savagery of a "final world war."

This peace momement, therefore, is the great, wide force at the heart of our country's political life with which the broad movement of the Black people for suffrage rights must seek bonds of solidarity and connections of mutual aid. The elemental Black suffrage movement of the South aligned with the peace movement of the country would mightily bolster the popular defense against the outbreak of world war and would be a brake upon the offensive of the reactionaries in government against the rights of labor and the democratic provisions of the Constitution.

What is now urgently required is to supplement the heroic, direct assault that the Southern Black people are making upon the sheriffs' registrars in the fight for the ballot, with a broadly based nationwide movement in behalf of the enactment of federal legislation to enforce the free suffrage provisions of the federal Constitution.

All the forces sincerely concerned with the preservation and extension of democratic practices and institutions in our country are challenged by the brave actions of the Southern Blacks to wrest the ballot from the mailed fist of the poll-taxers, to take measures now toward guaranteeing that a "Fair Registration and Voting Practices Bill" or an amendment to the Civil Rights Act—with strict enforcement powers—will be introduced and enacted into law in the early days of the 1959 legislative session of Congress. The popular and democratic forces in the labor and people's organizations throughout the country should undertake the convening of a *national conference for suffrage for Southerners*. Limiting itself to this one issue, the right to vote (the elementary hallmark of even the most primitive democracy), such a conference could initiate a program for uniting the overwhelming majority of Americans in support of the freedom to vote for the ten million Blacks and additional millions of disfranchised whites in the South.

The convening of such a broad conference, the launching of such a really mass and nation-wide crusade, is not just the concern of the Blacks alone; it is in the highest interest of all who cherish what remains of their own freedom and all those who look forward to the enrichment and extension of democracy in our land.

It is of urgent concern to, and the responsibility of all labor unions and of the progressive unions particularly. It is in the direct interest and the responsibility of the growing organized peace camp. It is the solemn responsibility of the bloc of progressive voters and aspiring progressive office seekers in our country. It is the obligation of the Communists to aid in every way the elevation of this vital democratic demand of the Black people and oppressed poor whites into the consciousness of the organized American people, that it might develop the necessary scope and power to achieve success.

Communists, who are orientated by the compass of Marxist-Leninist science, above all others, must appreciate and energetically fight for such a partial democratic reform as this: because it is right, and just and would represent some measure of dignity to an outrageously oppressed people. But this does not yet exhaust the vital significance of this particular development in the freedom struggle of the Black people. This development takes place in the historic epoch of the general crisis of world imperialism, in the particular conditions of a sharpening world-wide struggle between the forces of peace, anti-colonialism and democracy on the one hand, and the forces of war, fascism and rapacious imperialist expansionism—the monopoly ruling circle—on the other. Therefore, in such a setting, every really popular movement of the people for democratic reforms—no matter how elementary the demands—is pregnant with the seeds of enormous possibilities for favorably altering the social forces in the direction of sweeping progressive advancements for the working class, the Black masses and all their democratic allies.

"Universal suffrage is thus the guage of the maturity of the working class." Frederick Engels, the co-founder of scientific socialism, i.e., Marxism, pointed out this basic truth some 68 years ago. He stated, furthermore, that "It cannot and never will be anything more in the modern state, but that is enough. On the day when the thermometer of universal suffrage shows boiling-point among the workers, they as well as the capitalists will know where they stand." (F. Engels, *The Origin of the Family, Private Property and the State,* New York: International Publishers, 1973. p. 232)

Memo to Southern Regional Committee, C.P., USA, June, 1955

22   Class Forces in
The Black People's Movement

U.S. capitalism's more "efficient" and thorough-going super-exploitation of the Black masses has transformed the Black people from primarily an exploited peasantry into a more productive base of super-profit—into basically an exploited and oppressed working people. It is this working class strata of the Black people—dominant for the people as a whole and constantly increasing in the South as well—which will progressively stamp the Black people's freedom movement with its own image. The high proportion of the Black people who are working people means that the Black Freedom Movement will increasingly reflect in its program, policies, leadership, alliances, immediate and long-range goals the influence and will of the working class.

This is a feature in the prospects for development of the Black Liberation Movement which is quite different from that usually associated with national movements of colonial economies, wherein the weight of the petty-bourgeois peasant class groupings is very heavy, if not decisive. The proportionate numerical strength of the class forces within the Black movement is decisively on the side of the workers. This circumstance favors that *ultimate* dominance of the policies of the working class and the leadership of the working class in the Black people's movement, which is indispensable for the triumph of the cause of Black liberation over all manner of oppression.

As Lenin observed: "The world-wide experience of bourgeois and landlord governments has developed two methods of keeping the people in subjection. The first is violence. . . . But there is another method. . . . That is the method of deception, flattery, fine phrases, numberless promises, petty sops, and concessions of the unessential while retaining the essential. . . . But from day to day trustful naivete and naive trustfulness will diminish, especially among the proletarians and poor peasants, who are being taught by experience (by their social and economic position) to distrust the capitalists." (V.I. Lenin, *Collected Works,* Moscow: Progress Publishers, 1965. Vol. 24, pp. 63-64)

This key fact, in the final analysis, will determine the basic orientation and ultimate character of the Black people's movement for equal rights and liberation. It will propel that movement in the direction of conscious anti-imperialist, anti-monopoly, anti-capitalist struggle in combination with and under the leadership of the working class.

At the present stage of its development, the Black people's movement puts forth a program of elementary democratic demands for equality of citizenship rights, economic opportunities, and social justice. It struggles against all forms of racial segregation and discrimination, and demands full political, economic and social equality for Blacks as individual citizens and as a people. It seeks to organize the united strength of Black people of all classes in active struggle for these immediate common demands. Likewise, it strives to enroll the active participation and support of the broadest strata of white people in the struggle for these equal rights demands of the Black people.

The common bondage of racial and national oppression to which the whole of the Black people are subjected makes possible the coalition of the diverse class strata of the Black people in struggle for their freedom.

The working class strata of the Black population is the first and most important of the social forces which make up the Black people's freedom movement.

The workers are the most numerous strata of the Black people and are constantly increasing their proportion in the total Black population, as the petty-bourgeois class strata of the rural masses suffer decline.

The social action of the Black workers is the most potent force in the Black people's movement because the Black workers, like their white class brothers, are strategically positioned at the very vitals of the oppressing capitalist class production system—in the mines, mills and factories.

The Black workers are an integral part of the U.S. working class—brothers with the white workers in toil and struggle against capitalist exploitation. Black workers seek the support of the entire working class for the struggle of the Black people for equal rights and freedom from racial oppression. They are an important integral part of the working class, being 31 percent of all industrial workers—the number of Black workers in such key industries as steel, auto, transport, longshore are of decisive importance. Consequently they are able to help insure the participation of large sections of the working class in the Black people's freedom struggles.

Because of their dual identity—with the struggles and aspirations of the Black people for freedom from racial oppression, on the one hand, and with the struggles and aspirations of the working class for freedom from capitalist exploitation and political domination, on the other—the Black workers represent that numerically dominant force within the Black people's freedom movement which insures the correlation, the partnership, the development of deeper and closer relations of alliance and solidarity between the Black people's movement and the working class movement on issues of immediate interest and, ultimately, on questions of strategic objectives.

There is no greater task for the Communists and advanced workers to fulfill in connection with the working class than that of furthering the bonds of class unity between Black and white workers. At all times Communists must stand in the forefront of the struggle to smash every remaining color bar and anti-Black prejudice, practice, or manifestation of racial prejudice in the trade union and other working class organizations. Communists must always stand forth as tireless fighters for full equality of Black workers in the life and affairs of the trade unions. Communists must ceaselessly work to influence the trade unions to struggle for full equality in job rights in all branches of industry for Black workers—in employment, equal pay for equal work, job classification, upgrading, training and promotion. All racial exclusiveness in the employment and job classification practices in the industries and enterprises must end. Communists must be outstanding in influencing and sharing in the completion of the urgent work of the labor movement to organize the millions of unorganized Black and white workers —particularly in the South—into the trade unions.

Communists must be tireless in organizing and stimulating the labor movement to champion the freedom demands of the Black people, and to render every material and moral support to the concrete struggles of the Black people for political, economic and social equality and freedom from national oppression, segregation, disfranchisement, and discrimination.

The strata of the Black population which is of the urban middle class are indeed a small percentage of the total Black people. Yet, individuals from this strata play an uncommonly important role in the Black people's movement. The professionals, small business people—by virtue of their greater articulateness and technical proficiency—largely dominate the leadership of the various organizations which constitute the Black people's freedom movement at the present time. This segment of Black people, in the main, live in much more favorable material circumstances than the masses of the Black workers and farm toilers. However, when compared with the status of the urban middle class strata of white people—in every category—the Blacks are bound down in an inferior and unequal status by a fierce pattern of discrimination, segregation and racial oppression. Illustrative of this condition of the Black middle-class strata is the situation which Black physicians confront. They are admitted to only a few medical schools and can practice or use the facilities of a negligible number of the tax-supported hospitals; they are barred from membership in most medical societies where knowledge of a scientific nature is exchanged. Consequently, their median income is less than one-half that of the median income of white physicians and their numbers are but a token of the need. For example, in all of Mississippi, where a million Blacks live, there are only 62 Black doctors, or one for every 15,900 Blacks. (In the country as a whole, there is only one Black doctor for every 3500 Blacks.)

The positive and valuable role which the Black urban middle class play in the cause of the struggle for the rights of Black people flows from the discrimination visited upon Blacks in this strata. However, their role within the Black people's movement is neither uniformly progressive nor consistent, for they also represent the propertied and higher income strata of the Black people and reflect all the conservative and compromising influences that are associated with protection of vested property interests vulnerable to the pressures of the banks and big business dictation.

The middle class strata of the Black people will remain a very significant associated component of the social base of the Black liberation movement. However, the present dominance of their policies and leadership in the Black people's movement is a temporary phenomenon; eventually they must give way to the leadership and policies of the workers and farmer-toilers, and especially the leadership of the workers.

Black capitalists number only several thousands. They are small capitalists largely limited to the service fields of enterprise—that is, insurance, small loan companies, undertaking establishments, tonsorial enterprises, newspapers and magazine. There are no Black industrial capitalists engaged in manufacturing commodities on a large scale. Only a fraction of one percent (20,000) of the total number of Black working people are exploited as wage earners in the enterprises of Black capitalists.

In addition to all the general problems besetting small capitalists in an economy geared to the interests of and dominated by the big monopolists, Black capitalists also fall under the yoke of racial discrimination. Their investment opportunities are largely limited to that segment of the Black consumer and service market which the white monopolists have not elected to seize. In matters of securing bank credits, marketing and merchandizing products or services, securing licenses and franchises to do business, acquiring necessary types of insurance for their enterprises, the Black capitalist confronts barriers of national exclusion and race discrimination on every hand. Although there are a token number of "mixed-capital" (Black and white investors) enterprises operated by Black capitalists, generally speaking, no Black compradore bourgeoisie exists. The Black market is exploited *directly* by the big white merchants and capitalists, and not through the agency of Black "compradores," as is often the case in colonial countries.

Such is the broad class spread, the social base of the Black people's movement.

The content of the inner struggle within the Black people's movement is reflected in the strivings of representatives of the bourgeois classes on the one hand, and representatives of the working class on the other to establish the dominance of the leadership and policies of their respective class viewpoint.

Memo to National Committee,
C.P.USA. December, 1955

23   Black Liberation and
Working Class Unity

Essentially, the Black liberation movement in the United States is constituted to secure and safeguard the rights of a people to be free from all oppression. To be effective, it must amass power equal to its task. For this purpose it strives to unite the great mass of Black Americans so that the strength of their numbers and the weight of their alliances with other anti-monopoly groupings of the population can best be employed to fight for new positions of political strength, a larger economic share, social justice, and cultural recognition and opportunity. It struggles to gain a just share of political strength in order to acquire a fair share of the economic means needed to eliminate ghetto poverty and racist misery.

The political struggle of Black people, therefore, is for a national political situation of genuine representative government, wherein they seek to exercise their right of majority rule in those areas and communities where they are the dominant constituency, and for a maximum democratic share of power in those situations where they are in the minority. And, for the elimination of all those racist proscriptions and prejudices which bar eligible Blacks from high office regardless of the ratio of Black people to the total population.

In northern ghetto and southern community, the population centers of the Black citizens of this nation are boiling points of militant passion and launching pads of sky-rocketing social struggles. The Black people of all classes, of town and country, North and South, are to one degree or another suffering a common burden of racist oppression. It is manifested by a pattern of special economic exploitation, political disfranchisement, cultural denial and social ostracism.

Racism is not only a depraved ideology that violates the human dignity of Black citizens, it is a body of practice, prescribed by law and customs, which assaults and ravishes the human and civil rights of Blacks; it is an instrument of divisionism between Black and white toilers; a device for compounding profit taken by the ruling class from the extraordinary exploitation of Black people.

The basis for a broad spread of unity of the Black people across class lines lies in this fact of the all-class national character of the racist oppression which Blacks are subjected to regardless of station in life. However, the weight of racist oppression does not fall equally hard upon all classes. The Black workers and farmer-toilers suffer the severest consequences, bear the heaviest burdens of the racist system. And it is the Black workers—concentrated as they are in the pivotal centers of the production process within the capitalist economy—who, in unity with their white class brothers, have the potential power to compel real relief of the immediate situation, and for effecting strategic changes in the social system itself.

The ratio which the urban working class strata and the rural working people occupy in relation to the total Black population emphasizes the determinative, the decisive aspect of the role of the working class in the leadership, program, strategy and tactics of the Black people's liberation movement. Maximum internal unity of the Black liberation movement is forged in the course of struggle for freedom and against the influences of anti-working class policies within and upon the movement.

Racism in the United States is sustained and nourished by the monopolists in the interest of boosting their profit lust and power greed. Consequently, every blow struck against racism, every advance secured by Black Americans on the way to unqualified equality and freedom, strikes at the system of the ruling power of the monopoly capitalists.

The practice of white supremacy and racism is at once brazenly flaunted and subtly insinuated. Genuine revolutionaries—Marxists-Leninists—above all, must set sterling examples of sensitivity to even the slightest manifestation of racist discrimination, bigotry or national chauvinism, and to be models of initiative and courage in the untiring struggle to rid the labor movement and popular movements of this alien force. Racism, like anti-communism, is a powerful and dangerous virus designed to disintegrate the needed unity of Black and white working masses and to blind the masses to the interests they have in common: working class unity and people's alliance for victorious struggle against the common foe.

The river of the U.S. working class is not white, nor Puerto Rican, nor Chicano, Indian, Asian or Black; the working class is international.

It is composed of all the differentiated national and racial elements that exist in our country, and on a global scale.

What is the problem? There is ice on the river of the working class. It forms on the largest body of water in the river of the working class, that of the white workers. These ice blocks of chauvinism, racism, of white supremacy and prejudice in the river-bed of the working class impede its flow and diminish the torrential revolutionary power inherent in the waters of the whole working class. Therefore, the *ice of racism* must be melted to unleash the energy of the river of the working class.

But something has to be added, and that is, the function of the conscious force in the working class. It has to melt the ice of white supremacy that blocks the torrential waters. There is vast revolutionary potential in our working class. And we have to put an end to what is in some areas still lingering disdain, a writing off, of the numerically largest category, the most numerous physical component of the American working class—the white workers. Whoever sees only the ice of prejudice, racism, white supremacy in the mainstream of the workers and not the potential power of the waters of this mighty river is blind to revolutionary reality.

There is more in the river bed of the working class than the ice floes of prejudice, of racism, of racial backwardness. The ice is temporary; the river is enduring. The task is to introduce into this river of the working class the heat of revolutionary consciousness, to convert the ice floes into torrents of revolutionary working-class force. Whoever denigrates the white workers does not understand the simple arithmetic of the requirements of unity of the whole in our country. Without *class* unity there can be no real outlook for radical, revolutionary transformation.

There would be no victory prospect for national freedom for Black Americans, for Puerto Rican Americans, for Chicanos, for Native Americans, for the specially oppressed nationalities of our country save as their struggles are related in the first instance to the class struggle of the majority among the workers who are white in our country. If the white workers are written off as hopelessly frozen in their prejudices of white supremacist racism, then social revolution as well as freedom for the oppressed nationalities must be judged hopeless. Such a position objectively becomes counter-revolutionary.

Genuine revolutionary leadership always demands the highest standards of sensitivity and vigilance against the penetration of influences of white supremacy prejudices. It must be intolerant of the slightest chauvinist assumptions of national or racial exclusiveness or superiority.

Memo to the National Committee,
C.P.USA. February, 1956

24 On the Theory of
Black Liberation in the U.S.

The struggle waged by the Black people in the United States for equality and freedom is growing and playing an ever bigger part in the general struggle for social progress both in the United States and in the anti-imperialist movement of all oppressed peoples.

This struggle, unfolding in the citadel of world capitalism, in direct and intimate association with the working class and popular movement, is all the more significant because it is directed against the common oppressor—the monopolies. The efforts to cement a labor-Black people's alliance by mass action for equal rights of Black Americans are designed to lay the cornerstone for a broad anti-monopoly coalition on which the progressive future of the country depends. At the same time the struggle for the rights and equality of Black people, taking place against the background of the upsurge of the national-liberation movement in Africa, Asia and Latin America, undoubtedly furthers the cause of world peace and security.

These points were emphasized in the political resolution adopted at the Communist Party's 16th National Convention. In the section headed "Rally to the Banner of Struggle for Black Freedom—Key to Strengthening American Democracy," it is stated: "The question of

Black peoples freedom, then, is the crucial domestic issue of the day, and a factor of growing international consequence."

The fact that today, almost 100 years after Lincoln issued the famous proclamation abolishing slavery, the Black people are meeting with fierce resistance from reaction in their fight for freedom, equality and elementary rights, reveals the hypocrisy of those who extol the "free world" and "American democracy."

The Black people are the most severely oppressed and exploited of all the peoples who make up the American nation of the United States.

The Black people in the United States are not constituted as a separate nation. Rather, they have the characteristics of a racially distinctive people who are a historically determined component part of the United States. This American nation is a historically derived national formation, an amalgam of more or less well differentiated nationalities.

Though deprived of their just and equal rights and freedom to fully participate in all aspects of the affairs of the nation, the Black people nonetheless have contributed to and have an inseparable stake in—no less than its other national components—this nation's common territory, economic life, language, culture, and psychological make-up.

At the same time, compounded out of their singular historic experiences—from yesterday's slavery to today's aspirations and struggles for complete freedom—the Black people retain special characteristics which manifest themselves (among other ways) in a universal conception and consciousness of their identity as an oppressed people, with a common will to attain a status in the life of the U.S. nation free of all manner of oppression, social ostracism, economic discrimination, political inequality, enforced racial segregation, or cultural retardation. To conclude that the Black people in the U.S. are not a nation is *not* to say that Black liberation is not a national question. *It is indeed a national question. The question is, however, a national question of what type, with what distinguishing characteristics, calling for what strategic concept for its solution?*

"An abstract presentation of the national question is of no use at all." These words from Lenin's famous letter of December, 1922, on the "Question of Nationalities," (Lenin, *Ibid,* Vol. 26, p. 607) represents the key to the Leninist approach to the national question. In establishing the theoretical representation of Black liberation in the United States from the Marxist standpoint, it is necessary to appreciate the scope of the national question in Marxist thought. Marxism on the national question is concerned with the liberation of the oppressed nation and the relationship of that cause to the liberation of the working class from the yoke of capitalism in a given country and on a world scale. But this does not yet exhaust the scope of the national question.

The national question exists in an infinite variety of forms, and Marxist science provides guide lines for the theoretical representation and solution of each particular manifestation and formation of the national question. Within the scope of the national question, there is included not only the question of the nation, but the question of national minorities, national and ethnic groups, national-ethnic minority questions and national-communal (religious) group questions, etc. Marxism provides a guide to the characterization and developmental outlook for each of these manifestations of the national question.

It is first necessary to determine precisely the particular variety or type of national question one is confronted with. It is obligatory to examine the distinctive features of that question in its development, not statically, and in its actual and potential relationship to dominant historical development of a given time. In reference to the national question, one must above all be guided by Lenin's admonition that no problem can be presented for practical solution in isolation.

The particular national question must be viewed and represented at all times in the context of its total relationship to the historical primary social forces. That is to say, it would be a feckless exercise to present the question of Black liberation in the United States divorced from the historical and social national and world influences and relationships which bear upon and in large measure decide the frame in which it can achieve resolution.

It is incorrect to focus upon the distinctive "nation-like" features and characteristics of the Black people as *the thing* of almost *exclusive* importance to Black liberation in the United States. Of *no less importance* in the life as well as the history of the Black people in the United States are *the integral features and experiences,* common history and aspirations of this people to secure their unfettered identification with, and inclusion in, the full rights and privileges of the country. This includes the centrality of the Black people's rightful claim to an equal stake and participation in the country's total economy—built with more than 350 years of unpaid and underpaid labor, during and since slavery—while being the most exploited, most oppressed, deprived and denied component part of the nation.

It is not at all necessary to deny the fact that the Black people in the area of their former majority in the deep South exhibit to one degree or another some aspects of the characteristics common to distinctive nations in order to establish the fact that such partial "nation-like" attributes are not an objective determinative for either the solution or representation of the Black condition in the United States. Such characteristics cannot of themselves mark out the course of development and pathway to Black freedom.

The path of development of the Black people toward individual and "national" equality does not take the route of struggle for liberation in the form of political-geographical sovereignty and statehood. This *decisive* attribute for nationhood is not present. The Black people in the United States historically, now, and most probably for the future, seek solution to their national question in struggle for equality of political, economic, and social status *as a special component part of that amalgam of nationalities* which historically evolved into the nation—the United States. This course of development conforms with the first law of Marxism that "mankind sets for itself only those tasks it can achieve." (K. Marx, *Contribution to the Critique of Political Economy*, New York: International Publishers, 1972. p. 21) It corresponds to the sociological and economic forces *operating objectively* upon the course of development of the Black people.

These latter objective forces are centrifugal. They operate against the progressive build-up of closed areas of settlement on the countryside or in the towns (Black Belt). They correspond to the overbearing tendencies of industrial society to invade, diffuse and amalgamate peoples and dislocate sectional and regional populations. (Monopoly employs racism in its attempt to block the natural course of history and liberation.) But the course of development and outlook corresponds to the central political reality of our historic period: the solution of all democratic tasks is worked out in conformity with, and on the basis of, the primacy of the working class struggle to transform modern society onto a socialist base—the key task in the solution of the overall problem of human oppression and exploitation. It places the struggle for the solution of the Black condition in direct and strategic relationship to the movement and main social force—the working class, Black, Brown, red, yellow and white—for progress in our age.

If the Black people are not a nation, then how does one characterize their status in the United States? The Black people suffer a special form of racist oppression. This common experience is national in the sense that all class strata of the Black people are subject to a common yoke of oppression and social ostracism, are victims of social, economic, and political inequality. They are racially identified and set apart by racist laws and customs, social existence and by actual ethnic identifications.

If the characteristics of a nation are not the determining factors or indicators of the course of development of the Black people, then what is their significance for the Black people's freedom movement? That there are sizeable areas of the country where the concentration of Blacks in the population is large or a majority is of great importance for the political struggle and economic and cultural development of the Black people. These areas are bases where the Black freedom movement can organize and assert the mass power of its numbers to secure political authority in proportion to Black numerical strength in the population. Such areas of large Black population allow for the continued development of the distinctive in the culture of Black Americans.

In general, the large areas of the Blacks' concentrated numbers become the centers where mass actions of the Black people are generated, the vortices of the Black people's movement which draw into the freedom struggle Blacks everywhere. They represent the big wheels of the Black people's struggle which move the whole.

What are the objective factors which operate and have operated against the development of the Black people in the South as a nation? The accepted Leninist definition of a nation is that "a nation is an historically evolved, stable community of language, territory, economic life and psychological make-up manifested in a community of culture." *A key word in this definition is "stable."* Capitalist development in the United States generates forces which assail the stability of communities. In the past, two factors gave a certain durability for a time to the Black Belt area of Black majority in the deep South. First, the fact that the overwhelming bulk of the Black people were attached to the land as sharecroppers, tenants, and impoverished farmers; and second, the racist barriers erected against Black integration in the economic, political, and social life in the country.

As late as 1930, 70 percent of the Black people were counted in this "peasant" category. The factor of a large land-bound ratio in the Black community's total population gave that community a certain stability. But the demands of industrialization and the development of mechanization and technology in agriculture combined to command and expel the population from the countryside into the cities. *This process considerably shrank the areas of Black majority in the South and furthered the distribution of the Black population at the expense of a "stable community on a common territory,"* until today there remains in the old areas of Black majority some five million Blacks, of whom less than 5 percent are economically attached to the land. One half of the Black people, however, make their homes in the South. The Black people, therefore, are in the main an oppressed urban working people. Thus the decisive leadership in the solution of the Black question shifts to the Black working class. The poor farm masses and their economic demands and struggles relative to the land question remain an important component in the total cause of Black freedom—but they clearly do not occupy the strategic position as of old, when the bulk of the Black people were farmers.

Hence, the operation of the elemental forces of economic changes have driven the Black people from their paternal grounds. The improvements in the area of economic and cultural opportunity (wrested in long and fierce struggles on the part of the Black people and their allies) opened small doors of opportunity to Blacks, particularly in the non-Southern metropolises and the larger Southern cities.

In formerly characterizing the Black people in the Black Belt as a nation, we failed to properly plumb the import of that subjective attribute of nations which is one of the determining features, namely, "a common psychological make-up." If we had, we would have more seriously inquired into the history of the Black people's movement and freedom endeavor in our country and drawn the requisite conclusions. The main currents of Black thought and leadership in the struggle for advancement and freedom historically and at the present time have projected their programs for Black freedom from the premise that Blacks individually and as a people have a claim to the country's total land and economy, no less than any other U.S. claimants. They have ever sought to identify the aspirations of Black people for freedom and equality of citizenship status with the broadest national interests of the country. They have not by choice sought a separate path of development in opposition to the main forward trends in American national life.

The Black people related their cause of Abolitionism to the interests of national survival and democratic fulfillment prior to the Civil War. In the Civil War years, the Black people made their alliance with Federal authority against counter-revolutionary secessionism. Today, they invoke their constitutional rights as citizens of the United States in demands upon, and in alliance with, Federal authority against the tyranny of "state's rights" Southern governments. The *red thread of strategic conception running through the whole history of the Black freedom movement is that of amassing the maximum self-organization, unity and strength of the Black people, and allying their forces with the major progressive causes and developments in complementary struggle for full equal rights for the Black people and progress for the nation.* Only in describing the dimensions of their oppression have the Black people represented themselves as a people apart from the American nation. Their whole struggle has been to secure their historically due and just recognition as Americans with all the accompanying perquisites of such national identification.

It is true, of course, that objective being is not conditioned upon subjective recognition of one's status. A particular working class is the gravedigger of its capitalist class historically whether the workers are aware of this at a given time or not. So if objective factors and the line of historical development were operating to enhance the maturation of the national attributes of the Black people and compound their features in nationhood, the Black people would have a separate national destiny whether or not they manifested this consciousness. But *the objective factors operating in relation to the Black people in the United States are working not in the direction of national insularity or separate development but in the direction of self-organization within a broad multi-racial coalition of the oppressed and exploited to put an end to the rule of the monopoly successors of the slave power.*

By *not* placing Black liberation as a question of an oppressed nation fighting for national-state sovereignty, are we thereby diminishing the revolutionary import of the Black people's struggle in the United States? *No!* A special feature of the U.S. road to socialism is revealed in the fact that the requisite preparations of the forces for fundamental social change in the system necessitates the completion of the bourgeois-democratic norms of political, economic and social development for the South in general and the Black people in particular. Furthermore, a condition for accomplishing the prerequisite unity of the American working class with its class allies for advanced social struggle is to level the main rails of the color bar. *The struggle of the Black people for the democratic goals of political, economic and social equality feeds into the general stream of the historic working class cause, of which the Black workers are a decisive component. The Multi-racial working class is a powerful and decisive current which raises the torrential power of the whole cause of social advance.* The elementary democratic demands of the Black people can be met only at the expense of the monopolists and Dixiecrats, by strengthening the popular forces and depriving the monopoly ruling circle of the means of political oppression and economic superprofits. The fact that the Black people's struggle for freedom and equality unfolds *within* the United States in direct and intimate association with the working class and popular struggles, the fact that it is directed against the common class oppressor (the white monopolists and ruling circles) and not through a compradore class of "native" agents, the fact that the scene of the Black people's struggle unfolds within the bosom of U.S. imperialism—on the main stage and not in a faraway land or insular holding of U.S. imperialism—means that the full force of even the least activity of this movement has its direct impact and consequences in challenge to the class enemy and support to the broad forces of social progress.

Furthermore, the purging of white chauvinist and anti-Black prejudices from the thought and attitudes of the white masses is a vital aspect of the subjective preparation of the working class for undertaking the leadership responsibility in the struggle for a higher form of social order—for socialism. It is the way the U.S. working class must be educated in internationalism in the first instance. Lenin has written that:

"Internationalism on the part of oppressing, or 'great' nations as they are called (though they are great only in violence. . .) must consist not only in observing formal equality of nations, but even in an inequality of the oppressor nation, the great nation, that must make up for the inequality which obtains in actual life. Whoever does not understand this has not grasped the real proletarian attitude to the national question. . . ." (Lenin, *Ibid,* Vol. 36, p. 608)

The true proletarian attitude to the national question, Lenin stressed over and over again, consists of deeds performed to wipe out the inequalities and injustices suffered by the victims of national or racial oppression. As Lenin noted further:

". . . nothing so much holds up the development and strengthening of proletarian class solidarity as national injustice; 'offended' nationals are not sensitive to anything so much as to the feeling of equality and the violation of that equality if only through negligence or as a joke, to the violation of that equality by their proletarian comrades. That is why in this case it is better to overdo it in the way of flexibility and leniency towards the national minorities than underdo it. . . ." (Lenin, *Ibid,* Vol. 36, pp. 608-609)

The Black people's movement has a continuing vital interest in all general problems–the state structure, laws, etc., for this is the frame within which it makes its struggle for freedom. It is vitally affected by the nature of these general questions of State.

When we conclude that self-determination for the Black people in the Black Belt or in the ghettos scattered from coast to coast is not a sound or applicable characterization of the course of development in the cause of Black freedom and the solution of Black liberation in the United States, are we not saying, that the Black people have voiced their right of self-determination and chosen integration? No.

Developments beyond the will of the Black people to determine— objective economic historical factors — have primarily conditioned the course of development and solution of Black liberation in the United States. The reflection of these objective and material considerations and circumstances find their expression in the articulated programs, outlook and conclusions as to the course that the movement for solution of Black oppression will take. The basic objective of the Black people's struggle, in whatever forms required, is to secure full and equal means of decision on all questions affecting them and the country's welfare, to secure the right to vote and be elected to office, and to secure unfettered equality in all respects. These are the tools for decision for which Black people struggle now in order to be enabled to decide matters in their self-interest and in the national interest, as is consistent with democratic requirements.

* * *

In regard to the Black people's course of development and the land question: In theoretical considerations of the solution of the Black question in the United States, our Party in the past put first stress on the land question. As a matter of fact, the first strategic consideration for the solution of Black liberation was projected in terms of securing to the landless Black farmers land holdings at the expense of the plantation-owning landlord class and the land monopolists and banks. The thesis behind this approach was that by breaking up the plantation and turning the land over to the Black toiler, not only would the means of economic sustenance and development be secured to the Black people but this would also cut into the economic might of monopoly of U.S. imperialism. This approach had meaning in a situation in which the bulk of the Black people were economically exploited by and held in the grip of landlord capital, when the largest numbers of Blacks were attached to the land.

It cannot be viewed as the strategic approach to the solution of the Black condition today, when the emigration from agriculture has transformed past relationships to the land. *The vast changes that have taken place in the class structure of the Black people as a consequence of this occupational redistribution, with the resulting general urbanization, means that the strategic solution to Black liberation has to be worked out in terms of struggle primarily of an urban people against monopoly.* It is in an overall sense a struggle for the industrial rights of the Black people economically and their full social-political equality. *The strategic class force in Black liberation therefore, becomes firmly identified as the working class.*   This is not at all to say that the struggles of the Black farmers for the land and for a higher standard of living and democratic rights *as farmers,* and the need for all democratic forces to struggle against the farm trust and against the reactionary survivals of the plantation system is not of great economic and even greater political importance—both, for the solution of Black liberation and for the general democratic reformation of the South and of the country as a whole.

Is there a possibility of a significant return of Blacks into agriculture? No. The redistribution of the Black population will not reverse itself. Before the Second World War two-thirds of all American Blacks were Southern farmers and farm workers; only 5 percent are today. Now almost 80 percent of the Black people are living in Southern and Northern cities. The manpower needs of agriculture are in steady decline. As a result of big strides in technical progress, the agricultural sector of the economy produces greater quantities of food and raw materials with a steadily decreasing number of workers.

In 1957, farm population was only 12 percent of the total U.S. population, compared with 23 percent in 1940. (In 1972 only 6 percent of the population of the South lived on farms.)

Report to the Black Liberation Commission,
C.P.USA. January, 1957

25   Look Southward, Labor

In the South is to be found an exaggerated delineation of all the social problems—economic, political, cultural and racial —which beset U.S. capitalism. This fragment of modern exploitative society epitomizes the social problems begging solution in our times. Here are revealed the contending contradictions which at once arrest and propel the forces of social change and progress. In this sense, the South is the United States in microcosm; its past, its present, the challenge to, and harbinger of, its future. And more than this; the South is the essence of world capitalism entering upon the second half of the 20th century.

Those who would understand the tasks of the times for our country and who would divine the means and facilitate the accomplishment of these tasks, must study the Southern scene in all its turbulence.

Any programming for social progress in the United States which fails to take into account the challenge of the South is so much vanity fare served up for the divertissement of idlers and utopians and has no relation to social science applied to the new times and conditions of mid-century U.S.A.

The key to social advance in all basic areas of our national life is to be found in the enlistment of the maximum forces of social progress in activities designed to secure for the South those norms of economic, political and cultural practice obtaining in the country as a whole.

The working class and progressive strata of the nation will reap no significant new harvest of social advancement so long as the Southern quadrant remains a reactionary basin, a political-economic and cultural low ground draining off the springs of new life from the rest of the nation.

What accounts for this sectional lag in our national development?

Historically the anachronism of modern slavery was developed in the South as the social system in a labor-short economy which would insure absolute control by the exploiters over the Southern workers. Then, as Frederick Douglass noted in 1867, "The South fought for perfect and permanent control over the Southern laborer."

And today the ruling and owning oligarchy of the Southern states fights on against the national interests in the cause of maintaining "perfect control of its laborers." The animalistic malice which the official South displays (in statutes and customs) against the human and civic rights, the dignity and humanity of the Black people is not the object of the oligarchy but the means of attaining its objective: that objective remains as it has ever been—to hold the laborer "in perfect and permanent control," the better to command his super-exploitation so that southern capitalist and northern investors can enrich themselves.

In the slave-South the employer-employee relations and wage standards of the white workers were influenced disastrously by the inhuman relations which the master imposed upon the Black labor chattel. So today, the master plan for holding all southern working men and women "in perfect and permanent control" is hinged upon the general subjugation of the Black people—in binding them down into an inferior economic, political and social caste by means of hundreds of Jim Crow statues, discriminatory practices and racist calumnies.

It follows, therefore, that the secret of the solution of the "Southern Problem" is to be found in struggle by labor to realize its program of economic, political and cultural needs, so long buried in its hope chest. The solution lies in the buildup of its mass organizational strength on the principle of the primacy of unity of workers, not division of races, in a determined struggle to secure: (1) the right to vote and political participation for all; (2) equal pay for equal work without North-South or Black-white wage differentials; (3) state programs of social security and welfare benefits at least equal to those in Northern states; (4) the repeal of "right to work" laws and repressive statutes; (5) the full enforcement of the U.S. Constitution for all Southerners, Black and white; and (6) a just share of industrial jobs for Southern workers.

But the key to unlocking this hope chest of Southern working class struggle and socio-political initiative is the fight of the Black people to exercise their rights as full fledged and equal citizens. Without grasping this key, labor cannot open wide its hope chest—either in the South or the nation, either in realization of the opportunities before us today, or in timely fulfillment of our class destiny tomorrow. The Jim Crow bondage in general, and the disfranchisement of the Southern Blacks in particular, bear a relationship to labor's condition and aspiration today, much like that which obtained at another nodal point in our national development over 90 years ago. Karl Marx noted this historical fact and predicted this current challenge when he wrote, "In the United States of North America, every independent movement of the workers was paralyzed so long as slavery disfigured a part of the Republic." (K. Marx, *Capital*, New York: International Publishers, 1974. Vol. p. 301)

Labor must make the cause of the current great suffrage and equal rights battle of the Black people its own struggle. For it is being waged against labor's worst enemies and is therefore in labor's direct self-interest. With victory in the struggle, the newly enfranchised Black masses will constitute a powerful assist to the forces of social progress in the South and the nation. It is as true today as when Frederick Douglass noted it 90 years ago that: ". . . it is the good fortune of the Negro that enlightened selfishness, not less than justice, fights on his side. National interests and national duty, if elsewhere separated, are firmly united here."

There is, then, direct immediate force to Douglass' appeal: "Give the Negro the elective franchise, and you at once destroy the purely sectional policy, and wheel the Southern states into line with national interests and national objects." *(The Condition of the Freedmen, Harper's Weekly, Dec. 8, 1883.)* [*The Life and Writings of Frederick Douglass,* New York, International Publishers, 1955. Vol. IV; p. 403.]

The influx of new industrial plants into the South is not the result of any policy of the monopolists to proceed with the all-round development and exploitation of their traditional "reserve" region.

The expansion of industries into the South, such as textiles, chemicals, electrical and food has been motivated by the special inducements held out to them by the local and state governments of the South. Among such inducements are low cost sites (and in some cases rent-free), tax exemptions and/or low taxes and even the building of plants financed by public bond issues and then leasing them to the northern capitalists for a song. Above all other "inducements" which the South holds out to outside capital, the main persuader by far is its *lower wage scale*. The whole machinery of the state power in the South is arrayed on the side of maintaining this Southern wage differential in behalf of monopoly capitalist robbers. Therefore, capitalists continue to move their plants South in pursuit of maximum-profits; to take advantage of the invitations extended by the reactionary political regimes there who promise them protection against the demands of working men and women for a decent living wage.

The principal factor that is operating to undermine the wage standards and working conditions of the organized workers in the United States is the existence of the North-South wage differential within the same industries which discriminate against the southern workers in general and the Black workers in particular. Really effective labor unity cannot be realized until the trade union movement carries out the long-delayed task of knocking out, once and for all, the North-South and Black-white differential in wages for the same work performed. Such divisive differentials exist in every industry without exception. Unless the largely unorganized workers in the southern factories and on the southern plantations are brought into the general organized labor movement—and this can only be done on the basis of a fight against the North-South, Black-white wage differentials—the wage standards, working conditions and trade union organizations are in danger of being driven into the ground and wrecked. It will be utterly impossible for the trade union workers to defend themselves against the blows of wage cutting and unemployment without mobilizing, enrolling and uniting the full strength of its class. To head into the coming struggles with the potential great army of Black and white southern workers scattered and unorganized would be disastrous for the American labor movement and the nation.

Therefore, what is required is nothing less than a gigantic, full scale organizing offensive in the South *now*! The condition demands a campaign to organize the unorganized factories and plantations of the South, developing the greatest possible degree of mutual aid and cooperation on the part of the respective international and central bodies of the AFL-CIO, the independent unions, the RR brotherhoods and the United Farm Workers of America.

The strategic keys to the organization of the southern workers are in the largely unorganized old and new industries of the South. In addition to the main older industries such as textile and lumber, the new industries include, electrical, chemical, food, and garment. Among these expanding industries there are more than 600 unorganized chemical and 700 unorganized electrical plants.

A southern organizing drive cannot succeed if conducted again in the half-hearted, timid, professional organizer style of the past. It cannot be victorious if undertaken routinely as a pure and simple trade union chore. To win, it must unfold those tactics which will give it the fervor and character of a Southern people's crusade to wipe out the discriminatory wage rates paid Southern workingmen and women by the monopoly-owned southern mills and plantations. It must be conducted as a crusade for equal job rights and equal pay for equal work for the Black masses. It must be conducted as a crusade that brings decisive strength to the Black people's and white workers and poor farmers struggle to win full suffrage rights and legislative protection for their general civil liberties. To succeed it must draw upon the rewarding experiences and rich book of tactics developed during the initial CIO drive in the South of the late 1930's.

To insure its success, it must fully absorb the full import of the lessons of the defeats suffered over the years by the textile workers. The basic lesson that must be drawn from the long record of unionizing failures suffered by the textile workers for more than fifty years is this: *Effective* unionization with the elimination of the southern wage differential in textile and other lily-white industries and plants is quite impossible apart from successfully waging the fight for *introducing* nonracial, non-discriminatory hiring policies. This is the inescapable lesson of the history of textile union organization in the South. This axiom is drawn from the half-century experience of the textile workers—a lesson they must yet learn, recognize and accept before they can substantially improve their plight. Therefore, the first *cardinal principle* for success of a trade union organizing drive in the South is that it must be conducted in intimate union with the struggle of the Black masses for equal *job rights* and for the general democratic demands for suffrage rights and civil rights. Either unity with the Black workers to wipe out the wage differential or unity with the bosses in defense of white supremacy and the southern wage differential. (The price of unity with the bosses to maintain white supremacy prejudices is paid by the white workers accepting the wage differential for the "privilege" of being exploited separately from the Black workers.)

The South of today remains a classic showpiece of the divide and rule strategy of the monopoly ruling class. Old and new industries continue to flourish and make multimillionaires of their owners because of the North-South and Black-white wage differentials. To the extent that the white workers of the South have been influenced by the ruling class to bar Black workers from jobs in the mills under the white supremacist guise of "not exposing their women to the glances of Negroes" (sic!), to just such an extent have they conspired against themselves and have delivered up their women and children to generations of ravishing super-exploitation by the textile barons and other kingpins of industry. The white workers pay the price for their boss-inspired prejudices not only in terms of their weekly earnings (below the national average) but in the highest tuberculosis and illiteracy rate suffered by workers of any other major industry in the country. Not only is this the case, but in addition their boss-inspired white supremacist self isolation from political contact and unity with the majority Black masses of their area has deprived them of any effective vote or voice in the political life of their towns, counties, states and congressional districts.

Hence, it is evident that it is in the best self-interest of the white workers themselves to fight to establish Black-white working class solidarity by opening the gates to employment of Black men and women in their industry. For this is the necessary first step, the precondition, for forging a durable Black people-labor alliance for seriously unfolding the *political* struggle for greater democracy in local and national government, civil liberties and advanced public services. Hence, also, the vital stake that the Black liberation movement has in the successful organization of the unorganized workers in all industries on the twofold basis of elimination of the North-South wage differential and anti-Black employment practices.

The big, sprawling lumber industry is one of the largest employers of Black labor. Working conditions in this industry are as primitive and "labor relations" as barbaric, as can be found in any colonial country in the world. Wages are notoriously low and almost half of that in the Northwest and far West—the other two principal lumber producing regions.

The organization of the workers of this industry is not only a vital aspect of the fight to bring the trade union movement up to full fighting strength; not only is it necessary in the fight to wipe out the North-South wage differential in order to raise the wages of these workers and to protect the jobs and wage standards of the lumber workers of the West, but also, because it is of strategic importance for the further development of the Black liberation movement. The organization of the lumber workers would add to the organized proletarian base and backbone of the Black liberation movement additional and crucial scores of thousands of worker *who reside in the Deep South.* Also, because the lumber workers—like the bulk of the textile workers—have close ties with the rural masses and, in season, they themselves often double as farm workers on the big cotton and produce plantations.

In addition to the organization of these two major southern

industries—(which is the class obligation of the entire organized labor movement to guarantee its speedy accomplishment)—it is necessary for the respective international unions to fill in the gaping open-shop holes in their jurisdictions in the South. This means there is room for expansion southward for every bona fide trade union—AFL-CIO and independent. There are literally scores of thousands of unorganized workers in aluminum, sulphur, rubber, chemical, glass, farm equipment, farm workers, electrical, shoe, paper, apparel, tobacco, transport, department store and others in the South.

Such an insistent demand must go up from the rank and file in every union that the top labor leadership will be forced to move and fulfill their responsibility to their union members by undertaking the organization of the open shop, low wage plants in their respective jurisdictions in the South.

There is also the need for planfully undertaking the job of strengthening the unions which are already established in the South. Above all to improve the bonds of Black-white solidarity—in employment practices, in up-grading and job training, in wiping out discriminatory job classification practices, in the promotion of Blacks to a full share in the leadership of all aspects of union activities, etc. At the same time, to work to enlarge the progressive community role and legislative-political activity of the unions in the fight for free and equal suffrage rights, for the abolition of anti-labor laws, jim crow laws, anti-communist-anti-democratic rights laws, and for free and fair trade relations with the socialist countries and for internal union democracy, for fighting trade union tactics in handling grievances, and to secure advances in wage and working conditions.

There are in the South one-third of the farmers of the country, one-half of the farm workers, practically all of the sharecroppers and the bulk of the tenant farmers. For the workers to make *secure* their wage standards and working conditions, it is necessary to extend their trade union organizational activities into the Southern countryside, to organize the unorganized working farmers—the farm laborers, sharecroppers, and tenant-farmers; and also the small farm owner-operators. Because of the pressure of the rural population on the cities, really serious economic and political victories and advances calls for the urban working class to seek a fighting alliance with the *organized farm masses*—in addition to cementing its firm alliance with the Black people's liberation movement. This is the *strategic* necessity for the trade union movement to give leadership and every support to building militant organizations and unions of farm workers, sharecroppers, tenant farmers and struggling yeomen farmers.

The predominant mono-culture characteristic of Southern agriculture, means that the Southern farm masses engaged on the big capitalist farms (who suffer impoverishment and ruin in geometrical progression to the arithmetical fall in the commodity market) have no home produce self-sufficiency—no personal garden-crop, pigs, chickens, milk cows —with which to feed themselves. They do not raise their food stuffs; they are dependent on store purchases like other ordinary consumers. Crop failure or sharp declines in market prices spells untold misery, immediate impoverishment and imminent threat of starvation for the families of the farm toilers. They are unprotected by even the meager social security benefits and unemployment compensation of the city industrial workers. Hence, the very circumstances of existence tend to "radicalize" the bulk of the Southern farm masses. The working class must fully appreciate the Southern farm toilers as an especially prized and worthy ally for both today's economic and legislative struggles, and tomorrow's political victories.

Such is the present task before the labor movement in the South: to repeat—to undertake, without further delay the job of organizing the unorganized Southern workers in both industry and agriculture with particular emphasis on workers in the textile and lumber industries and on the cotton plantations.

The first insurance, the main protection that the workers of our country have against bearing the full and disastrous burdens of the profit lust of the monopolies and the developing economic crisis is in their ability to face the capitalist moneybags with maximum trade union solidarity—organized and united.

Political Affairs. December, 1959

26 Between Little Rock and Watts

As vitally necessary as it is to come to grips with and resolve in the interests of clarity and sound orientation the fundamental theoretical problems of strategic concept, characterization, and definition of the status and developmental outlook of the Black people's freedom cause, the urgent, pressing tasks of the living movement are not unrelated or irrelevant considerations in the correct achievement of this work. In connection with this latter point, there are certain developments of very special importance in the unfolding current struggle for the rights of Black people which require special action and a major exertion on our part to insure their success.

The 86th Congress will open on January 7, 1959 in a struggle to repeal Rule 22 and break the filibuster veto power of the Southern Senators over effective civil rights and other progressive legislation mandated by the people's vote in the November elections. Already the Johnson-Rayburn forces are working to split and weaken the forces pledged to support a clear anti-filibuster rule. With a crusading intensity, every day must be utilized to sustain the pressure upon the Douglas-Javits anti-filibuster block to brook no compromise with the appeasers of the Southern segregationists. Letters, telegrams, petitions, ads, participation in the January 5 Washington lobby of the 27 cooperating national organizations and trade unions should be encouraged from every mass organization and trade union, etc.

Following this battle will come the struggle for an enforcement amendment to the Civil Rights law. The most imaginative campaign must be sustained as long as required for victory in support of genuine civil rights measures in Congress. The clear intent of the politicians will be to push the matter over, to do nothing until the party conventions of 1960 and convert it into a competition in party platform writing and presidential campaign promises.

The Southern segregationists and the state governments of the South

have laid siege to the Supreme Court's ruling against school segregation. They have interposed over 200 state laws against the Constitutional right of the Black people to equal unsegregated education in the
Southern states. President Dwight Eisenhower, in flagrant contempt of
his Constitutional obligation, refuses to take any action to uphold the
law as ordered by the Supreme Court, to enforce the equal citizenship
right of the Black people to equal unsegregated education in the Southern states. Thousands of Black and white children are locked out of their
schools by the insurrectionary actions of Almond and Orville Faubus,
while other Southern governors contumaciously make no move in the
direction of honoring the orders of the highest court of the land or of
respecting the Constitutional rights of Black citizens in general.

In response to the challenge and affront of this situation, the Youth
March for Integrated Schools came into being. The great demonstration
that was held in Washington is scheduled to be repeated and multiplied
several times over on May 16. At this time the youth are pledged to
bring to Washington the signatures of a million young Americans who
support their pledge to forever combat discrimination and segregation.
This is a very big undertaking and the import and consequences of such
a successful action must not be underestimated. Certainly no effort on
our part should be spared in helping the young people to realize this
noble goal.

To secure the liberties and safeguard the lives of Southern Blacks
beleaguered by revenge-seeking local governmental and police authorities, Klansmen and White Citizens Council desperadoes, the Federal governmental law enforcement agencies must be compelled to in-
tervene and bring an end, once and for all, to the usurped rights of the
States to wantonly violate the Constitutional rights of Black citizens.
But to bring about such a turn in events will require that the Black trade
unionists commence to exert their own initiative in the struggle of the
Black people. Two million-strong Black trade unionists have a potential
power of action to bring to bear at the point of production in the cause of
Black freedom that has not yet been felt or fully perceived.

We welcome the news of a new beginning on the part of Black trade
unionists to give organizational expression to the special fraternity that
obtains among them, with the objective of playing a leading role in the
unfolding struggles of the Black people.

In all of the United States, there are less than 100 Black elected
public officials. This spells out most graphically the fact that the Black

people in the United States are the most disfranchised people in the world with the exception of South Africa. How significant, therefore, is the anticipated convocation of a Conference of Black Statesmen in Washington in the early spring! Such a conference will be a major podium from which the heartfelt aspirations and urgent demands of Black people for genuine representation in government, for real enforcement of the right to vote and to be voted for in the South, for the reapportionment of gerrymandered Congressional Districts, will be voiced to the nation. Also, it will give a dramatic push to the fight for enacting civil rights and fair employment practices legislation.

The prospectus is that a Washington Conference of Black Statesmen may become a new permanent institution of much promise. But if an assembly of Black elected officials is to be basically meaningful beyond its declamatory value, it needs to have as its backdrop an organized, nationally federated nonpartisan movement of Black voters for concerted independent political action. We look hopefully upon a current development in this direction which has taken root in one of the Midwestern cities. The political sagacity displayed by the Black electorate in New York in connection with the Adam Clayton Powell campaign, and elsewhere across the country, indicates that the mood of the Black voter is ripe for concerted independent political action on a national scale, even though still expressing itself within the electoral framework of the two party system. Certainly this development will be followed attentively, and progressives will find ways of rendering effective aid to its development inside and outside of the two-party structure. It indicates a maturing of political independence which cannot long be retained within the two-party straitjacket.

The municipal and state elections of 1959 will offer opportunity for Black people to advance the fight for Black representation as well as to further the local and state legislative measures necessary to secure freedom and equal rights. Our Party plans to participate in one or more Southern cities in the municipal and state elections. Certainly, elsewhere in the country, our comrades will not be amiss in doing all they can to aid the cause of Black representation both in a supporting role and, as with Ben Davis in Harlem, in putting forward where possible and proper our own candidates for public office.

An event of signal importance to furthering the advance organizationally of the Black people's movement is to be noted in the preparations being made for the June, 1959 Golden Jubilee of the National

Association for the Advancement of Colored People. These preparations are of a special character. They have to do with a most significant struggle within the Black mass organizations on matters of policy, scope of program, tactics of mass struggle, democratizing the structure of the organization, a youth program, among other issues. Personalities in contest for election as delegates to the convention and to local and national office will identify with definite positions on these matters. The membership of this vital organization of the Black people's movement wants basic reforms in the policy and structure of this organization. For our part, we identify with their aspirations and wish them success in rendering that organization a more effective instrument in the fight for Black freedom.

Various pressures are brought to bear upon the Black people's movement and especially upon its leaders to divert it from its course, to undermine its strength, to weaken its unity and effectiveness. Sometimes, some of the established Black leaders who are the victims of these pressures seek release by becoming purveyors of anti-Communism. But the lying propaganda of the "Communist danger" is itself one of the most damaging and weakening pressures within the Black people's movement. It threatens to ensnare the people in lies and mold hostile attitudes toward the world forces of anti-colonialism and socialism which are objective allies of the Black people's freedom cause at home.

In the second half of the twentieth century, in the age of the worldwide triumph of Marxist science in the liberation of oppressed peoples, there can be no successful end to any people's freedom movement whose leaders march under the Chamberlain umbrella of anti-Communism.

One of the important contributions our Party, and especially Black Communists, have to make to the task of ideological clarity as to who are the friends and who is the enemy of the Black people is precisely the exposure of all redbaiting preachments and practices. In conducting this ideological work against anti-Communist propaganda, we will make clear our support for every forward step of the movement. We will strive to enhance the unity and advance the cause of the movement at all times no matter how provocative and divisive the redbaiting indulgences of a part of its leadership.

The desperate antediluvian denizens of Dixiedom have unleashed an unprecedented propaganda barrrage in behalf of white supremacy and in defense of segregation. The centerpiece in their broadsides of racist pornography is to depict the offensive of the people and democratic forces for equality as a "communist-inspired plot" against the domestic peace, as a "Moscow-ordered gambit in the cold war." In their indecent diatribes the school room becomes the boudoir, and the enforcement of integration becomes "invasion." The Georgia Educational Commission is spending two million dollars in a slick Madison Avenue campaign to sell the case for segregation to the nation. A bill has been introduced into the Florida legislature for financing a similar project.

We are called upon to move the trade unions and religious organizations, colleges, and scientific societies to rise to the challenge of the racist ideological assault that has been developed anew against the minds and reason of the American people. Our Party has a special independent role to play in this connection. In a previous period, the works of Dr. Herbert Aptheker and other Communists scored significant victories against racist ideology in scholarship. Now, once again we must counter the propaganda waves of the racists with popularly presented revelations of truth, fact, self-interest, and social necessity for inter-racial unity and for the equality of Black people. The struggle against racism and white supremacy prejudices and practices must be carried to the white masses via the organizations in which they are to be found. Black people do not want the progressive white person spending his or her time commiserating with them over their oppressed status; they want to see the white progressives fighting alongside of and for them in behalf of their just rights in the white communities, among the white masses.

Now, as never before, there must be a keener sensitivity and vigilance against all manifestations of white chauvinism, of insensitivity to insult and injustice against Black people, of abstentionism in the struggle for Black people's rights, of paternalism and discourtesy toward Blacks.

*   *   *

On the African continent, a new sovereign state has been born, Guinea. Several other nations there have taken first steps toward independence. A great conference of the liberation fighters from the African world is now taking place in Accra, Ghana, and in attendance there are the outstanding Black internationalists and Marxists, Dr. Alphaeus Hunton, Dr. W.E.B. Du Bois, Paul Robeson, Mrs. Eslanda Goode

Robeson from the United States. Other Blacks from the United States are there too, such as Congressman Charles Diggs of Detroit, and news reporters. The bonds of fraternal solidarity among United States Blacks and the dynamic liberation movements of Africa are growing and create great popular enthusiasm within large sections of Black public opinion. This represents a vital and developing stream of anti-imperialist consciousness among Blacks. Furthermore, already in 1958 almost a hundred Black citizens visited the Soviet Union. The inspiration they received there and the discovery of the true world situation as a consequence of their first-hand "look-see" at socialism-in-being, is reflected in a growing body of Black periodical literature that is sympathetic to socialism and highly appreciative of the achievements and significance of the Soviet Union and other socialist countries to the cause of anti-colonialism and Black liberation on a world scale.

We welcome this significant beginning of inter-cultural communication. We are for the broadest development of tourism on the part of Black people, particularly the trade unionists, youth and women, to Africa, the Soviet Union and the socialist countries.

As a result of the outcome of the November elections, the trade unions have developed a new self-confidence. They should also have acquired a new and profound respect for their electoral partnership with the Black people, who held their ranks solid with labor in spite of every provocation from the Democratic Party chieftains and their southern cabal; but this they must yet learn to value properly. In any event, the opportunity has been created for recommencing a rank and file campaign to move the leadership into action on the question of the organization of the unorganized millions of factory and field workers in the South.

Finally, nothing we speak of here will succeed in attaining the dimensions and scope of real effectiveness in the months ahead if we do not simultaneously occupy ourselves with the upbuilding of the independent strength and influence of our Communist Party among the Black people —the workers, the youth, the intellectuals. The crisis of policy and leadership of the Black people's movement today is traceable in no small part to the absence of a conscious Marxist trend in the ranks and leadership of this movement. Our Party retains great latent credits among the Black people. We must multiply our influence and numbers among them.

A key opportunity to secure a new appreciation for our Party among broad strata of the Black people is offered us in the struggle for amnesty for Henry Winston and his colleague, as well as in the demand for the dismissal of the Claude Lightfoot case. Above all, Black Communists must take into their own hands the cause of freeing Henry Winston from jail in 1959. We must set up a special committee toward this objective, assemble such forces and secure such funds and resources as are necessary, and carry through this task to the end. Winnie belongs to the working class and to the Party as a whole, true enough, but in a special way he is ours. Let us do our Brother to Brother duty to him now. Never mind protocol and togetherness—let us take on this job and do it!

* * *

As we address ourselves to the subject of the theoretical premises for the representation and solution of the Black question in the United States—let us be mindful of the function and role of theory. Theory is not for the purpose of shielding or denying reality, or of arresting the development of phenomena. "Phenomena are richer than any law," said Lenin. Theory explains and illuminates the forces at work in a given phenomenon, and reveals its relationship to all surrounding phenomena. It distinguishes the new and vital from the old and dying. It provides a guide to action. Correct theory is the midwife of the possible and reveals the most favorable course for its development.

The question is not how to compress the phenomena of the Black people's movement in the United States into the conditions of a given Marxist category, but how to effectively use the science of Marxism-Leninism to serve the cause of Black people's equality and freedom.

Political Affairs. January, 1959

27   The Democratic Upsurge
of Black Americans

I t is not fortuitous that the Black people in the United States have mounted their magnificent struggle at precisely this time.

First of all, the new world relation of forces, which characterizes our epoch, provides a favorable and sympathetic international climate. Furthermore, the great advances made by the people of Africa, of Asia, of valiant Cuba in throwing off the chains of colonial bondage and striding along the path of free and independent development have acted as a powerful stimulus to the Black people in the U.S. Then, the growing awareness that there exists in the world a great country—the Soviet Union—whose success in securing to its many diverse ethnic and national peoples conditions of full equality and a truly open society in which all enjoy the right to maximum national development as well as complete integration in the political, economic and social life of the whole country, is a progressive and challenging alternative to the prevailing racist patterns in the U.S.

To appreciate fully the major political consequences which can flow from the American Blacks' present upsurge, it is necessary to have a full view of the place this people occupies in the nation in general, and in the working class of the United States in particular.

The nation, like the human body, does not permit the prolonged abuse of one of its parts without the whole suffering serious consequences. When one member of the body is subjected to injury, the bleeding and pain may be endemic or local but the effect is systemic or general, and the curative process requires that all the healthy forces of the whole system be brought into play. So, too, with a nation, its integrity and its viability as a political entity require conditions which ensure the fullest development and integration of its several ethnic and national components into one nation of equal peoples, communities, and citizens.

As the social and political circumstances and consequences of the oppression of the twenty millions of Black Americans are not endemic, neither can the solution of the problem be arrived at in isolation from the forces at play in the total economic, political and social milieu of the nation as a whole. There are particular social and class forces within the United States which benefit in certain ways from depriving Black people of their equal civil and political rights and which gain from their economic exploitation. There are other social forces in our class-stratified society which, objectively, suffer a depression of their own status, and a diminishing of their own rights, as a consequence of the abuses to which Black Americans are subjected. The essential strategy for victory for the Black people's movement for freedom lies in establishing maximum bonds of unity with the comparably deprived forces of the latter, in united struggle to defeat and break the power of the common exploiter.

There are more factors in the equation than the two principals—*i.e.*, Blacks and their oppressors—and these other factors will have their decisive bearing upon the solution of the problem. First of all, the solution of the Black question in the United States cannot be abstracted from the relationships which it bears to the general dynamic of the contradictions besetting the capitalist social system within the United States, that is, from the historically determined and restricted societal framework in which the particular struggle for Black freedom is being fought out. Secondly, the impact of world developments upon our country also influences the struggle for Black rights.

Progress in the socio-economic and political spheres in the nation as a whole and in the world at large which enlarges human liberty and diminishes exploitation, which strengthens peace and abolishes colonialism—such general developments favor and facilitate the advancement of the Black freedom cause. Therefore, the program and leadership of the Black people's movement must fully take into account the developments in the national and international arena of social struggle, and its leaders should be aware of the relationship between the progressive forces in struggle on these respective levels and the success of the unfolding struggle of the Black people for equality and freedom.

The Black is the Cinderella in this family of man that makes up the United States. Though put upon, deprived, denied and victimized by every outrage and indignity by others of the national household, he is no less a true-born member of the family than they. Black men and women were brought to America as slaves in 1619 from Africa to Jamestown colony, which had only been established as a permanent settlement in

1607. Africans were subsequently brought to America in great numbers as slaves, until the end of the African slave trade in the mid-1850's.

Both in numbers within the total population and in work performed in building his country, that part of the American people which stemmed from Africa was ever an important presence in the making of this great North American nation. Indeed, no national stream can have greater claim to first membership in this family-nation, compounded of so many national and ethnic streams, than that which flows from Africa. It was the unrequited toil of the African bondsmen that provided no small measure of the capital for the nation's tempestuous economic growth and accumulation of wealth. First the colonizers, and then the new nation of the United States, reaped a golden harvest from the slave chains that bound their Black brothers. Through this "primitive accumulation" of human labor power, immense values were wrested from the bountifully endowed virgin lands which was the territory of the United States of America.

Black oppression has been the question with which the politics of the nation has been occupied again and again. The main content of the political history of three-quarters of the last century was taken up with the question of the struggle against slavery and the problems that followed the necessary surgical operation of the Civil War. In our decade, the failure of bourgeois democracy to secure the Black's equal status in the nation constitutes an important article in its indictment by history and has become one of the major factors in its deepening general crisis.

As the Black's role in the history of the nation's economy is of undeniable importance, and as the political history of the nation is writ large in its own blood around the question of his status and presence, so it is with the spiritual-cultural history of this nation. Abraham Lincoln and the former slave Frederick Douglass made enduring contributions to American political thought through their responses to the challenge of the Black question; so it has been and continues to be unto the present, that in the field of letters, the most outstanding works in literature and poetry have found inspiration in the epic cause of the Black people's striving toward liberation. The noble theme of the life and struggle of the most brutally oppressed sister and brother in the nation's house (which they did so much to build and defend) has been one of the richest skeins in American literature.

In the field of music and the dance, it has been in great measure the

Blacks' contributions which have given works in these cultural areas their national distinctiveness.

As the mental and manual contributions of the Black have flowed into the making of the nation—economically, politically and culturally—so have the major currents of the mainstream of the nation swirled about him, becoming the major determinant of his values, standards, goals. True, there has never been a time when the Black received anything like a just measure in return for that which he has given, or which has been robbed from him; (indeed, that is the sum of his problem); nevertheless he has been shaped and fashioned by the general social milieu in which he has always been segregated and subjected to discrimination.

As the Americans whose forebears came from Africa were contributing to the making of the nation, they were in turn being moulded and modified by that experience.

This American-derived "new" people have grown up with and as a part of the nation. These, then, are the Black Americans, *people who have a proud history and a rich future as a specially identifiable member of the family of their nation.*

Having established the fact that *the Black people belong to the American nation that inhabits these United States, it becomes readily apparent that he suffers oppression in exact measure as he is deprived of his equal status with all others within the nation.* At the same time, the *goal of his struggle* is revealed as that of securing all the rights and opportunities which are common to the people of the nation.

The freedom struggle of the Black Americans, therefore, unfolds as a *struggle for a full and equal measure of the economic and political means for the satisfaction of their material, social and spiritual needs- -needs which are the common norms of the society as a whole.*

The failure of the Federal government to secure the full citizenship rights of the Black people, to provide them with the opportunity to secure a just place in the developing economy of the South as farmer, workers, businessmen and professionals, was in itself a motivating factor in the great population movements of American Blacks.

As a consequence of the Civil War, Blacks were freed from slavery, but a feudal pattern replaced slavery as a system in the South's agricultural economy. The former slaves were rebound to the plantations as sharecroppers and tenants with no more "free men's" rights than European serfs. As the 20th Century opened, 90 percent of the six million

Blacks then in the United States still lived in the South, and fully 70 per cent of these as peasants in the same countryside where their fathers and mothers had toiled as slaves. The inhuman relations which the plantation owner established to insure his exploitation of his tenant "serfs" and sharecroppers molded the pattern by which the white-supremacy elite of exploiters ruled the South. The iron law of the prison-like plantation economy became the Jimcrow law by which the whole South deprived the Black people of their rightful opportunity to share in the economic development of the region, and which effectively nullified their constitutional rights as free and equal citizens.

Blacks began to leave the plantations in ever larger numbers as job markets opened in the cities as a consequence of the gains in industrialization of the South. But life for Blacks in the southern cities was in many respects little better than in the countryside. The trek was extended to the North and Midwest where there were more and better jobs, some schooling, some dignity. Blacks who at the beginning of the present century lived in the South mainly as a "peasantry" on the plantations are now to be found as a part of the population of every large city in the country.

Denied the status of equal citizens and the opportunity for a fair stake in the economic life of the South, Blacks migrated in waves to the North and West in search of a livelihood and some liberty. The Black question was not solved by this; it was merely distributed throughout the country. This movement of the Black people, from the old plantation areas of the South to the industrual and commercial cities of the country, brought about important changes in the character of the Black condition. From sharecroppers, tenant farmers and toilers on the plantations, Blacks became engaged in urban occupations—as workers in industry and in the service trades. Their class composition and, correspondingly, the primary form of their oppression and exploitation, changed from that of rural peasant to that of urban worker. The now urban Blacks developed in some measure the class stratification characteristic of the population in the over-all capitalist society.

The population movements of the Blacks furthered the process of integration of the Black question into the general social problem inherent in capitalism. Likewise, the needs and aspirations of the Blacks became as one with the great mass of all other Americans, as variegated and as complex as theirs. If, at the beginning of the reconstruction of the old slave states of the South following the Civil War, the demand raised in the Congress by Thaddeus Stevens that the ex-slaves be granted "40 acres and a mule" of their former masters' properties had been granted, along with the full complement of civil and political rights of equal citizenship, the Blacks would have been provided with an economic base for the solution of the problem of their oppression. If "40 acres and a mule" was the bargain basement price the ruling class *could have* paid to solve Black oppression a hundred years ago, the price which must be paid to solve the Black condition is infinitely higher today.

For the Black is no longer a peasant hungering for a strip of land—he is a worker, in union with his fellows, in struggle for a full social share in the mighty industrial plant of this country in which he toils: he wants it in terms of full employment at the highest wages paid at his maximum skill; he wants it in unfettered access to all outlets for cultural enjoyment. And, more than this, he wants full voice and his rightful share in the exercise of political power.

Indeed, Black oppression has become a part of every social problem of the nation. The nation's problems cannot be solved without solving the Black condition, and the Black condition cannot be solved without profoundly affecting the nation's social system.

As their existence inside the family of the nation determines their goals and defines the objectives of their freedom struggle, so it is that the distribution of the Black people within the social class structure of the society as a whole determines the pattern of the struggle to attain those goals.

Analyzing the social composition of the Black people is of the greatest importance for an understanding of the Black condition.

With a working class composition of approximately 90 percent, Blacks are the most proletarian of all the large nationality–ethnic groups who make up the United States. There are still a considerable number of Blacks on the farms of the South, but they own little land and are mainly farm laborers. The Black people's urban middle class accounts for less than five percent of the total Black population. Blacks have few representatives in the capitalist class and these are in the category of small capitalists.

Whereas Blacks are about 10 percent of the total population, they make up approximately 20 percent of the working force. The proportion of Blacks in the labor force of a number of key industries is still greater than their ratio in the working force nationally. Among the industries in which Black workers constitute a significant proportion of the labor force are: mining, lumber, meat-packing, longshore, auto, steel, garment, building trades, and transport.

So we see that, whereas Black Americans are a relatively small part of the total population (10 percent), they are a *major force,* approximately 30 percent, in the *industrial* working class.

Black Americans are most heavily represented in the working class base of the class stratified pyramid of U.S. capitalist society, with a small percentage in the middle-class brackets and a numerically sparse representation in the strata of small and marginal capitalists. Their struggles to level all barriers to an attainment of a status and condition of equality with their fellow Americans introduce a *special* social dimension into the *common class struggle.* The question of Black oppression manifests itself as a particularly rapacious *form of class oppression* and is being fought out on a national scale, particularly in the cities of maximum working class strength.

The fact that the Black people are primarily of the working class is at once a characteristic feature of their oppression and a determining factor of the greatest strategic significance in the solution of the problem of their oppression. This means that what is good for Black people is good for the working class. It means that in a qualitatively new way the struggle for Black freedom cannot be in conflict with, but conforms to, the interest of the working class as a whole. Indeed, *the freedom struggle of the Black people is a specialized part of the general struggle of the working class against deprivation and class exploitation and oppression.*

Likewise, such programs as meet the needs of the working people, and conform to the interest of the working class, correspondingly serve the cause of Black freedom.

From a recognition of his basic working class identity in the class structure of the society, the Black worker can readily locate the class source of his oppression. As he occupies a status at the base of the class-stratified pyramid of the society, his enemy is that class which occupies the apex of the society's pyramid, for that is where the exploiters' power resides.

The struggle of the Black people for freedom from oppression is not a horizontal struggle but a vertical struggle. It is not directed against better-advantaged white working people in the exploited class strata but against the common exploiter class at the top of the pyramid.

Therefore, the freedom struggle of the Black people reinforces the struggle against the exploiting class of the white capitalists and joins with those strata of the population upon whom the privileged apex weighs so heavily.

Furthermore, the very patterns of discrimination against the Black worker in industry which have largely segregated him into the hardest, heaviest and hottest jobs, have produced a situation in which Black workers are the dominant majority at the primary stages of the whole production process. On the other hand, the traditional economic deprivation of the Black masses has become unbearable now as a consequence of the displacement of Blacks *en masse* from their jobs as automation is extended. All this, added to the weight of his numbers in the working class, is the objective basis of the strategic importance of the Black worker to the working class as a whole.

But there is another factor which endows the Black worker with a special quality of premium value to the working class as a whole: the Black workers are doubly motivated as fighters of their class, for they are not only exploited as workers but are workers who are additionally victimized by racist proscription and discrimination. The struggle to reduce the degree of their economic exploitation results in a measure of relief from racial oppression,and the breaking down of racial proscriptions in turn facilitates their battle for economic advancement.

Indeed, the presence of so large a proportion of Black workers, so especially motivated to militancy, in the American working class can be likened to the addition of manganese to iron ore; when the two elements are united and fused in the furnace of class struggle, the metal of the U.S. working class acquires a new quality, a quality vastly superior to either of its components—the quality of pure steel.

Elimination of the racial barriers between Black and whites in the United States will greatly enhance the unity of the anti-monopoly front of struggle for general social progress, democracy and peace. Above all, the leveling of the color bar in industry and political life will make it possible for our working class to achieve a new quality of class unity wherein Black worker will stand with white worker as brother to brother, and the class will be enabled to give its undivided attention to its true class enemy, the monopolists.

With the right to a political life secured for the Black masses of the South, the popular base of the electorate will be strengthened by an influx of three to five million Black working men and women. These new voters who will have won their right to vote in long, fierce battles against the Dixiecrats, these veterans of the Civil Rights revolution, will be fighting partisans of social progress all down the line. They may well contribute to a basic transformation in the relation of forces both within and independent of the Democratic Party, and they constitute the requisite force for the ouster of the Dixiecrats from Congress and for breaking the stranglehold of reaction over the South.

From its earliest days the Communist Party of the U.S. has given major attention to the struggle for the economic, political and social equality of the Black people. It has done so not only because the racist oppression of the Black people in the United States was itself a shameful violation of the dignity of human beings, but also because the racist proscription of the Black people stood athwart the path of social progress of the class and the nation.

At its 16th Convention in 1957, the Communist Party clearly pointed out that the main line of march of the Black people's movement was that of opposition to all forms of separatist "solutions" to the question of their oppression and toward full and complete equality in the life of the nation. It estimated the significance of the Black question then as being "the crucial domestic issue of the day,"(*Political Affairs,* March 1957, pp. 31-42), the struggle for the solution of which would accelerate social progress along the entire anti-monopoly front.

Events have fully confirmed the major theoretical and programmatic resolution on the Black condition which our Party adopted at its 17th Convention in December, 1959. In this convention, we stated:

". . . The main unrealized task of bourgeois (capitalist) democracy in the United States is revealed in the special oppression of the Black people. The bonds of Black oppression can and must be shattered. . . . Victory on this sector would open the way to rapid developments along the whole front for radical social advancement of the entire nation."

In the current stage of the massive advance of the Black freedom movement, our Party has given full support to the broadly based united front of the Black people's organizations which give leadership to the direct actions of the Black people's rising against segregation and for full equality. Our Party fosters the widest unity of action by the broad political spectrum of participating organizations and leaders which make up the Black freedom front. Our Party promotes in every way the involvement of white masses—labor, youth, peace forces and religious people—in the struggle for the rights of the Black people. At the same time, our Party exposes the diversionists, adventurists, provocateurs, and opponents of Black-white unity who seek to poach upon and disrupt the Black people's freedom movement.

Through the victorious development of the Black people's freedom struggle, the Party perceives the reinvigoration of the whole front of social action and struggle for new levels of social progress in our country. As Gus Hall put it:

"The removal of the cesspool of racism with its practices of discrimination in the South will also eliminate one of the main sources of ideological contamination of our people. Racism and white chauvinism have stunted the growth of class-consciousness and working class ideology in general. They remain among the most effective weapons in the hands of the employers for diverting the rise of class unity, class consciousness and militancy. . . . Victory in the South will enable the healthy ideology of the working class to take its rightful place in our midst."

And he added,

"The struggles [of the Black people] in the South to rid our land of the shackles on freedom are giving an injection of new strength to all our democratic institutions. They are broadening the popular base of democracy in our land. They are cleansing the political base of democracy in our land. They are cleansing the political and social atmosphere of our country."

World Marxist Review, September, 1963

28 Blacks Want Cooperation,
Not Permission

The Black masses, joined in battle on a wide front against discrimination and racism, appeal to their white countrymen for cooperation and participation. Hard pressed Black citizens in battle for their freedom solicit and welcome a fighting fellowship with all strata of justice-loving white citizens. Especially is labor looked to, to take a firm stand in support of the just demands for equality which the movement advances.

What Blacks are asking of their fellow-Americans is cooperation in their freedom struggle, not permission to fight it.

One would think that this elementary aspect of the relationship of "liberal white opinion" to the militant thrust of the Black freedom movement would be apparent to all. But not so, as seen by the cacaphony of condemnations of the stall-in action called by a detachment of the movement for the opening day of New York's World's Fair.

All manner of liberals and erstwhile "friends of the Blacks" queued-up before television cameras to publicly rebuke Blacks for impatience and "the employment of rude tactics" in pursuit of their objectives for equality of rights with white citizens.

Those white friends of the Blacks who presume to designate the "permissible" ways and means by which the victims of segregation may fight for their rights would do far better by stepping up their own personal participation in the struggle to secure these rights.

It is not those who militantly conduct the struggle to secure the rights of the Black people who are imperiling the cause, but those consecrated Confederates in the Senate who are engaged in a filibuster on the Senate floor, week after week, and who have converted its august assembly hall into an echo chamber for the recitation and dissemination of every possible racist calumny against U. S. citizens.

It there are alarms to be sounded, let them sound against the filibuster of the Senate Dixiecrats and their Everett Dirksen-Republican collaborators who are waging a sit-down against the will of the people for the prompt enactment of a genuine Civil Rights bill.

If there are appeals to be made, let them be made to the true friends of the Black people—and consequently the real patriots of the national interests—in the trade unions, in the churches, in the schools, in the communities, for all to come forth now in greater unity and far more vigorous struggle, to compel the Senate to pass the Civil Rights law in particular and bring the government into action at every level to secure and enforce the full equality of rights of Black Americans in all aspects of the nation's economic, political and social life: in matters of schooling, housing, employment.

The struggle for Black freedom is a dead-serious pursuit. Its justification is not to be sought in the decorous manner of those who fight its battles, but in the death-dealing slum conditions which have been produced from a profit-motivated segregation and discrimination system which grinds in its maw over 20 million North Americans who are Blacks. The only question of relevancy in the area of manner and forms of the struggle is the question of whether the particular tactic allows for mass expression for both the Black victims of discrimination and for mass solidarity on the part of their white allies.

In this connection, there can be no principled objection to supporting the stall-in initiated by a segment of the civil rights movement. The only question of principle involved here is that of the necessity for both Blacks and whites, working people in the first place, to recognize and then act upon that recognition, that the conditions for a general social advance in our country call for an allout struggle to shatter the walls of segregation and discrimination which have operated to divide brother from brother along the color line to the furtherance of an unequal measure, but equally insufferable, deprivation and exploitation of both.

The Black freedom struggle has come now to the point where there can be no vision of peace in the land until its simple democratic, Constitutional, and human rights' demands are fully attained. Therefore, there will be no abatement in the militancy or scope of the struggle. The struggle will rise to embrace ever higher democratic actions and at the same time will attract increasingly wider popular support among white masses.

We believe it possible to secure economic, political and social justice to the Black people short of bringing all the wheels of the country to a halt. But if that should be what it would take to secure to the Black people their rightful share in the democracy, that is what it will be. But should the stubbornness of the nation's ruling clique compel such a general stoppage in the country before securing to the Black his equal rights, one thing will be sure, the economy will be starting up again under a new management, and the plain people will have displaced the privileged scions of the establishment in government at all vital levels.

The Worker, April 19, 1964

29   Watts Burns with Rage

After you have read all about the "riot" in Los Angeles, you will have to weigh all of the thousands of words of the newsmen's "battle scene" stories against one solid statistic: the head count of the dead. The uncontestable fact is that of the 36 people who died in the six days of wrath, 33 were Blacks.

In addition to the number and color of the dead, other statistics have been dutifully compiled. There were 900 persons hospitalized for injuries, and almost all of them were Blacks. Blacks arrested in the Watts area of Los Angeles were jammed into every available space in the city jails—of the more than four thousand people arrested in the area all were Blacks.

The papers reported in some detail how the National Guardsmen operated in "the field" while another 8,000 in reserve awaited their turn. An Associated Press man wrote that on Sunday morning "about4:30 a.m., a woman motorist approached a National Guard blockade at 59th Street and Vermont Avenue. When she failed to stop on command, guardsmen opened fire with a machine gun. A policeman who helped carry her to an ambulance said, 'Her legs were almost cut off.' She was identified as Mrs. Lerner Cooke, 47, a Black."

A staff man for the *New York Herald Tribune* told of the teamwork between Lt. Richard Bogard's police from the Venice district and Col. Tom Haykin's 1st Battalion, 100th Infantry, 40th Armored Dovision of the National Guard. The combined force occupied the firehouse on 103rd Street (Watts) as its command post.

"The Guardsmen hit two men they figured were snipers. Maybe they were; maybe they were just curious," the reporter wrote. They were dragged into the firehouse and propped against the wall. One resisted as a doctor probed in the hole in his shoulder for the bullet lodged there.

" 'Choke him till he blacks out,' a policeman said and somebody choked one of the suspects till he blacked out. He revived in a minute, coughing blood, and the fight was out of him." Again the reporter told how—

"The National Guardsman had fired a perfect shot. He hit a man in the middle of the forehead, the shot had ripped off the back of the man's head. He was dead upstairs in the firehouse. 'It was a beautiful shot,' a detective said. 'We've killed two here so far, wounded a lot of others,' someone said."

Who were the white victims of the riot? There was a sheriff's deputy—Ronald E. Ludlow, 27. Another white man died of a wound that could have come from a police riot gun; a white fireman died when a wall of a burning building fell upon him.

Most of the 33 Blacks who were killed were gunned to death by police wielding riot guns. The National Guardsmen, of course, also machine-gunned a woman driving in her car. Then there was the four-year-old Black "looter and rioter," Bruce Brown, who was shot to death in his front yard. His riotous 3-year-old brother was wounded by the spray of police bullets and Guardsmen's 30 caliber machine-gun fire, but at last reports he was still alive.

Not so with 18-year-old Charles Shortridge who was all set to enter Los Angeles City College in September; he lay there dead as his uncle stared unbelievingly at the huge punched-out places the riot-gun shells had left in his nephew's head, neck and cheek.

They say it was a "race war," "an insurrection." But how come it turns out that 33 Blacks were killed to one white deputy sheriff?

This was no "race riot." This was an elemental scream of outrage from a violated people entombed in a prison house of social deprivation and economic impoverishment. No one has a right to expect that those whom the men of power and privilege, the capitalist ruling circle, have rendered reliefless in their wretchedness will forever slumber silently in the lower depths where they have been consigned by this society of bourgeois and billionaire.

Only those ignorant of history; only those blinded to the sight of injustice and the daily degradation of the Black detainees of the slums of this country's great cities, ringed all about as they are by towering walls of white-supremacy, hatred and exclusion; only simpletons can assume that prisoners will not generate out of the fury of their circumstance the fire with which to ignite their cages. And so they set fire to their prisons, these unattended, denied, abused and degraded ones. They burned their prisons as did the desperate ones who followed Spartacus. Like the ragged ones who marched and sang with Villon. Like the slave chain breakers who lived to hang with Nat Turner.

So they made other statistics—500 stores of absentee-owners were set afire.

One of those who lost a store to the angry uprising of the downtrodden of Watts of Los Angeles (the City of the Angels it says in the Chamber of Commerce ads) was a certain Richard Gold. Mr. Gold has many stores, a chain of furniture stores, so he will simply write that burned one off of his income tax returns next year.

But the point is that Mr. Gold knows more about the time of day in the world we all live in than most of the men of his class and all of the Los Angeles city fathers. Said Mr. Gold: "I cannot condemn these people. These people should not be shot down like dogs. White people who were as poor as they would burn and loot if they saw the chance. What's behind this is pentup anger over poverty and miserable housing."

Mr. Gold, the Watts businessman, is white and right on this score.

Watts is the city center of a Black population which numbers some 523,000 in the whole of metropolitan Los Angeles. Watts is indeed the most poverty-ridden area of lush, plush, tinseled and glittering Los Angeles. Into its 150 blocks are jammed 67,000 Blacks. They pay high rents for deteriorating houses. They shop in neighborhood enterprises in which they are not employed.

There in Watts, income is lowest in all of Los Angeles, save the "skid row" district. Unemployment is several times higher in Watts than for the city as a whole. More than one-third of Watts Blacks are unemployed. Unemployment among its youth is almost twice that of whites. Close to 60 per cent of the Watts population depend on relief.

The New York Times told it as it was when it said that—"The fact is that the new Civil Rights Laws—and the related anti-poverty program—have not yet greatly improved the lot of the Negroes in the teeming ghettos of the cities of the North."

The welkin sounds that came from Watts last weekend were loud and angry enough to have shaken the complacent into a wide-eyed confrontation of the reality of the challenge by the slum-confined millions who have come to the point where they were determined not to live any longer in the same old way.

Billy Graham, the head of a Crusade for Christianity Movement, called the Watts explosion a "dress rehearsal for revolution," and blessed the clubs and guns of the police for crushing it lest it spread to other cities and "require the nation's armed might to quell it."

Fortunately, the frenetic fulminations of Billy Graham did not set the pattern for the commentary of notables upon last week's social explosion in the Black ghetto of Los Angeles. There were thoughtful observations and conclusions being suggested by many prominent personalities.

Senator Robert Kennedy, formerly Attorney General, scored the philistines who think the answer to Watts-like outbursts lies in applying more police muscle. He is quoted as saying: "There is no point in telling Negroes to obey the law. To many Negroes, the law is the enemy. In Harlem, in Bedford-Stuyvesant (Brooklyn), it has almost always been used against them." He emphasized that "the only real hope for ending the violence is in speeding up social programs directed at the problems of slum Negroes."

Dr. Ralph J. Bunche, Under Secretary of the United Nations, in a statement to the press, said: "The ominous message on Watts is that city, state and national authorities must quickly show the vision, the determination, and the courage to take those bold—and costly—steps necessary to begin the dispersal of every Black ghetto in this land."

And he warned that continued social neglect and police abuse of the most oppressed and exploited Blacks, shoved as they are into ignored corners of the cities—"Black ghettos"—are the tinder for future explosions "in every city in this country with substantial population."

Prof. Frank Hartung, sociologist of Southern Illinois University, asserted:

"It will be as difficult—but not more difficult—to eliminate this sort of violence as it is to eliminate poverty . . . Major social reformation, going far beyond the passage of civil rights laws will be required to eliminate the threat of future upheavals from the Negro slums.''

Herbert C. Ward, Machinists' District 727 business agent and chairman of the Community Labor Committee, spoke for Black labor leaders in the Los Angeles area in demanding the immediate removal of the Los Angeles police chief William H. Parker as the most universally hated symbol of the continuous and wanton police brutality and terror which the Black people are subjected to. Furthermore, he called for the immediate starting of slum clearance and new housing projects with public and private resources; the construction of a fully equipped hospital; the cooperation of all levels of government; and an intensive program of placing unemployed and underemployed Black young people in jobs or training for jobs at standard rates of pay.

Burt Lancaster, the Hollywood actor, derided the hysterical reaction of some whites and their exclamations of alarm. Said Lancaster, ''I'm just surprised it didn't happen sooner.'' And the screen writer, Abbey Mann, added, ''I don't condone rioting, but anybody who doesn't understand it has no heart.''

A man in Watts said the word in a television interview:

''We ain't going to just stand and look while they beat us.

''We ain't going hungry and ragged when they got more'n they can eat and wear either.

''Those fires lit something inside my soul too.''

The challenge of the Watts explosion can be met only by a truly massive program to extend genuine material equality of opportunity to the Black masses in particular and to those who dwell in poverty and social deprivation.

It means a vast increase in investments in the War Against Poverty Program, an increase that can only come about through a proportionate decrease in the expenditures in the criminal diversion of national resources and men to the dirty work the Johnson Administration is carrying out in Vietnam, where U.S. soldiers are busy killing people who have risen in behalf of freedom for themselves as did our forefathers in the Revolutionay War.

In Watts itself, what is called for is not only a total economic opportunity program for wiping out unemployment and for proper job-training, but a program for the total reconstruction of the area. All the blight of slum conditions must be eliminated in accord with a plan speedily implemented. Housing, educational and recreational facilities must be provided for in full measure.

In addition, Watts requires that Blacks, who are more than 90 per cent of the population, shall be predominant in the police department, fire fighting, and other city service jobs and functions for the area. Merchants doing business in the area must employ Blacks in their establishments in proper ratio.

With such an approach for Watts and for all the ghetto cities of the country, guarantees can be established against recurrences of such tragic outbursts of primitive protest and outrage at injustice.

As Rep. Augustus F. Hawkins, Los Angeles Black congressman, said, "The trouble is that nothing has ever been done to solve the long-range underlying problems."

Watts means that the time for stalling and demagogic promises and good will platitudes has run out. It has come down to this: Either wipe out the conditions that produce the slums, or the slums will wipe out the cities.

The Worker. August 16, 1965

30   Black Oppression as a Function of U.S. Capitalism

The monopoly capitalists' domination of the country is characterized by the merciless exploitation of the working class, the ruination of the farmers and the savage oppression of the Black people.

Though only one-tenth of the nation's population, the Black people supply nearly one-fourth of its industrial working force.

It is a mark of their special oppression that the Black people have been bound in the main to the bottom rungs of the ladder of social classes. They are the most proletarian of all the peoples or ethnic groups who make up the population of the nation. About one-half of the number of white workers are engaged in occupations classified as white-collar jobs, but only one-fifth of the Black are employed at jobs above the blue-collar level. Less than five percent of the Black people can be classified in middle class and professional employee categories. Among the small capitalists there are only the barest representation of Blacks and none are to be found in the higher rungs of big capitalists and monopolists.

In the total population the farmers are a small part of the whole—about seven percent. This ratio also holds true in respect to the Black people, where just eight percent of the Black working force are employed in various kinds of farm work.

The special racist character of the economic exploitation of the Black people by monopoly is disclosed in the fact that Blacks are paid less than whites for equivalent work in every category of employment, from unskilled laborer to university-trained professional.

As the Black Americans have been ruthlessly exploited and robbed of their rightful share in the U.S. economy, so have they been deprived of their just share of social services, educational and cultural opportunities. Racist laws, discriminatory customs and poverty have conspired to force the mass of Black people to dwell in the most depressed areas of the cities. The big city ghetto and rural slums are everywhere, North and South, the home communities of the Black people. They are segregated parts of the larger communities, and are systematically cheated of their just share of housing, parks, transportation, hospitals, schools, and cultural centers. They are supplied only with an abundance of police by the local government authorities. The police who patrol the Black sections and communities operate as defenders of property and the privileges of the "downtown" ruling class interests. They are committed to defense of the "establishment" through subjecting the people of the slums to endless and brutal assaults upon their dignity, their lives and liberties with billy and pistol and arbitrary acts of arrest of innocents.

The greatest indictment against the social system of the U.S. monopolists is revealed in the fact that the Black people have been deprived of the minimal political rights associated with the Constitutional guarantees of citizens and the basic criteria of democracy and human rights. In the southern states even the elementary right to vote is still a cause to struggle for and not yet a universally won and exercised right of the Black citizen. Throughout the country, South and North, Black Americans are deprived of their rightful share of the political power, of fair representation in government from the local to the national levels. Along with the political, economic and social discrimination which expresses the fundamental nature of the oppression of the Black people in the United States, they are also confronted on every hand with the ideological assault upon their human dignity and self-esteem by the barbarous doctrine and practices of white supremacy, of racist prejudices and chauvinist arrogance.

It is such circumstances which characterize and define the conditions of Black people in the nation and which have given rise to the present movement for freedom and equality of the Black people. During the past decade especially, this movement has conducted wave after wave of heroic mass actions which have set millions of Black Americans and white masses in motion in support of its goals. The ceaseless struggles of the Black people have attracted the active support of ever-larger sections of the rest of the nation. Furthermore, world public opinion has rallied to the cause of the Black Americans in battle for their just rights. As a consequence, some declaratory measures have been won from the government, which affirms the justness of the Black people's demand for an end to the discrimination system—but the *system remains* as oppressive as ever.

In the present and developing phase of the Black people's struggle for equal rights and freedom, a new quality of emphasis must be placed on the question of the interaction and interdependence of this battle with the historic working class obligation to lead the entire nation in struggle to break through the barrier of the capitalist social system itself. It becomes increasingly evident to the Black freedom fighters that the real enemy is the big business-dominated society, which is structured primarily to serve the profit interest of the monopolists rather than to satisfy the ever-expanding needs and requirements of the masses of the people.

Lenin noted that it was necessary to be mindful of the wide range of the correlations between the movement of the oppressed and the proletarian emancipation movement of the oppressor nation; to help each in turn to identify its cause and goals with that of the other. He saw the convergence and mutual reinforcement of these two movements as essential for the victory of either. This concept has special validity for our time and the struggle in our country; emphatically so, when we give consideration to the overwhelming working class composition of the Black people.

In the period ahead the Black freedom movement will increasingly develop a consciousness of the objective fact that *the struggle for Black equality and freedom is a specialized part of the working class strggle*; that ultimately the Blacks' oppressive condition is perpetrated by the capitalist-monopolist class which is able to gain additional profit advantage from the super-exploitation of Blacks as a consequence of their deprivation of equal rights.

More and more clearly the Black freedom movement will draw anti-monopolist conclusions from the experiences of its struggle. The heavy proportion of working people to the total Black population dictates such a course of deveopment for the Black freedom movement.

What is more, capitalism in the United States has historically victimized Black people, even as capitalist-imperialism victimized their ancestral kinsmen of the African continent.

From its earliest establishment, U.S. capitalism has been guilty of enriching its private fortunes out of the most savage robbery of the Black people and most ruthless exploitation of the labor power of the Black working people, both during the era of chattel slavery and throughout the span of the century since emancipation.

Capitalism instituted the dreadful system of human slavery to translate "the blood, toil and tears" of Blacks into personal profit and corporate capital and maintained it by terror and law and savage racist social customs for over 300 years.

The operation of the slave system in the United States then, like the discrimination system against Blacks now, was a development of capitalism and a function of this nefarious system of human exploitation for private profit-making.

Notwithstanding, all the disabilities and oppression—the excluding and the denial, the segregation and the discrimination—the Black people are an integral part of this nation.

The Black is an American and this United States is his native land.

Other than the Indians, all peoples in the United States have ancestral origins abroad. Black Americans' ancestors stemmed from Africa, from peoples who today are playing a great role in the world cause of emancipation from the bondage of colonialism and imperialism.

The struggle of the Black people for full economic, political and social equality with all other Americans *is a struggle to enlarge democracy in the entire nation.*

Blacks of all classes are compelled to enter into the struggle against racial discrimination and its social consequences. However, the fact that the Black people are predominantly working class will increasingly influence the program and goals of the Black people's movement, the strategy and tactics of the struggle, as well as assure the permanent nature of the alliance with the organized labor movement. Indeed, labor and the Black people are destined to march together in pursuit of a common future, free of capitalist exploitation and capitalist racial oppression.

Because of the high working class composition of the Black people and the strength of the Black workers in key areas of the economy, *the freedom struggle of the Black people presents itself as a vital front of the anti-monopoly struggle.* It is geared into the tasks related to the fulfillment of the historic goal of the working class, that is, to effect the transformation of society from capitalist to socialist. The freedom objectives of the Black people directly benefit the working class and serve the democratic interest of the whole nation.

The Black people's fight to eliminate political discrimination is, in essence, *a struggle for genuinely representative government.*

It entails full freedom to vote and to be voted for. The *majority* must be secure to exercise its *right to the power* in local political subdivisions—precincts, wards, counties, Congressional Districts, Assembly Districts. The *minority* must have the right to *its just share of the power,* to proportional representation at all levels of the three branches of government—the legislative, administrative and judicial as well as an equal share of the police authority.

The struggle of the Black people for full access to the political arena in the southern states and the northern ghettos is a struggle to oust the worst reactionaries, Dixiecrats, racist warmongers, anti-labor servants of the monopolists from the Congress and from the state and local governing bodies, and to place in public office genuine representatives of the people chosen by and from the Black people, the labor movement and the progressive forces generally.

The struggle of the Black people against economic discrimination is a major front in the real *war against poverty.*

It requires the trade union organization of the unorganized, especially in the factories and the fields of the South.

It necessitates the development of the economy in the South in particular and in the other areas of blight and poverty as well. The reconstruction of agriculture on a modern scientific basis and big expansion of industry in the southern region is needed.

The economic needs of the Black people require a vast and countrywide program to wipe out the shame of the slums of the metropolitan centers and rural areas and to erect in their stead unsegregated, open-occupancy, controlled low-rent and low-cost housing, recreational facilities, playgrounds and parks, as well as all necessary schools and hospital facilities.

Capital for the financing of such development programs, which are needed to reduce the accumulated discrimination gap in the economic status of the Black people, must be supplied by the government out of the profit hoards of the monopolists and from the savings that would flow from a drastic reduction of the military appropriations.

To secure the scale of anti-poverty programs needed to wipe out the economic discrimination and social deprivation of Black Americans is to make an assault upon the profit-grabbing of the corporations and the trusts, is to enter into struggle against the economic and political pillars of monopoly capitalism itself.

Central to the solution of all problems that present themselves in the area of strategy and tactics for the Black freedom movement is the necessity to identify the Black people in terms of their relation to the nation as a whole, as well as their relation to the working class, whose destiny it is to lead the nation to its classless future. In this regard:

1) Blacks are an integral part of the nation, though suffering special oppression and racial discrimination.

2) The number of Black capitalists is minimal and none are big capitalists; the middle class category is a small percentage of the total; the *mass* of the Black people is of the working class.

The approach to all policy questions, to all matters of tactics and strategy in respect to the developing struggles of the Black freedom movement must take into account the necessity that all policies and tactics must correspond to both the immediate as well as long-range interest of *the basic numbers* of the Black people, that is, to its working class majority.

During the past decade the young generation, especially, of the Black people, have gained a wide experience with the *class* nature of the capitalist *state* and how its police and court system defends its privilege and power. They have gained much experience in the matter of building organizations, cultivating unity, reaching out to forge alliances with wide strata of white people. They have out of their experience, grown profoundly critical of the whole nature and structure of capitalist society. They seek a progressive alternative to capitalism. Now, as at no other time in its history, the Communist Party of the United States has the opportunity and duty to disclose the socialist alternative to the young generation, to bring to the Black militants the science of Marxism-Leninism to help illumine the way to lasting victory for the masses in the struggle for freedom, equality and justice.

Political Affairs. February, 1966

31   To Amass Power

For the oppressed to secure the goals of freedom, they must acquire the power to compel the oppressor to yield to their demands.

The statement of the freedom goals is merely the beginning of the tasks of leadership; its main function is to give direction to the striving of the masses to produce a situation wherein they have the power to gain and defend their freedom.

The strength of the oppressed is based upon the unity of their own numbers, reinforced through a system of alliances with other strata and sectors of the population.

As this is so generally, it is particularly true in respect to the struggle of Black Americans for freedom, equality and justice in the United States. A valid concept behind the phrase "Black Power" is that of the need of Black people to secure sufficient means of power to free themselves from the yoke of discrimination and deprivation. The struggle for the power with which to gain freedom has to be waged in several areas.

It is a struggle for the political self-expression of the Black people; for Blacks determining the choice of candidates, elected officials and appointees in all those situations in which they constitute the majority. And where Blacks are less than a majority, it is a fight to secure a fully just share of the political power—at least proportionate to their numbers. In addition, there must be a continuing struggle to obtain and enforce the right of individual Blacks, regardless of their proportion, to exercise the right to seek and be elected or appointed to posts of responsibility on the sole basis of merit and without reference to "a fair racial share."

It is likewise a struggle to gain a just share in the economic life of the nation. First of all, it is a fight for a proportionate share of jobs and for job training in industry and the professions.

It is a struggle against all manifestations of racist indignities, for recognition and respect for the cultural, material and ethnic contributions which Black Americans make to the national culture and history of the country.

To accumulate the power necessary to secure full freedom, more than Black Power, more than the self-organization and militant action by the Black people themselves are required.

It is necessary to win broad strata of white masses to active participation in struggle for the freedom rights of Black people. On the basis of mutual advantage and advanced self-interest, it is necessary and possible to establish a fighting partnership between the Black liberation movement and the organized labor movement, as well as with various associations with the peace movement and other organized categories of the population who are victimized by the monopolists' establishment.

Discrimination against and oppression of Black Americans are in fact super-exploitation and robbery of the most under-privileged of working class people, the Black people, by the capitalist owners of the economy.

Therefore, the struggle of the Black people for freedom can be viewed as a specialized part of the general struggle of the jobless and working poor against the monopolies, *i.e.*, of the working class against the capitalist class. It is a part of the revolutionary processes rending the old social system, and a major part of the struggle for bringing into being a new society—socialism.

From the Montgomery, Alabama, Bus Boycott which the Reverend

Martin Luther King led in 1956 to the Freedom March through Mississippi, the struggle of Black Americans to secure their citizenship rights
to full political, economic and social equality has been the most visible
battle banner on the frontier of social progress in our country for a
decade.

Enormous energy has been expended in great mass actions of the
Black people and their white supporters in dramatizing the demands for
equality and freedom and for an end to segregation and discrimination.
In these struggles, men, women and youth of the Black freedom movement have made staggering sacrifices: scores have been martyred,
thousands have been imprisoned; their schools, churches and homes
have been bombed. When contrasted with the situation that prevailed in
the past, the Black freedom movement can take justifiable pride in the
significant gains which its militant struggles have forced the ruling class
to yield. However, when measured against the rights which white
Americans take for granted as their birthright, and when weighed
against the suffering and sacrifices exacted in the last decade of hard
fought battles, the advances which Black Americans have made toward
the goal of equality and freedom have indeed been insubstantial. All of
the key indices of their special oppression remain as before: Blacks are
the most disfranchised politically, the most jobless and underemployed,
economically; in terms of social well being they are the most
deprived—ill-housed, medically uncared for, educationally and culturally denied; their dignity as human beings is constantly violated by
anti-Black slurs and defamation, by the practices and precepts of the
racist doctrine of white supremacy.

After a decade of pragmatic pursuit of objectives obviously essential
for the attainment of a status of equality with all other citizens, the need
for a summing-up of experience and a definition of the theory of Black
freedom as an aid and guide to the further development of the movement has become a matter of concern to the leadership.

The catch-phrase or slogan of "Black Power" has emerged as a
rather sensationalized by-product of the new endeavors by Black leadership to formulate a strategic and tactical pattern of guidelines, to elaborate a theory for advancing the Black freedom movement.

The primary use of the term "Black Power" was in connection with
the campaigns to boost the registration by Blacks for the right-to-vote. It
was also used to describe the consequence of Blacks withholding their
purchasing power from stores which discriminated against them; it was

used to describe the potential power of the economic boycott in the tactical armory of local Black communities. Stokley Carmichael, who was then President of Student Non-Violent Coordinating Committee (SNCC), put the phrase "Black Power" into sloganized form during speeches on the 260 mile Mississippi Freedom March. In doing so, he was seeking to generalize certain positive experiences of the Lowndes County, Alabama, Freedom Organization which had fielded an all-Black (Black Panther) party in the local elections that year. (Since then, Stokley Carmichael has attempted to turn the "Black Power" concept from a unifying into a divisive, separatist concept.)

Elaborating on the original positive concept behind the phrase, Black Power, the Mississippi Freedom Democratic Party leader, Mrs. Victoria Gray, said in a press interview that "The MFDP is interested in consolidating a base of power in the Black community. This is our concern.

"But we are not interested basically in color—and we have said this in our campaign. Our interest is in changing the political and the economic system of this entire state and this ultimately involves white people as well as Blacks."

In a declaration printed as an advertisement in *The New York Times* of July 31, 1966, a National Committee of Black Churchmen issued a statement on "Black Power" signed by some 30 prominent Black clergymen of major denominations. They expressed themselves as follows: "Powerlessness breeds a race of beggars. . . . Having no power to implement the demands of conscience, the concern for justice is transmuted into a distorted form of love, which in the absence of justice, becomes chaotic self-surrender. . . . A more equal sharing of power is precisely what is required as the precondition of authentic human interaction. . . ." What the "disinherited " must have, the clergymen pointed out, is an increased "capacity to participate with power—i.e., to have some organized political and economic strength to really influence people with whom one interacts. . . ." They declared, further, that "Negroes need power in order to participate more effectively at all levels of the life of our Nation."

Essentially, there is general agreement among Black spokesmen today that the chant, "Black Power," is reflective of a determination on the part of the Black Freedom Movement to build up maximum strength for united action in all situations in which Blacks are the preponderant number in the total population, to create local bases of political power and economic strength and thereby transform their isolated ghettoes into positions of influence, of Black Power.

This aspect of the concept of Black Power corresponds to what was stated in the Communist Party's resolution on the Black people in this regard. The Communist Party's position on the freedom cause of Black people adopted at its 17th Convention in 1959 and affirmed and further elaborated at its 18th Convention in June of this year, stated that: "Black Americans are determined to build ever closer their unity in order to wage the struggle even more militantly to break down all remaining barriers to their exercise of any and all political, economic and social rights enjoyed by any other citizens.

"The great masses of Blacks unite not in order to separate themselves from the life of the country. They unite to more effectively employ the strength of their own numbers and the weight of their alliances with other parts of the population to level all barriers to their fullest integration into all aspects of the economic, political and social life of the American people as a whole. They are forging an internal unity to facilitate their struggle for equality as free and equal American citizens."

And several years in advance of the current concern with this aspect of the problems of the movement, the Communist Party pointed out the dialectical relationship of the work to utilize local situations where Black voters constituted the majority as bases of local political power to strengthen the overall struggle *for genuine representative government.* We said: "The Black people in the United States must secure their rightful share of governmental power. In those urban and rural communities where they are the larger part of the population generally, and in the deep South areas where they are the larger part of the population particularly, they must constitute the majority power in government.

"In its essence, therefore, the struggle for the rights of the Black people is not merely a 'civil rights' fight, it is a political struggle for the power to secure and safeguard the freedom of a people.

"It is a struggle for a just share of representation nationally; it is a struggle for majority rule in those localities where Blacks are the dominant people in the population."

The Communist Party has long recognized that the struggle to create the conditions for Black people to exercise power in the areas of their majority is an important part of the full program for Black freedom. Yet, this does not and cannot satisfy the requirements of the whole of the Black people. In terms of the country as a whole, Black Americans are more often than not cast in a minority situation; therefore, the fight to guarantee fullest protection and enforcement of the equal rights of the minority is no less important to the cause of Black freedom. Also, the struggle against prejudice and racist practices and the fortification and enforcement of an adequate body of law against victimization and discrimination of individuals because of race and color remain an important part of the program for fulfilling the rights of the Black people. Indeed, the absence of prejudice means a Black should enjoy the right to fill any position which he or she is qualified for, regardless of the proportion of Blacks in the given situation.

The perspective and struggle to establish Black power bases of local political control in the deep South and metropolitan slums of the North ought not to be confused with any notions of Black exclusiveness or political isolationism. Such Black power positions of strength would prove useful to a total strategy for Black freedom only insofar as they enhance the capability of the Black movement to consumate more favorable alliance relations with comparably disadvantaged and objectively "anti-establishment" classes and forces among the white population. *The mass of Blacks who are poor and working class have no choice but to seek to effect alliances with the comparably disadvantaged whites who are exploited by the ruling class of monopolist interests which dominate the society. Black power of itself is not and cannot be sufficient to overcome the tyranny of the power of the monopoly capitalists.* In the final analysis, theirs is the power behind Black enslavement as well as working class exploitation. Theirs is the power that stands astride the path of progress toward freedom for the Black people and social advance for the nation. To win significant victories from it will require not only the maximum united action of the Black people, but Black and white working class unity in allied and coordinated struggle against the common oppressor and in behalf of the common goals of the poor and the exploited.

The National Committee of Negro Churchmen gave an excellent expression of this strategic necessity of seeking a fighting alliance with social forces in the population who are objectively "going our way" in order to fashion the scale of power required to win. They said: "We must organize not only among ourselves but with other groups in order that we can, together, gain power sufficient to change this nation's sense of what is *now* important and what must be done *now*. . . . We and all other Americans are one. Our history and destiny are indissolubly linked. If the future is to belong to any of us, it must be prepared for all of us whatever our racial or religious backgrounds . . . we are persons and the power of all groups must be wielded to make visible our common humanity."

There are other concepts associated with the discussion about Black Power which are of significance to the further development of the practical activity of the movement as well as relating to the theory of the freedom movement.

One of these is the reestablishment of Black hegemony over the leadership of all major departments of the Black freedom movement. This is a demand for a new quality of Black-white relations within the Black freedom movement; it demands an end to all paternalistic and privileged assumptions on the part of white participants in the Black freedom movement; that is to say, that the white supporters of the movement must not arrogate to themselves roles of super-advisors of the leadership as the price for their participation. The leadership of a number of Black people's organizations have called for a greater sensitivity to the mores of the Black community on the part of white workers in the movement, so as not to affront the dignity of those very people with whom they have joined for the fight. These organizations have called for their white supporters to make their first concentration work in the working class areas of the adjacent white communities. Especially do the Black leaders now challenge the organized labor movement to make their support to the cause of Black freedom more visible and more substantial by policing their own unions, their own areas of influence and authority for ending discriminatory practices in employment, housing, upgrading, apprenticeship and other training programs, and election to union offices. Above all, Black leaders demand of the labor leaders that they carry through the long awaited task of undertaking the organization of the unorganized Southern workers, Black and white, of factory and farm.

Another question which has been given widespread discussion in connection with the dialogue on the theory and practice of the Black freedom movement, which the Black Power issue triggered, has been that of the effect of the foreign policy of the government upon the goals of the Black people.

Never before has so substantial a section of the Black leadership come out in vigorous opposition to a war in which the U.S. government was engaged. In the past, individual Black leaders have opposed various foreign policies and particular acts of aggression by the government, but never before have entire organizations of the Black people unequivocally denounced a war in which a high proportion of Black soldiers have been impressed to kill and be killed. In addition to the Student Non-Violent Coordinating Committee (SNCC) and the Congress for Racial Equality (CORE), the Nobel Peace Prize winner and best known Black leader, Dr. Martin Luther King Jr., condemned the war in Vietnam. The resistance of Blacks to the genocidal war against the people of Vietnam is not only disclosed in the position of their civil rights leaders and clergymen but in the growing number of Black youth who defy the draft boards, the army induction centers, and in the number of Black soldiers in Vietnam who have resisted serving on "hunt and kill" missions against the people of Vietnam.

Dr. King and others have raised the banner of anti-imperialist solidarity between the Blacks of the United States and the victims of U.S. imperialist aggression in Vietnam, the Dominican Republic, as well as in African and Latin American countries, as a vital strategy for uniting the cause of Black freedom with the interest of the majority of mankind. They have pointed out that for American Blacks to adopt a position of support to U.S. imperialist policies of aggression and war would be to isolate themselves from the overwhelming majority of mankind. This represents not only a meaningful contribution of Black Americans to the growing power of the world peace front to force the U.S. government to quit Vietnam, but it also represents a new depth of comprehension of the true nature of the social and class forces within the country and the world arena on the part of an important sector of the Black freedom movement. It has demonstrated by its opposition to the Vietnam war that it associates the destiny of the just cause of Black freedom with the main social tendency of our epoch and is not beguiled by the apparent overriding power of U.S. imperialism.

Seeking sensations and fostering all opportunities for divisionism and conflict among the component sections of the Black freedom movement and between Black and white, the press and television have been waving the phrase "Black Power" before the eyes of the nation with alarming interpretations. It is represented as a Black nationalist answer to white supremacy and as the doctrine for ghetto uprisings of Blacks against whites in the great cities of the country.

The ideological provocateurs of the press find some encouragement for their sensationalizing the "Black Power" phrase in some speeches and articles of certain Black spokesmen, who sometimes endow the two words with powers that they cannot and should not possess. At times they even suggest that by uniting their own strength, Blacks can go it alone, by virtue of the fact that whey would "control" politically a score of metropolitan centers of the country.

What these poorly informed speakers and demagogic commentators forget, or don't know, is the actual nature of the "power structure" in this country—the corporate elite of monopolists whose power over the Congress, the White House and the Pentagon rests on the solid material base of de facto ownership of the whole economy. Also, in responding to the atrocities of the police against Black marchers struggling to push back the walls of their ghettoes in order to enlarge living space and secure some job opportunities, some people have suggested that Blacks could organize their own policing system to counter the violence of the racists and the police.

The concept of self-defense is a well established practice in life on the part of American working people; furthermore it is given official sanction in the Constitution of the United States. The right of the Black community or of an individual Black citizen to armed self-defense in face of wanton assault by mobsters, racists, or other lawless elements is one of the inalienable rights of citizens of this country and does not need the advocacy of anyone. The fact that circumstances have prevailed where Blacks have been abandoned to mob terror by law enforcement authorities—and indeed in many situations the officers of the law, sheriffs and policemen have themselves committed "the deeds most foul"—does not make the responsibility of the Federal Government any less for the protection of the lives and property of Blacks, while securing them the full exercise of their Constitutional rights and a non-segregated, participating share in public affairs anywhere in this country. Blacks have in the past and will in the future defend themselves against racist violence; but their demand remains for the government to discharge its duty to safeguard the lives and property of all of its citizens in the exercise of their Constitutional rights.

The widespread discussion which has developed about the several interpretations of the cry of "Black Power" that was raised by marchers on the walk from Memphis to Jackson, is part of a seeking for sound theory to illiminate the pathway of progress for the Black freedom movement.

The Communist Party has made important contributions in elaborating theoretical problems and strategic concepts of the Black freedom movement. As the leadership of the mass movement now addresses itself to the problem of historic direction and relationship of the Black people's cause to the goals of peace and the change of the system of society itself, the Communists will continue to make key contributions.

Political Affairs. September, 1966

32   Proud Heritage

E ven the worst racist defamers of the Black people bear witness to the fact that the past decade in the United States can only be described as "the decade of the Black people's mass upsurge for freedom and equal rights!" From Montgomery, Alabama to Watts in Los Angeles, California; from Chicago, Illinois to Grenada, Mississippi, mass actions for freedom have been waged by Black people in a variety of forms—forms which correspond properly to the requirements of the goals and the circumstances in which the battles have unfolded.

The ways and means of the conduct of a given struggle are influenced by the goals and purposes of that struggle. The object of the Black people's struggle in the United States is not to blow out the brains of the white masses, but to rid their brains of race hatred and legally and physically prevent them from committing anti-Black racist acts of prejudice.

Writing about the matter of nationalist, racist prejudices which created many barriers to the unity of the working class and its allies in Czarist Russia, Lenin underscored the necessity for Marxists never to forget that: "The masses have a future, besides a past, and reason, besides prejudices." (V.I. Lenin, Collected Works, Moscow: Progress Publishers, 1965. Vol. 9, p. 18) Lenin taught that the more enlightened workers must constantly appeal to the reason and the advanced self-interest of the prejudiced ones with confidence in their ability to overcome their prejudices.

Marx and Engels in their day were acquainted with the almost unbroken chain of slave revolts which periodically rocked the slave-holding oligarchy of the southern part of the United States. They joined their voices to that of the great Black strategist of abolitionism, Frederick Douglass, in appealing to Lincoln to enroll Blacks into the armed forces as the quickest route to military victory over the slave-holders' rebellion of the Confederacy.

The epic story of the struggle for freedom of the Black people is as glorious a part of the history of the United States as is the near-genocide of the American Indians a measure of its shame.

How many martyrs? How many casualties? How many hanged? Lynched? How many imprisoned?

The 5,000 Blacks who were lynched since 1900 were put to death to discipline those who were stirring from "their place." Buckets of blood oxidized black and hard on the concrete floors in hundreds of jails throughout the southern routes of the "freedom riders" and "demonstrators" over these past ten years when some 30,000 Blacks were jailed for defying segregation laws and resisting the police.

The matter of the strategy and tactics of the struggle for Black people's freedom and equality has been a subject of voluminous works by Blacks in the struggle for more than 200 years: The 19th century opened with the moving appeal by David Walker. It produced the great heritage of the literature of abolitonism—dominated by the writing of Frederick Douglass—on the strategy and tactics of the freedom struggle. The 20th century opened with W.E.B. Du Bois' ringing Niagara Appeal, and there has continued, unabated, an on-going elaboration of policy and theory based upon the experiences of the struggle of the Black people for their freedom. This particular people's struggle is certainly one of the most complicated and intertwined and interrelated national struggles known to history—being both a national question and a class question, a minority question and a race question.

The whole world has applauded the heroism displayed by the current upsurge of Blacks in bare-handed confrontation with police and soldiers across the country. Honest and responsible revolutionaries have marveled at their ingenuity and studied their creation of forms of mass actions in circumstances in which they were vastly outnumbered and forced to find a form of struggle in the midst of a veritable armed camp.

Indeed, the history of the Black Americans' struggle for freedom constitutes one of the most courageous and glorious books in the library of humanity's struggles to overthrow tyranny. The Blacks' 400 years of uncrushable resolve and fight for freedom, first as a slave and then as racially oppressed freemen, is an inspiring epic of mass heroism.

Memo to the editorial staff of *The Worker*. October, 1966

33   Black Identity and Class Unity

In a recent article, Comrade Roscoe Proctor writes: "The lack of emphasis now placed upon integration by the Black Power advocates should be interpreted only as applying to Black people's national and community development, not to the American society as such. Economically speaking, the Black people are not only reliant upon, but are bound to the American economy as a whole. The struggle for Black inclusion into the trade unions, the various shops, the schools of higher learning, the political life of the country, etc., constitutes the very basis upon which the struggle for unity between the oppressed Black people and the broader American working class and progressive movements can be realized in practice.

"The fact that the Black people are primarily of the poor and of the working class means that the struggle for Black liberation cannot be directed against the white working class and the white poor who are also exploited, but rather against the American ruling class which exploits the poor Black and white workers in common." (Roscoe Proctor, *Notes on "Black Power" Concept,* New York: *Political Affairs,* March, 1967)

These are sound conclusions.

They have been substantiated in the unfolding experience of the practical movement for Black freedom and equality. They accord with the Resolution on Black Liberation at the 18th Convention of the Communist Party USA, held in June 1966 and, prior to that, in the Resolution on the Black Liberation question adopted at the 17th National Convention in December 1959.

In his report to the December 1966 National Committee meeting (published under the title *Black-White Unity),* Henry Winston documents this thesis from a rich variety of current experiences and events.

Despite the present upsurge of the nationalists, we perceive that on a world scale there will take place a growth in internationalism—an internationalism based on an ever-ascending role of the working class within the affairs of each nation as well as within the world community.

In our day it is impossible to perceive of serious advances for the labor movement, or for the working class in the sphere of economics or politics, save on the basis of the further advance of the Black people along the path toward full equality in all spheres of life. One cannot foretell a decade of Black isolation without at the same time prophesying a decade of defeats and setbakcs for the working class as a whole.

Henry Winston pointed out in his pamphlet: "The growth of national pride is an expression of the new level of consciousness in the struggle against segregation which combines a recognition of the special problems of the ghetto with a recognition of the imperative necessity for unity between Black and white. It follows that the growth of this tendency cannot but help to strengthen all efforts towards unity of the Black people in struggle."

Whereas national pride is a positive and welcome tendency, black nationalism is something else again. It is, as Winston indicates, "a minority tendency in the Black movement" that "stems from the Black bourgeoisie whose program is based upon the internal market of the ghetto." Winston points out elsewhere in the cited work, "that a struggle is developing among the Black people, not for separation from the democratic white masses, but for separation from the economic, political and social oppression imposed upon them by Wall Street and Southern Bourbon Dixiecrat rule."

Communists stress the basic distinction between these two tendencies. We are for the fullest expression and development of national
pride as a force for the struggle against chauvinism, which is the main
tool of division between Black and white working masses. By the same
token, we are unrelenting opponents of bourgeois nationalism whose
danger to the struggle of the oppressed peoples and the working class is
not relieved by adjectives of color. Black nationalism is not and can
never be the negation of white nationalism or white chauvinism. The
opposite of racist nationalism is interracial equality and justice; it is the
elimination of nationalism and racialism, not the change of brand from
white to black.

Oscillation between an orientation of separation from, versus an inclusion in, the United States nation exists as an historical fact only in
relation to the more basic fact that the Black people adhere to a determination to secure their full place within the nation, for their full integration in the total national experience.

Even Black professionals suffer a discrimination in earnings and
employment opportunities as compared to their white colleagues in no
less, and often greater, measure than the working class category of the
Black population. The Department of Labor and the Department of
Commerce current reports document the long-established fact that, contrary to popular belief, discrimination does not diminish in proportion as
educational attainments increase. Blacks have not even begun to secure
a just share of high-paying jobs.

Here one must point to an odd distinction that recurs in the writings of
a number of "radical" analysts and commentators on the Black movement in the United States. They tend to set a special low ceiling on
income for Blacks before assigning them to the class categories of the
Establishment. White Americans with $10,000 annual incomes are
bonafide proleterians, but according to the calculations of the "new
radicals," Blacks earning $10,000 a year are "black bourgeoisie" and,
therefore, part of the Establishment.

If we relegate to the ruling class all those with incomes of $10,000,
the camp of the enemy would be formidable, capitalism would be
secure—and not only for the next decade. This is nonsense, of course,
American bourgeois captains of industry, monopolies, members of the
establishment, have million-dollar incomes. Those with $10,000 in-
comes are properly a substantial and vital strata of the anti-monopoly

forces. It is precisely the economic consequences of the caste system of anti-Black racism, which has deprived all class categories of the Black people of their economic due, that constitutes the material objective basis for broad class unity among Black people in the struggle for genuine freedom and equality. This is not to deny that the class struggle has its reflection within the Black people's community. Indeed, the all-class character of much of the freedom struggle at this stage is a unity of diverse classes—therefore, in a certain sense, a unity of opposites. Where there is a unity of opposites, there has to be also a struggle within the opposed tendencies for leadership. Within the Black people's freedom movement, there takes place a struggle on policies, tactics and strategic concepts, which reflect the striving of the working class forces to establish the dominance of its leadership, and that of its class opponents to restrict, minimize or deny the leading role of the working class in the freedom movement.

They are in error who contend that Black unity is represented as a stage in the Black freedom development that is in conflict with and in opposition to the broad progressive movement—the labor-liberal-civil rights coalition.

They are in error who hold that almost everything, including Black-white unity, should be sacrificed at the present stage to further Black people's unity; that only on the foundation of a solid unity of the Black community would meaningful Black-white alliances be possible. This schematic stage approach to the effective organization of the Black freedom movement does not take into account the actual reality that these two parts of the development of the Black people's freedom cause go on simultaneously and are complements of one another.

As the struggle advances to higher levels of consciousness, standing on the shoulders of minimal gains and limited successes, Black people's unity will increase and Black-white unity—centered upon Black-white working class solidarity—will also greatly expand. This question goes to the very heart of our basic analysis and understanding of the pattern of development of the road to Black freedom in the context of the over-all struggle for social progress within the nation. The basic resolution of our Party on the Black Liberation states:

"Black Americans are determined to build ever closer their unity in order to wage the struggle even more militantly to break down all remaining barriers to their exercise of any and all political, economic and social rights enjoyed by other citizens. . . . They are forging an internal unity to facilitate their struggle for integration as free and equal American citizens."

New developments are posing some new questions of great theoretical interest and of practical importance. One such question is the impact and consequences for the total freedom struggle, of the entry of large sections of the Black freedom movement into the struggle to compel the United States to end its war in Vietnam. This development of the formal integration of the two movements—that for peace in Vietnam and that for Black freedom—posits in a new way a variety of questions bearing upon the strategic problem of the relationship between the democratic struggle for equality of peoples, within the frame of capitalist relationships, and the working class, socialist objective of replacing the capitalist system of exploitation, of changing the social system itself.

The experience of the past decade, of massive actions in behalf of advancing the freedom front of the Black people, attest to the fact that maximum mobilization of the Black people themselves and the widest attraction of support from white masses occur around issues wherein the particular interests of Black Americans as Blacks are related to and bear upon the general interests of the masses of all Americans.

The task of successful and effective Black leadership is that of defining the particular interests and fighting objectives of the Black people, and of skillfully relating and combining the particular with the general. Only in this way can maximum forces be mobilized from the whole nation to join actively in the struggle for Black freedom, with the oppressor ruling class isolated and deprived of support from the majority population of the nation at large.

Speech to trade union activists. November, 1967

34   From Detroit to Newark

From Detroit, Michigan, to Newark, New Jersey, to Tucson, Arizona, the flames of rebellion give a red glow to the night shadows shrouding the vast ghettos of poverty and misery long characteristic of our great cities.

We said it after Watts. We said it before. We say it again:

"The time for stalling has run out. It has come down to this — Either wipe out the conditions that produce the slums, or the slums will wipe out the cities!"

At this very moment, some ten cities are the scenes of upsurge by the most downtrodden and deprived of the poor and the jobless. The Black communities, suffering the most outrageous discrimination in matters of jobs, decent housing, educational and recreational facilities, are targeted for massive police occupation.

The murderous police-terror attacks upon the persons and dignity of Blacks in their segregated communities have been the instant provocation for violent strike-backs on the part of the crowds of outraged citizens.

But before the provocations there was the unrelieved misery of the impoverished and abused victims of ruthless ruling-class exploitation and racial prejudice.

In a land where affluence is boasted of as commonplace in every TV cigarette ad, millions are jobless and hunger dwells among them. Half of all Black Americans and a fifth of the whole nation have endured an agony of poverty and neglect for years on end.

Their appeals and petitions have received mocking responses and empty demagogic promises from local politicians and the Johnson Administration.

Such is the background to the Detroits and Newarks. The demonstrators display rage against the fat indolence and deaf indifference of the ruling class to their call for opportunities to work and live in health and decency and dignity.

Detroit signalizes a new stage in the rebellion of the poor. Though the Black people played a major role in the demonstrative protest against the crimes of the Establishment there, for the first time Detroit witnessed an upsurge of the poor which features the united and fraternal action of Black and white together!

The rebellion of the slums of Detroit, like all previous upsurges, was marked by the "liberation" of food-stuff and much needed household appliances and furniture. The picture windows of the stores with their opulent displays of the enormous accumulation of a super-abundance of goods, of which the millions of needy Americans—Black and white—are deprived, taunt and challenge the prisoners of the slum to an act of redistribution of some token "sharing of the wealth," as it were.

In truth, the uprising in the slums of the big cities during this month—historically revolutionary July!—renders a dramatic service to the country. It has administered what should be a timely shaking-up of all thoughtful people. The rebellion of the poor has served warning to the nation to stop its drifting toward disaster in the wake of the L.B. Johnson dreamboat of a Southeast Asian empire, and to strike out on a new course in national policy.

The rebellion of the poor signalizes the fact that a deep-going national crisis is upon us which calls for the emergency reappraisal of ongoing policies. Above all, it demands that the $50 billion a year Operation Graveyard that the Johnson government is digging in Vietnam be ended forthwith and the funds now being wasted in this madness be routed into vast investments for eliminating slums in America.

The national emergency which Detroit and Newark highlight calls for an extraordinary response on the part of the people. It calls for the convocation of an emergency conference of all peoples and labor organizations in Washington, D.C. to demand that Congress convene in special extraordinary joint session to stop the Vietnam war, and put in force a multi-billion dollar program of slum clearance rehabilitation and jobs to lay the material base for ending the poverty and prejudice crises that threaten the nation with catastrophe.

We urge mass demonstrations to aid the victims of the brutal and heartless military suppression throughout the country, and to demand the government stop the Vietnam war and mobilize all resources to meet the poverty crisis at home.

We urge all material and moral aid to the struggle for equality and justice for the Black people. No one has the right to challenge the form of their struggle, after hundreds of years of abuse and absence of relief. Brothers in struggle with the Black people ask only that the forms be effective. No racial bar must be left standing to divide the poor one from another!

Editorial, The Worker. August 12, 1967

35   Martin Luther King, Jr.

These days have heard the thunder and seen the flash of the terribly swift sword of historic Justice shifting the balance in her scales: the freedom-loving peoples of the world are looking at the United States with eyes of wonder and discovery. For there, yesterday's sullen and segregated—the sable sons of her Southern fields and factories, of her Northern ghettos and jobless rolls—have grasped liberty's torch from the upraised hand of the barren Lady and fired cities as flaming sacrifices, candles burning —as it were—as offerings on the altar of an unaltered racist society.

The drama of these days awaits its rendering by a worthy artist of words and insight. For tragedy, like the chill and starless hour of night when the stars have gone out and dawn not yet arrived to lift the veil of sorrow with gentle fingers of light, hovers over the land. Its focus is on a new grave in a cemetery "for colored" in Atlanta, Georgia. For the life of the great preacher and partisan of peace has been taken. That one who stirred the hearts and best expressed the burning wants of most of the Black people and, indeed, of almost all of the poor people—Black and white.

The murder of Martin Luther King, Jr. was a desperate deed to destroy that one who seared the souls of those who dared sit in silence while the sounds of sirens are roaring in the ears, and napalm bombs, sticking and sizzling napalm bombs, are falling upon the village huts, the children's schools, the hair and flesh of Vietnam's fathers and sons, mothers and daughters, the new-born and the aged.

But already there can be seen that early light of the new day aborning in the outpouring of mourners, by waves of converts to his cause and call to battle—for ending the war in Vietnam, for digging out racism and destroying it, and for labor unity.

Thirteen years is a minor segment in the life of a man, with longevity being what it is in this modern time. Still, that was all the working time at the disposal of the Reverend Doctor Martin Luther King.

Memorial meeting message. April 5, 1968

36 Separatism—a Bourgeois Nationalist Trap

Lately there has been much discussion concerning "the right of Black America to create a nation." This is an unscientific, subjectivist concept. It rejects the Marxist-Leninist view of a nation as being a material community of people with very definite features. The classical definition states that:

"A nation is a historically constituted, stable community of people, formed on the basis of a common language, territory, economic life and psychological make-up manifested in a common culture." (J.

Stalin, *Marxism and the National Question,* New York: International Publishers, 1942, p. 12)

A nation comes into being only when a community of people has evolved a combination of such characteristic features. One feature or another may be stronger than the others—this gives to each nation its peculiar national identity—but each one of the above stated characteristics must be present or the community cannot be a nation. A nation is a historic phenomenon—it arises, develops and declines; it undergoes constant change.

A community of people may evolve into a nation by acquiring precisely those characteristic features listed in the given definition.

But it is not something that can be willed or chosen. A nation exists as an objective fact, or it doesn't exist because of mitigating historical circumstances which left it deprived of the requisite attributes. For instance, both Lenin and Stalin in their respective works on the national question made favorable references to the illustration given by Otto Bauer in his book, *The National Question and Social Democracy,* of the point that the concept nation is not an ethnographic or racial category but a historical category that conforms to definite objective criteria. Bauer wrote that in general, capitalist society makes it impossible for them (the Jews) to continue as a nation, because they had no closed territory of settlement causing them to assimilate with other nations and because no nation is possible without a common language.

The Jews in Czarist Russia were certainly oppressed—experiencing the kind of savage discrimination and persecution and being subjected to the horrors of lynching pogroms which are so analogous to the worst features of Black oppression in the United States. Still they were not a nation. Therefore, the character of their condition defined to an important extent the route they could take in the struggle for freedom. Had they been a nation oppressed, they could have taken the route of struggle for *self-determination, for political secession* from the Great Russian oppressor nation. But since *they were not constituted* as a nation but rather—in Lenin's phrase—*"a persecuted and oppressed minority caste,"* they had to struggle under other slogans—against discrimination, segregation, the pale, separatism; and in alliance with the working class and others for equality, for democracy, for the overthrow of the system that bred anti-Semitism: against capitalism and for socialism.

Basically, in its scientific usage, the slogan of self-determination of nations means that nations, large or small, developed or underdeveloped, have the right to sovereign existence, to complete secession and the establishment of a independent state. The right of self-determination means that only the nation itself will decide how it will arrange its internal affairs and its external relations with other nations. But these are slogans for the orientation of the fighters against national oppression when the oppressed are constituted into a specific socio-historic formation—a nation. These slogans are not necessarily apt or correct or useful guides to action for the communities and groups of oppressed people who do not constitute nations. National and racial oppression often falls most heavily upon peoples who are not oppressed as whole nations, but as fragmented communities, or minorities. The slogans appropriate for oppressed nations often ill-fit the demands and prove contrary to the requirements and the circumstances of the struggle and the goals confronting the *oppressed nationalities,* such as Blacks in the United States.

There can be nothing wrong with "tying into" a certain popularity that the term self-determination currently has among circles of radicals of various hues, providing one makes clear that it is not intended to convey the Marxist meaning in political science. When we give a term from political science a *special* meaning, we must accompany it with *our* definition and explanation. For example, I made use of the term self-determination in its popular, broad, non-scientific sense in writing on this question in the following way.

"It seems to me that such relevance as the general principle of self-determination has to the reality of the status and outlook for the Black people's struggle in the United States can be expressed as:

"The right of a people—irrespective of their level of, or direction of, development as a national entity—to act in concert, or in alliance with fraternal classes and peoples, under the direction of their own leadership, after the fashion they may choose, in pursuance of their own goal of freedom as they so conceive and construe it to be at any given moment, is an inalienable democratic right of that people which can neither be ceded or withdrawn by any other power. In this sense, the right to self-determination is to the national community what the right to freedom of conscience and freedom of political choice is to the individual." (*Theoretical Aspects of the Negro Question in the USA,* February, 1959.)

What is at issue is more than a popular usage for the now fashionable term of self-determination; what must be countered is the demand for the revision of the Marxist-Leninist definition of both *nation* and *self-determination*. And to qualify these scientific definitions and concepts opens the way to replacing a Marxist-Leninist analysis with a confused accommodation to the "revolutionariness" of the petty bourgeois Black nationalists.

Some express the view that we should be mindful of the fact that, "We live in an advanced age of science, both natural and social" and call for approaching this question "scientifically." But it is precisely this, a scientific approach to the problem, that is lacking on the part of those who revise the Marxist-Leninist presentation of the question of national oppression and how to solve it in the diverse forms in which it occurs—such as in the form of an oppressed *nation,* and oppressed *nationality* of people within a nation, an oppressed national minority, an oppressed caste, an oppressed group, and so forth. Ironically, some whose presentation of the question of self-determination and of the nation do not accord with Marxist-Leninist science, deride "an approach which is based only on subjective desires . ..." and ". . . will lead exactly nowhere."

Of course, it leads exactly nowhere to assert, as does one writer, that self-determination "must be applied to the people as a whole and not to a territorial unit . . . the right of self-determination applies to Black Americans independently of whether there is territorial unity in the black belt or elsewhere. It was wrong from the beginning to have restricted the use of this slogan on the basis of territorial approach."

This assertion not only is in glaring contradiction to the definition of a *nation* but is the exact opposite of the same writer's view that "of course, the concept of common territory is one of the fundamental features of a nation and without it there is no nation."

People suffering common oppression—racial, ethnological, caste, religious, language, cultural—who nevertheless do not occupy a common territory do not add up to a nation. This, of course, is not to say that the victims of oppression are any less oppressed because they are not oppressed in the category of *nation,* but it does *say something* about *how* the struggle can be waged for freedom from oppression. And it demands a correct appraisal (the facts of the case) of the particular type of national oppression that one is dealing with. Only in the most general sense can the slogans and strategy of struggle of a nation for liberation illuminate the tasks, the ways and means by which oppressed people in other or lesser social political formations can advance along the correct path to freedom.

The mistake of the "nation builders," wrote Lenin, is not their concern for objective conditions but "their incorrect appraisal of facts—they grab hold of trivialities and do not see the main thing." He followed with the affirmation that "We Marxists have always been proud that we determined the expediency of any form of struggle by a precise calculation of the mass forces and class relationships." (Lenin, *Ibid,* Vol. 20, p. 440)

In our studies of *"Theoretical Aspects of the Negro Question in the United States"*—the major conclusions of which were embodies in the 17th Convention *"Resolution on the Theory of the Negro Question"*—we established that *the representation of the question as that of an oppressed nation seeking state sovereignty was not a correct orientation* for the development of the necessary forms of struggle for the solution of *the particular* national question of Black Americans.

But those who would depart from Marxism-Leninism are apparently undaunted. Once again they insist that "The slogan of self-determination today means the struggle for the right of Black America to form a nation if it elects to do so." Still, we must ask: where will this nation be living—in what area of the country will it be located?

This view simply takes out of the Leninist definition of a nation the essential characteristic—that of "a common territory"—the most important attribute, the base upon which the other features could take shape!

To eliminate "common territory" from the characteristics of a nation is like taking the mainspring out of a watch. It may then still look like a watch, have a watch's face and hands, but will it truly be a watch?

The nation thus proclaimed for Black Americans would have the geographic profile of several strings of love beads! It would be a *conglomerate* Black nation which could view "the ghettos across the land" as a part of itself.

One writer misinterprets some fine lines of distinction which G. Starushenko in his book, *The Principles of National Self-Determination in Soviet Foreign Policy,* makes between foreign policy, national groups, peoples and nations in respect to their relating their cause to the slogan of self-determination. The aforementioned writer constantly uses the term "nation" when it is evident from the context that he is speaking of a "state." For instance, he writes of ". . . the possibility of Black America to establish a Black nation (state? J.J.) within continental United States." Again, he looks forward to a "new system which would permit a reorganization of our entire society, a condition basic to carving out a Black nation (*i.e.* Black *state*? J.J.) in continental United States."

When this writer describes the Marcus Garvey nationalist fantasy, at some points "nation" is used for "state" and vice versa. But lest the reader get lost in some fast semantical footwork here, the writer leaves no doubt about where he stands on the strategic concept for the Black people's liberation movement: He comes out as an advocate of a separatist nationalist solution. He declares, "The slogan of self-determination today means the struggle for the right of Black America to form a nation (a state? J.J.) if it elects to do so." And he urges that "We should call for a plebiscite of all Black Americans on whether they want to remain in the general commonwealth or to establish another nation (state? J.J.) within continental United States."

It makes no difference that the separatist outlook is presented in terms of the Black Panther Party's demand for a plebiscite; it is still a boost for a separatist way out. Such a thrust in emphasis is disorienting to the Black freedom movement and is confusing to the anti-monopoly allies in the struggle. When the progressive movement is confused, only the reactionary ruling circles benefit.

It must also be said that Communists cannot determine policies and make political decisions on the basis of the outcome of a plebiscite nor a Gallup poll, nor by reading tea leaves for that matter, but only by the careful assembly of all relevant facts and by submitting them to a thorough analysis, illuminated by the guiding principles of Marxism-Leninism.

Exhuming the corpse of a variant of the old slogan of *self-determination for the oppressed Black nation in America,* is self-defeating. We think life has affirmed the correctness of our Party's decision to retire that slogan a decade ago. And furthermore, better it be left there in its grave impaled with a wooden stake than be set abroad to divert from the new and vigorous current reality.

The theoretical foundation for our Party's ever vital, programatic policy concerning Black people in the United States, and its basic approach to the problems of the Black liberation movement, were set forth in the documents of the National Committee (N.C.) and the 17th Convention. They have proven their Marxist mettle and strategic and tactical value over the span of a decade, and have withstood all challenges. The 17th Convention Resolution and the N.C. documents on which it was based will continue to cast light on the road ahead in this field. This is so because our Party's position on this national question flows from a continuous and profound study of the ever-changing reality, and is deeply grounded in the scientific works of Marxism-Leninism.

Lenin's work in this area is full of illuminating insights into the complex, and variegated patterns of the national question, and, at the same time, is a dependable compass in pointing out a proper dialectical pattern of movement and struggle for its resolution.

Lenin said:

In regard to *"a democratic state with a mixed national composition, with sharp differences in the geographical and other conditions, Marxists defend autonomy as a general, universal principle."* (V.I. Lenin, *Ibid,* Vol. 20, p. 441) Autonomy meaning here not merely "community control," but real political power in areas of their majority, and maximum representation everywhere.

The above formulation of Lenin is deserving of the most careful contemplation. I consider it the *key* idea in Leninism in dealing with a general strategic concept and the direction of development for the solution of the national question in the United States.

While defending various forms of territorial political autonomy as a necessary aspect in the solution of the national question where there is "a mixed national composition," Lenin pointedly opposed notions of "extra-territorial or cultural-national autonomy." He called such schemes "segregation" and declared they were incompatible with Marxism, that they "spread ideas of bourgeois nationalism among the working class in a refined form."

Lenin said that:

"The theory and program of 'cultural-national autonomy' is petty bourgeois, for it converts bourgeois nationalism into an absolute category, exalts it as the acme of perfection." Furthermore, Lenin shows that "Under the slogan of 'national culture' the bourgeoisie of *all* nations . . . are *in fact* pursuing the policy of splitting the workers, emasculating democracy and haggling . . . over the sale of the people's rights and the people's liberty.

"The slogan of working class democracy is not 'national culture' but the international culture of democracy and the worldwide working class movement." (Lenin, *Ibid,* Vol. 20, p. 22)

Leninism teaches that:

"Marxism cannot be reconciled with nationalism, be it even of the 'most just,' 'purest,' most refined and civilized brand. In place of all forms of nationalism Marxism advances internationalism, the amalgamation of all naions in the higher unity, a unity that is growing before our eyes with every mile of railway line that is built, with every international trust, with every workers' association that is formed (an association that is international in its economic activities as well as in its ideas and aims)." (Lenin, *Ibid,* Vol. 20, p. 34)

"The principle of nationality is historically inevitable in bourgeois society and, taking this society into due account, the Marxist fully recognizes the historical legitimacy of national movements.   *"But to prevent this recognition from becoming an apologia of nationalism, it must be strictly limited to what is progressive in such movements, in order that this recognition may not lead to bourgeois ideology obscuring proletarian consciousness.* (Emphasis mine. J.J.)

". . . It is the Marxists *bounden* duty to stand for the most resolute and consistent democratism on all aspects of the national question. This task is largely a negative one. But this is the limit the proletariat can go to in supporting nationalism, for beyond that begins the 'positive' activity of the *bourgeoisie* striving to *fortify* nationalism." (Lenin, *Ibid,* Vol. 20, p. 34)

"To throw off . . . all national oppression, and all privileges enjoyed by any particular nation or language, is the imperative duty of the proletariat as a democratic force, and is certainly in the interests of the proletarian class struggle, which is obscured and retarded by bickering on the national question. But to go beyond these strictly limited and definite historical limits in helping bouregois nationalism means betraying the proletariat and siding with the bourgeoisie. There is a border-line here which is often very slight and which . . . nationalist-socialists completely lose sight of.

"Combat all national oppression? Yes, of course! Fight for any kind of national development, for 'national culture' in general?—Of course

not. . . . The development of nationality in general is the principle of bourgeois nationalism, hence the exclusiveness of bourgeois nationalism, hence the endless national bickering. *The proletariat,* however, far from undertaking to uphold the national development of every nation, on the contrary, warns the masses against such illusions . . . and *welcomes every kind* of assimilation of nations, *except that which is founded on force or privilege.*" (Lenin, *Ibid,* Vol. 20, p. 35)

". . . The proletariat cannot support any consecration of nationalism; on the contrary, it *supports everything that helps to obliterate national distinctions* and remove national barriers; it supports *everything that makes the ties between nationalities closer and closer,* or tends to merge nations. To act differently means siding with reactionary nationalist philistinism." (*Ibid,* Vol. 20, p. 36)

The Soviet academician T. Stepanyan, writing on the subject, *"Socialist Internationalism and Nationalist Ideology,"* (*Pravda* of January 15, 1969), underscored the fact that, "The ignoring of the tendency of *internationalization,* of the unity of nations, gives rise to diverse forms of nationalism." (Emphasis added. J.J.)

The tendency toward the uniting of peoples and nations, toward the formation of conglomerates of nationalities and peoples into large single states, is one of two objective trends in respect to the national question under capitalism. The other objective trend being the further development of national features of the respective peoples and of nation-type attributes in the sphere of economy as well as culture (not to take note of this companion tendency becomes a deviation toward national nihilism).

The two objective trends: one toward uniting the diverse parts of the multi-nationality state into a firmer whole; the other being the impulse *given* to the separate peoples to develop toward nationhood and seek national independence and state sovereignty.

"The Leninist principle of achieving a proper blend of class and national interest is as topical as ever," the Soviet scholar writes, "because part of the strategic plan of the ideological struggle of international reaction is *the promotion of nationalism* against proletarian internationalism." (emphasis added. J.J.)

"Nationalism under present-day conditions is above all expressed in ignoring the main contradiction of our epoch," Stepanyan continues, "the contradiction between socialism and capitalism, in giving up class positions when analyzing social phenomena, in giving up the ideas of the unity of all detachments of the world revolutionary movement and above all of the socialist countries in the struggle against the common enemy—against imperialism." (T. Stepanyan, *Ibid*)

Lenin said:

". . . On the national question, opportunism will naturally express itself differently among the oppressed nations from the way it will express itself among the oppressing nations.

"The bourgeoisie of the oppressed nations will call upon the proletariat to support its aspirations unconditionally for the sake of the 'practicalness' of its demands. It would be more practical to say a plain 'yes' in favor of the separation of *this* or *that* nation, rather than in favor of the *right* of separation for all sundry nations!" (Lenin, *Ibid*, Vol. 20, p. 411)

"The proletariat is opposed to such practicalness, recognizing equality of rights and an equal right to a national state, *It values most the alliance of the proletarians of all nations,* (Emphasis added. J.J.) and evaluates every national demand, every national separation *from the angle* of the class struggle of the workers. The slogan of practicalness is in fact only a slogan of non-critically adopting bourgeois aspirations." (Lenin, *Ibid*, Vol. 20, p. 411)

". . . *To the extent* that the bourgeoisie of the oppressed nation struggles against the oppressing one, *to that extent*, we are always, in every case, and more resolutely than anyone else, *for* it, because we are the staunchest and most consistent enemies of oppression. Insofar as the bourgeoisie of the oppressed nation stands for its own bourgeois nationalism, we are against it. (We are for) a struggle against the privileges and violence of the oppressing nation and no toleration of the strivings for privileges on the part of the oppressed nation." (Lenin, *Ibid*, Vol. 20, p. 411)

". . . The bourgeois nationalism of *every* oppressed nation has a general democratic content which is directed *against* oppression, and it is this content that we *absolutely* support, strictly distinguishing it from the tendency towards one's own national exclusiveness, fighting against the tendency of the Polish bourgeois to oppress the Jews, etc., etc." (Lenin, *Ibid*, Vol. 20, p. 412)

Lenin observed that;

"From the point of view of the theory of Marxism in general, the question of the right of self-determination presents no difficulties. . . .

"The difficulty is created to a certain extent by the fact that in Russia the proletariat of both the oppressed and oppressing nations are fighting and must fight side by side. The task is to preserve the unity of the class struggle of the proletariat for socialism, to offer resistance to all the bourgeois and Black Hundred (KKK-like, J.J.) influences of nationalism. Among the oppressed nations the separation of the proletariat as an independent party sometimes leads to such a bitter struggle against the nationalism of the respective nation that the perspective becomes distorted and the nationalism of the oppressing nation is forgotten." (Lenin, *Ibid,* Vol. 20, p. 451) ". . . The more slowly the democratization of Russia proceeds, the more persistent, brutal and bitter will national persecution and quarreling among the bourgeoisie of the various nations be. The particular reactionary spirit of the Russian Purishkeviches will at the same time generate (and strengthen) 'separatist' tendencies among the various oppressed nationalities which sometimes enjoy far greater freedom in the neighboring states." (Lenin, *Ibid,* Vol. 20, p. 453)

". . . in the interests of the successful struggle against the nationalism of all nations, in all forms, (the proletariat) sets the task of preserving the unity of the proletarian struggle and of the proletarian organizations, of amalgamating these organizations into an international community, in spite of the bourgeois strivings for national segregation.

"Complete equality of rights for all nationalities; the right of nations to self-determination; the amalgamation of the workers of all nations—this is the national program that Marxism, the experience of the whole world, and the experience of Russia, teaches the workers." (Lenin, *Ibid,* Vol. 20, p. 454)

Pointing up the continuing importance of the struggle against all varieties of nationalism, V. Afanasyev, in his book, *Scientific Communism,* writes:

"In order to disunite the peoples, shake the unity of the forces of democracy and progress and thus safeguard their domination, the imperialists use a tested weapon of the reactionaries like *nationalism.* Marxism-Leninism is intolerant of all manifestations of bourgeois nationalism and requires that a distinction should be made between the nationalism of the ruling nations (dominant-nation chauvinism and racism) and the nationalism of oppressed nations. The unquestionably reactionary ideology of dominant-nation chauvinism and racism, which justifies the domination of one nation by another, is flatly rejected by scientific communism. On the other hand, the nationalism of oppressed nations is directed against imperialism and contains elements of struggle for independence and is, therefore, progressive and supported by the proletariat. . . . On this score Lenin wrote: 'The bourgeois nationalism of *any* oppressed nation has a general democratic content that is directed *against* oppression, and it is this content that we unconditionally support.'

"At the same time, nationalism always harbors the threat of being stripped of its democratic content and turned into dominant-nation chauvinism and racism. For that reason, while supporting the liberation trend in the nationalism of oppressed peoples, Communists consistently champion proletarian internationalism, which consolidates the international solidarity and friendship of the working people of all races and nationalities. By demonstrating that the class struggle plays the decisive role in any social movement, including the national movement, and calling for unity among the working people of all countries, Marxists-Leninists combat the ideology of bourgeois nationalism and win the masses over to proletarian internationalism." (Afanasyev, pp. 117-118)

What Lenin taught in respect to the Russian and Ukrainian proletariat holds deep meaning and rich lessons for Black and white workers in the U.S. today.

Lenin said:

". . . Naturally, every democrat, not to mention Marxists, will strongly oppose the incredible humiliation of Ukrainians, and demand complete equality for them. But it would be a downright betrayal of socialism and a silly policy even from the standpoint of the bourgeois 'national aims' of the Ukrainians to weaken the ties and the alliance between the Ukrainian and Great-Russian proletariat that now exists within the confines of a single state."

". . . The national cause comes first and the proletarian cause second, the bourgeois nationalists say, with . . . would-be Marxists repeating it after them. *The proletarian cause must come first, we say, because it not only protects the lasting and fundamental interests of labor and of humanity, but also those of democracy; and without democracy neither an autonomous nor an independent Ukraine is conceivable.*"

"There are two nations in every modern nation—we say to all nationalist socialists. There are two national cultures in every national culture (that of the bourgeoisie and that of the proletariat). There are *the same two* cultures in the Ukraine as there are in Germany, in France, in England, among the Jews, and so forth." (*Ibid,* Vol. 20, p. 28)

"The Great-Russian and Ukrainian workers must work together, and, as long as they live in a single state, act in the closest organizational unity and concert, towards a common or international culture of the proletarian movement, displaying absolute tolerance in the question of the . . . purely local or purely national *details* of that propaganda. This is the imperative demand of Marxism. All advocacy of the segregation of the workers of one nation from those of another, all attacks upon Marxist 'assimilation' or attempts, where the proletariat is concerned, to contrapose one national culture as against another is intolerable. . . is *bourgeois* nationalism, against which it is essential to wage a ruthless struggle." (*Ibid,* Vol. 20, p. 33)

"Bourgeois nationalism and proletarian internationalism—those are the two irreconcilable hostile slogans that correspond to the two great class camps throughout the capitalist world, and express the *two* policies (nay the two world outlooks) in the national question. In advocating the slogan of national culture and building up on it an entire plan and practical program of what they call 'cultural-national autonomy,' the Bundists are *in effect* instruments of bourgeois nationalism among the workers.

"The Marxists' national program . . . advocates, firstly, the equality of nations and languages and the impermissibility of all *privileges* in this respect . . . secondly, the principle of internationalism and uncompromising struggle against contamination of the proletariat with bourgeois nationalism, even of the most refined kind. Marxists work to realize the demand for the unity and amalgamation of the workers of all nationalities in a given country in united workers' organizations." (*Ibid'* Vol. 20, p. 27)

"Whoever does not recognize and champion the equality of nations and languages, and does not fight against all national oppression or inequality, is not a Marxist; he is not even a democrat, That is beyond doubt. But it is also beyond doubt that the pseudo-Marxist who heaps abuse upon a Marxist of another nation for being an 'assimilator' is simply a *nationalist philistine*." (*Ibid,* Vol. 20, p. 28)

Lenin pointed out:

"That *'the right to advance separate demands to supplement a single general Social-Democratic program and to satisfy local needs and requirements arising out of the special features of Jewish life.'* is, of course, to be assured. However, *in everything else there must be com-*

plete fusion with the Russian proletariat, *in the interests of the struggle waged by the entire proletariat of Russia.*

"Autonomy in matters pertaining specifically to the *Jewish* movement, while in matters pertaining to the struggle against the bourgeoisie of Russia as a whole, *we must act as a single and centralized militant organization, having behind us the whole of the proletariat, without distinction of language or nationality, a proletariat whose unity is cemented by the continual joint solution of problems of theory and practice, of tactics and organizations; and we must not set up organizations that would march separately, each along its own track; we must not weaken the force of our offensive by breaking up into numerous independent political parties; we must not introduce estrangement and isolation and then have to heal an artificially implanted disease with the aid of these notorious 'federations plasters'."* (Lenin, *Ibid,* Vol. 6, p. 335)

"Marxism teachers the working class of the dominant nationality in the state that it must not forget the yoke of national oppression under which the so-called 'subject peoples' groan. That no matter how hard their struggle for a bare livelihood becomes, 'the conditions of life of this vast population are even harsher.'

"Marxism stands for complete equality. The policy of oppressing nationalities is one of *dividing* nations. At the same time it is a policy of systematic corruption of the people's minds . . . to poison the minds of the ignorant and downtrodden masses.

"But the working class needs *unity, not division.* It has no more bitter enemy than the savage prejudices and superstitions which its enemies sow among the ignorant masses. The oppression of 'subject peoples' is a double-edged weapon. . . .

"That is why the working class must protest strongly against national oppression in any shape and form.

"Millions and thousands of millions . . . are spent on poisoning the minds of the people." (*Ibid,* Vol. 20, pp. 237-238)

". . . the interests of labor demand the fullest confidence and the closest alliance among the working people of different countries and nations. The supporters of the landowners and capitalists, of the bourgeoisie, strive to disunite the workers, to intensify national discord and enmity, in order to weaken the workers and strengthen the power of capital.

"Capital is an international force. To vanquish it, an international workers' alliance, an international workers' brotherhood is needed.

"We are opposed to national enmity and discord, to national exclusiveness. We are internationalists. We stand for the close union and the complete amalgamation of the workers and peasants of all nations in a single world Soviet republic.

"He who says A must say B; one who has adopted the standpoint of nationalism naturally arrives at *the desire to erect a Chinese Wall around his nationality, his national working-class movement;* he is *unembarrassed even by the fact that it would mean building separate walls in each city,* in each little town and village, unembarrassed even by the fact that by his tactics of division and dismemberment *he is reducing to nil* the great call for the rallying and unity of the proletarians of all nations, all races and all languages." *(Ibid,* Vol. 6, p. 521)

Almost 100 years ago Karl Marx, in a letter of April 9, 1870 to Meyer and Vogt in New York, spoke on the question of consequences of national oppression to the proletariat of the oppressor:

"Every industrial and commercial center in England now possesses a working class population divided into two hostile camps, English proletarians and Irish proletarians. The ordinary English worker hates the Irish worker as a competitor who lowers his standard of life. In relation to the Irish worker he feels himself a member of the *ruling* nation and so turns himself into a tool of the aristocrats and capitalists *against Ireland,* thus strengthening their domination *over himself.* He cherishes religious, social and national prejudices against the Irish worker. His attitude towards him is much the same as that of the 'poor whites' to the 'niggers' in the former slave states of the U.S.A. The Irishman pays him back with interest in his own coin. He regards the English worker as both sharing in the guilt for the English domination in Ireland and at the same time serving as its stupid tool.

"This antagonism is artifically kept alive and intensified by the press, the pulpit, the comic papers, in short by all means at the disposal of the ruling classes. It is the secret of the impotence of the English working class, despite their organization. It is the secret by which the capitalist class maintains its power. And of this that class is well aware.

". . . The special task of the Central Council is to awaken a consciousness in the English workers that for them the *national emancipation of Ireland* is no question of abstract justice or human sympathy but the first condition *of their own emancipation.*" (Marx and Engels,

Selected Correspondence, Moscow: Progress Publishers, 1955, pp. 236-237)

In a letter to Marx (October 24, 1869) Engels had already pointed out that:

'Irish history shows one how disastrous it is for a nation when it has subjugated another nation. All the abominations of the English have their origin in the Irish pale.'

"Socialism alone provides for the combination of the development of each nation with the rapprochement and cooperation of nations on the basis of the principles of internationalism, thus creating opportunities for combining international and national tasks of the Communist Parties, the unity of their strategy and tactics in the struggle for building a new society.

"The proletarian party strives to create as large a state as possible, for this is to the advantage of the toilers; it strives to bring about a *rapprochment* between nations and the *further fusion* of nations; but it desires to achieve this aim not by violence, but *exclusively through a free, fraternal union of the workers and the toiling masses of all nations."* (T.Stepanyan, *Ibid*)

"The more democratic the . . . Republic is . . . the more powerful will be the force of *voluntary* attraction to such a republic felt by the toiling masses of *all* nations."

We Communists who are members of the oppressed Black people's nationality have the special responsibility to be vigilant against the impact of bourgeois nationalist influences, just as white Communists must stand tallest against great-power chauvinism and white supremacist racist corruption. We need to be ever mindful of the ideas of Lenin when he wrote.

"Bourgeois nationalism and proletarian internationalism—these are the two irreconcilably hostile slogans that correspond to the two great class camps throughout the capitalist world and express the two policies (nay, the two world outlooks) in the national question."

"The working class should be the last to make a fetish of the national question, since the development of capitalism does not necessarily awaken *all* nations to independent life. But to brush aside the mass national movements once they have started and to refuse to support what is progressive in them, is in effect pandering to nationalistic prejudices, viz., recognizing 'one's own' as the model nation.

"We fight on the basis of the given state, to unite the workers of all nations in the given state, we cannot vouch for this or that path of national development, we advance to our class goal by *all* possible paths.

"But we cannot advance to the goal without fighting all nationalism, without maintaining the equality of the workers of all nations." (Lenin, *Ibid,* Vol. 20, p. 413)

Political Affairs. March, 1969

37   Lenin and National Liberation

We are on the eve of one of the most notable historic events, the centenary of Lenin's birth.

This century, indeed, will be identified with the name of Lenin, as *The Lenin Century*—because probably no individual in all of history has been at the helm of comparable great events which so changed the face of the world as Lenin. People all over the world during this Lenin centenary year will be inquiring into the life and works of this extraordinary man, and examining and studying the Lenin heritage. Lenin's legacy is manysided and complex. It is a combination of profound, scientifically evolved ideas standing on the shoulders of vast knowledge.

A cardinal aspect of Leninism is that it weds the idea to the deed. There is no gap, no wall of separation between the Leninist ideas. They are brilliant in their conception, eloquent, penetrating and moving, and yet at the same time, they are fitted appropriately to actions just as monumental.

Lenin is one of the great seminal figures in history. His fertile work has split history into two parts: before and after the October Revolution of 1917. Mankind took a very long step toward an age of civilized conduct and rational relationships when the October Revolution occurred, because it opened the pathway, a model route for all mankind. It was Lenin's hand that was on the latch of that gate to real humane and civilized history. It was an opening for mankind to find at last a scientific road that inexorably must lead, on a world scale, to the emancipation of mankind from oppression by man.

Lenin's work was based on a solid foundation—the creations of Marx and Engels, who were the first to elaborate the scientific principles of modern socialism, on the basis of a searching, scientific analysis of historical development. They generalized the main laws of social development. Basing himself upon this Marxian heritage, Lenin profoundly studied his age and time. He analyzed capitalism in the period of its ultimate development and its decline—moribund capitalism, already dying even as it blossomed and bloomed to the ultimate point of its historic capability. It was capitalism grown into monopoly, capitalism in its imperialist phase. And Lenin defined the contemporary phase of capitalism as the eve of the socialist revolution, the ultimate, final phase of capitalist development, or imperialism.

Lenin perceived that the road to the liberation of the working class inevitably would draw into the vortex of this struggle all peoples striving to be free, no matter at what level of social development they found themselves.

Therefore, it was Lenin who perceived a world revolutionary process: that is to say, that revolutionary development was not a national phenomenon, not an exclusively European phenomenon, but the international working class struggle attaining its crest in first one country and then another or group of countries. The quest for power on the part of the oppressed and deprived working class was a battle that drew into its vortex all peoples throughout the world—thus making of the strivings for social change one international global struggle, with the particular efforts of the working class as its primary highway and its main motor force. Still the vehicle of social revolution has other wheels, first among them being the wheel of the struggle of the oppressed colonial masses, the unfree nations and peoples who suffered exploitation and oppression. Therefore, Lenin perceived that the national liberation movement would inevitably come to represent an extension of the class struggle into the arena of the colonial world, transforming that reserve base of capitalism into a militant front against imperialism.

Up until Lenin's time most of those identifying with the working class, including socialist thinkers and activists, hardly conceived of tapping the great potential for human revolutionary change that was represented by the oppressed tens of millions of the East, of Africa, of South America. These areas of the world were considered outside the province of sophisticated urban politics, and consequently there were "socialist" theorists who said: "Beyond the borders of Europe is an inert mass." And therefore decision would be wrought solely in the heart of western civilization, with the colonial provinces, the outlying unfree areas of the world, playing no role in overthrowing capitalism.

It was Lenin's *theory of uneven development* which served as a scientific instrument for divining social forces in respective countries and for making it possible to achieve a breakthrough in the shell of imperialism, which encompassed the whole world in one or another form of its oppressive embrace. This concept of the theory of uneven development explained rationally the inequality in the status of peoples in different parts of the world, and by the same token, disclosed how the whole world of the oppressed was objectively coupled to the main locomotive of history, the working class. Lenin added to Marx's foresight on the primary strategic concept of how the world would be changed, how imperalism would be cast off and how a new class would come to power, a class which would be truly capable of using all the creations of mankind—of science, of spiritual values, of humanistic values—and of applying them to the needs of man.

Lenin appraised the question of the struggle against national oppression as *a big part* of the world revolutionary process.

For us there is important material for thought in the following citation from the *Collected Works* of Lenin. It was written April 16, 1914. At that time, which was after the Stolypin reaction in old Czarist Russia, the Bolsheviks had succeeded in having a bloc, along with other labor and progressive candidates, elected to the Czar's Duma. It was the Czar's Duma because it was his hand-picked parliament. It had the facade of a democratic parliamentary body, but actually this Duma had little or no power to make changes in the life conditions of the masses. Nonetheless, Lenin called for participating in the Czarist Duma as a platform and a forum to rally the masses and involve them in struggles. And one issue that had come before the Duma was the question of a civil rights bill. Czarist Russia was considered the tomb of nations. Over a hundred distinct nationalities were imprisoned in this tomb. It was in this setting that these words were written by Lenin:

"The policy of oppressing nationalities is one of *dividing* nations. At the same time it is a policy of systematic *corruption* of the people's minds. The Black Hundreds' plans are designed to foment antagonism among the different nations, to poison the minds of the ignorant and downtrodden masses. . . .

"But the working class needs *unity, not division*. It has no more bitter enemy than the savage prejudices and superstitions which its enemies sow among the ignorant masses. The oppression of 'subject peoples' is a double-edged weapon. It cuts both ways—against the 'subject peoples' and against the Russian people.

"That is why the working class must protest most strongly against national oppression in any shape and form.

"It must counter the agitation of the Black Hundreds, who try to divert its attention to the baiting of non-Russians, by asserting its conviction as to the need for complete equality, for the complete and final rejection of all privileges for any one nation.

"The Black Hundreds carry on a particularly venomous hate-campaign against the Jews. The Purishkeviches try to make the Jewish people the scapegoat for all their own sins.

"And that is why the R.S.D.L. (Russian Social Democratic Labor) group in the Duma did right in putting *Jewish* disabilities in the forefront of its Bill.

"The schools, the press, the parliamentary rostrum—everything is being used to sow ignorant, savage, and vicious hatred of the Jews.

"This dirty and despicable work is undertaken not only by the scum of the Black Hundreds but also by reactionary professors, scholars, journalists and members of the Duma. Millions and thousands of millions of rubles are spent on poisoning the minds of the people.

"It is a point of honor for the *Russian* workers to have this Bill against national oppression backed by tens of thousands of proletarian signatures and declarations. . . . This will be the best means of consolidating *complete* unity, amalgamating all the workers of Russia, irrespective of nationality." (V.I. Lenin, *Collected Works*, Moscow: Progress Publishers, 1962. Vol. 20, pp. 237-238.)

This is an example of the high priority and importance that Lenin attached to involvement with the problems of the oppressed nationalities within the country, whose dominant population was the so-called "Great Russians." Of course, Lenin's point of departure and ending always centered upon the working class, not only with the largest section of the population, the Russians, but with *all* the oppressed peoples. And Lenin had an absolute rule-of-thumb standard which he demanded that any revolutionary worthy of the name abide by: that *the workers of any and all nations, nationalities, ethnic backgrounds, of all color tones and of all climes, shall seek to establish organizational ties in a common class organization.*

He insisted that the working class must pursue an overall common strategy and cultivate common bonds. Lenin was an absolute foe of what was then popular—"Bundism"—which introduced the idea of the organization of the working class along national lines, that is, of splitting the working class into national components, of atomizing the working class. He insisted that *class organizations must be common organizations,* and the striving of every revolutionary must be to foment and *fashion maximum unity within the class, to smash the color bar,* to eliminate the walls of distinction and difference on all class questions. *On the other hand, Lenin was not a national nihilist.* He was not for contempt for the national heritage, the national identity, the national form. Lenin advocated utilizing the national form in areas of other than class questions—to preserve the progressive aspects of culture, to use the language, to delve into and utilize the militant traditions of the oppressed of various nationalities, colors and identity. In such areas, separate organizations in which the theme of brotherhood and the extended hand to all other nationalities prevailed would be good. But they would be possible and could play a progressive role in the struggle for democratic objectives, in the struggle against national oppression and discrimination and violation of dignity in all forms, *only* if there was a solid class organization on which these national organizations could rest, and therefore could give the connecting link to the dominant, leading, vanguard role of the class of each national organization bound together in the universal fraternity of the working class.

Even in approaching the national question we must remain clear about the "main thing," Lenin said. "Our principal and fundamental task is to facilitate the political development and the political organization of the working class." The working class is multinational; the working class is international; the working class can understand that not every aspect of a national heritage is worth preserving. The working class has bonds, as Abraham Lincoln said, that are stronger than any other bonds, save those that link members of the same family. *The workers, indeed, are members of a class family, regardless of what nation or nationality they may belong to, irrespective of what ethnic mark of physiognomy they may bear.*

There are many good, progressive, legitimate national interests and causes, and the serious revolutionary will approach these activities and causes from the standpoint of moving the decisive social forces on issues, of moving the workers. If you have a good message, which you want to present to the population, present it to the workers, and it will go somewhere. Therefore, if you want to get rid of national oppression, the point of departure and the first audience, the first door, is the door to the workers. Because that's where it is. The working class is at the vitals of the total economy. The working class is the indispensable social force whose destiny it is to become the governing class, by objective, historical development, as well as by the conscious learning process from life experience. Lenin placed the question most sharply. He wrote:

"Those who push this task into the background, who refuse to subordinate to it all the special tasks and particular methods of struggle, are following a false path and causing serious harm to the movement. And it is being pushed into the background, firstly, by those who call upon revolutionaries to employ only the forces of isolated conspiratorial circles cut off from the working-class movement in the struggle against the government. It is being pushed into the background, secondly, by those who restrict the content and scope of political propaganda, agitation, and organization; who think it fit and proper to treat the workers to 'politics' only at exceptional moments in their lives, only on festive occasions; who too solicitously substitute demands for partial concessions from the autocracy for the political struggle against the autocracy; and who do not go to sufficient lengths to ensure that these demands for partial concessions are raised to the status of a systematic, implacable struggle of a revolutionary, working-class party against the autocracy." (Lenin, *Ibid,* Vol. 4, p. 369.)

Here, Lenin addresses himself to one thing: the primacy of the working class as the mover which can be relied upon to overturn the old order of things. But, at the same time, he gives a lesson in tactics. He scorns "Left" adventurism on the one hand, and he warns against Rightist complacency of smug satisfaction with petty reform on the other. While addressing himself to one main point, he takes care of the variation in the actual reality with supporting arguments, because Lenin is never the "professor in a muffler," talking for effects or resorting to a clever turn of phrase to get a laugh from students. He is a social engineer, bent on speeding the overthrow of an oppressive order. He is ever the scientist and doctor bent upon bringing to birth a new world with the least bloodshed and pain. Therefore, he knows life is complicated. It is not a simple confrontation. There are side effects. There are supporting and detracting issues. Just as it is necessary while driving down a busy thoroughfare to keep one's eye on the road, it is also important to look to either side, watching the other drivers. So Lenin does not divorce the question of who are the allies of the working class from the question of tactics.

It is necessary to say a word about the scope of the national liberation movement, the scope and the extent of national oppression. Colonialism is both a creation and an evidence of imperialism. As a creation of imperialism, it is evidence that imperialism still retains considerable power in the world. It is a creature of imperialism and it helps to sustain imperialism. It is still a reserve for imperialist superprofits out of which it uses its stolen largesse further to corrupt segments of "elite" workers and to buy governments and officials by the dozens. Therefore, it is in the advanced self-interest of the working class, of all Black and white working people, to help the colonial people to get rid of the yoke of imperialism. The success of the working class itself in contending with capitalism in the "home country" requires it.

Lenin called on the working class to address itself to the possible transformation of this reserve base of superprofit for imperialism into a major front of tens of millions of anti-imperialist fighters for the world revolution. Lenin showed how imperialism has united all peoples through its own exploitative system regardless of the technical level prevailing in different countries. Imperialism, by extending its tentacles over the entire capitalist world, *has united the victims,* bound them one to another, and given them a common target—so that it does not matter whether it be shoeless peasants in the African veld who fight imperialism, or city workers in a metropolitan sector fighting imperialism. They *meet together* by the acts of the common oppressor and by the processes of the oppression. Therefore, it is not an act of charity, nor paternalism, nor a Sunday goodwill deed for the working class to come to the aid of the oppressed colonial masses, the unfree, those suffering national oppression. *It is the indispensable obligation* of the working class seriously bent upon liberating itself.

It can never be free, it will never have the strength to face its capitalist class in an even contest, so long as that capitalist class still is able to draw sustenance from draining the blood of colonial tens of millions. Therefore, the struggle to finally do away with capitalism, the battle to usher in a humane and just social order, socialism, is a fight which has a priority in our time. That priority is to join and victoriously consummate the war of the colonial millions against imperialism, to put an end to colonialism. In order to transform the reserves of imperialism into active fighters for the revolution, and to enable the colonial masses to join directly the fight for socialism, the working class must do everything in its power to help the colonial masses wage this struggle victoriously.

Some 40 years ago, 70 per cent of the world's population was counted among the unfree subject peoples and 77 per cent of the territory of the earth was classified as colonial holdings of a handful of western powers. Imperialism expanded colonialism to its outer limits. At the same time, it created a colonial army of resistance which is destined to bring about its downfall. Correspondingly, the age of imperialism gave rise to the present-day national liberation movement, and this movement, in turn, is linked to the world working class movement.

So, the scope of the colonial liberation movement, the scope of the national liberation movement is massive and extensive, and second in importance only to that of the world working class movement. It is one of the three major components of the world revolutionary process which is, day-in and day-out, on one level or another, in battle with world imperialism. The two systems confront one another; now the struggle is open, now hidden, now taking one form, now another. The form taken is that appropriate to the circumstances; that is, what advances the revolutionary cause as against what deflects the arrow from the target, what broadens or narrows the front of engagement.

In the wide world of the anti-colonial struggle, in the wide world of the national liberation movement, stretching from Latin America to Africa, to the Middle East, to Asia, the forms of struggle vary from parliamentary and non-civil war mass actions producing advances of a qualitative character, to the heroic epic-making poem of valor that the

Vietnamese people are writing in a titanic and unequal struggle against the gargantuan powers of the U.S. aggressors. Never in history have so few stood against so many with such courage for so long.

And they do so because they represent the future of the world.

They do so because they are an extension of the world revolutionary process which is led by the working class, inspired and guided by the scientific contributions of Leninist science.

In addition to the external relations between the world working class struggle and the national liberation movement, the relationship and merger, as it were, between the two fronts of the worldwide revolutionary process opposing imperialism, the colonial revolution and the socialist revolution of the working class, there is that sector of the second front represented by national oppression. Within a number of capitalist states, there are oppressed nationalities in various aspects of distinctive national identity, in various stages of national formation. The national question is very wide in scope. It embraces everything from full-formed nations, nation-states, dominated by conquerors, by foreigners, by alien forces as in Mozambique and Angola and Rhodesia and South Africa today, to nationally oppressed peoples. These are peoples who suffer national oppression as minority forces within a larger nation, as an oppressed national component, a nationality, a people with various degrees of separate identity and various degrees of distinctiveness, defined as a community of people. Such a form of national oppression is that to which Black Americans are subjected.

Black Americans are a distinct component of the U.S. nation, which itself is a more or less solidified complex of many nationalities. Among the nationalities making up the U.S. nation the Black people are a distinct national component, no less American than any other, save the Indian people. The Black American has been compelled to contribute most to the wealth of the country, in terms of his unrequited toil. The Black man's bondage was a source of superprofit; it was a source of primitive accumulation.

Where did the young American state get the capital to leap from a primitive colonial holding into a modern industrial giant so quickly, when older, more sophisticated European countries did not advance at such a pace? It had to find readily available capital, and this capital was compounded out of the blood and the sweat and the toil and the lives of Black Americans for three and a half centuries in this country as chattel slaves, and after that time, as unequal, discriminated-against, abused, and persecuted citizens. Even now, Black citizens earn only one-half the national average. The Black citizen is deprived in all things, from human dignity to political representation in any fair measure.

With all great capitalist states, such as the United States, there is national oppression. The subjugation of nationalities or minority peoples is a hallmark of monopoly rule, of capitalism. It is part of the mechanism of the processes of capitalistic exploitation. It requires the special exploitation of minorities. If there were no Blacks in the United States, capitalism would import their equivalent or put the brand of oppression on some other people, because the persecution of minorities is needed to rob $37 billion a year in hard cash from the victims of segregation, racism, white supremacy. It is not the poor white workers who benefit from this robbery. It goes to the monopolists who steal and exploit from all. But Black workers, Black people, are robbed especially. Thirty-seven billion dollars is the racist loot from the conversion of blood and misery into dollars.

Exploitation is a hallmark of monopoly rule and such a racist pattern of special national oppression was elaborated and continues to be sustained by capitalism in order to maximize the rate of exploitation of all workers. To carry out more efficiently the multiple robbery of the poor and racially despised, the various devices of racism are made use of. But this fakery, this myth of race superiority and inferiority is a device not only for robbing the so-called "inferior people" by God-given right, or for white supremacists to rob Black people; it is designed to set up a competition within the white working class majority of the population.

To the whites it says: "See, there is yet another floor below you, so don't push too hard, or you can be put in the sub-basement, where the Black workers are." The ruling class would not, even if it could, deport all the Black people from the United States. No, they need this scheme, this mechanism that has been very profitable—because not only does it bring direct accumulation from the unpaid labor of the Black workers, but it sets up a system of competition which feeds on itself and grows and deprives the whole working class of a decent share of the values it creates. It is from such circumstances that new forms of resistance of the oppressed people arise.

What gives rise to the present-day national liberation movement? Is it the genius of the personality of a Lenin, of a Martin Luther King? The oppressed Black people will generate new Kings, new movements of struggle.

The ruling class is always dumber not wiser as it approaches its grave. It dies first in the head and the heart. Have no doubts, that it *does* approach its grave! Capitalism will never make it out of the 20th century.

All classes of oppressed people can find to one degree or another a point of involvement and identification with the goal of the national liberation movement. The decisive activists of the national liberation movement come, first of all, from the working class, the poor and oppressed farmers. In addition, the youth are in rebellion against the war they did not make and will not buy.

Women, of course, play a special role. Even women of the upper classes oftimes play a role in the liberation movement, because where there is national oppression, women—including those from upper classes—have no status, no dignity, no adequate protection of their rights. They are especially abused by the oppressor, and therefore women always play a major role in the national liberation movement.

I was the last U.S. visitor to talk with Ho Chi Minh before he died. He said there were so many things he wanted to do, but he had been fighting for twenty years, always having to postpone things for peaceful days—until next year. I asked: "Are there ever signs of war weariness?" He said: "A fortunate thing happened to us. We, at first hesitantly and not very confidently, wrote a Charter of Rights for equality of women, unprecedented in Asia. Nobody in the West has such a Charter of Rights. But our women believed it and acted on it, and therefore our resistance to U.S. imperialism rides not only on patriotism but on the rails of the women's liberation movement. It is impossible to stop it! Just impossible!" He added: "They may force our generals to retreat on occasion, but they will never stop the women's liberation movement, and you can't separate the resistance to U.S. imperialism in Vietnam from the new rights won by the women of Vietnam."

Therefore, the question of the class composition of the national liberation movement is very important. Do small businessmen, doctors, lawyers, teachers, for example, have a place in it along with workers? Yes! All who feel the slight, the heel, the insult of the oppressor have a place in it. Who will be more reliable than others? Will all be equally reliable? Will all play the same role? No! The class interest is very powerful, and we know that the rich sometimes do humiliating things for money, including the rich oppressed.

Nevertheless, "native sons" are unreliable for the ruling class. Therefore, when a ruling class has to appoint Black men as police and as judges and ambassadors and so on, it is already in trouble. To use even the alienated sons of an oppressed people as part of the mechanism of their class rule is to already admit to a certain cadre bankruptcy in operating their exploitative system. And it is an unreliable stratagem that can backfire. The history of India and of Africa proves it.

Now, given this broad spread of class composition that we have indicated, of the classes who make up the national liberation movement, it is absolutely necessary that the working class and the party of the working class play a very special role in that national front. *There is unity to be molded within the national liberation front, but there is also class struggle within the national liberaion movement.* The independent role of the workers and the party must be maintained to ensure correct leadership of the national liberation movement and of all democratic and reform movements. Leadership and direction should not be left to capitalist elements, because while they seek emancipation from the yoke of oppression, they want freedom not only for dignity and personal relief from oppression, but to do the business of capitalism, to exploit their own. Therefore, it is necessary to wage a skillful struggle to assure proper class leadership of the liberation movement.

In regard to tactics for the national liberation movement, it is good to bear in mind the ideas advanced by Lenin in his book, *What the Friends of the People Are and How They Fight the Social-Democrats.* This book was written in 1894, when Lenin was in the process of shaping up a vanguard party to lead the working class. Lenin criticized the Narodnaya Volya, called "The Friends of the People," for their advocacy of individual terrorism. Lenin considered such tactics harmful to the revolutionary movement, for they substituted the struggle of individual "heroes" for the struggle of the working class. Therefore, whatever poetic inspiration might be gained by the derring-do of individual terrorists, they alientated masses and unstructured the necessary maximum unity of the people.

It is not the heroic, or conceited, deeds of individuals that will move history to a higher plane, but the elemental movement of masses. Therefore, serious revolutionaries, concerned with making their maximum contribution to the national liberation movement, must guarantee that their tactical program is related to moving the masses in general, and the working class in particular.

Those who would be free themselves must strike the first blow. It cannot be struck for them. The working class wants to be free and will pay whatever price is necessary to be free. Black Americans want to be free and will pay whatever price by whatever means necessary to be free. The question is one of having patience and confidence in the masses. That is not to say that every day in the week the working class sees its own class interests. It does not, because it is no more free of the propaganda barrage laid down by the tools of capitalism than any other section of the people. Nevertheless, for the oppressed people, the national liberation movement marches forward to certain victory because it marches in company with the world working class.

The world working class today is in two component parts.

First is the world working class holding state power, using all that science has to offer in the means of production, developing military defense, possessing a vast territory with great institutions—a great power indeed. This section of the world working class is a fortress, a bastion, an arsenal of power for the world revolutionary movement. There can be no national liberation movement worth its name anywhere in the world which does not find a relationship to that section of the working class that holds state power.

Second, there is the section of the world working class movement which is in the capitalist countries, fighting at one level or another, with one degree of consciousness or another, on the economic, social and political fronts against capitalism for the advancement of the working class, for democracy and socialism.

Therefore, there can be no such thing as an independent national liberation movement that is not objectively a component part of the world revolutionary process. *Since the October Revolution of 1917, there has been developing one world anti-imperialist process.* The head of this world-wide, international movement against imperialism is that section of the working class which has taken political power. It is the main reservoir, the main defender, the bastion of strength and support to all other sections of the world anti-imperialist front: that of the colonial revolution and national liberation movement from Latin America to Asia to Africa to the Middle East to our own country, as well as that of the world working class in the capitalist countries, fighting for democracy and socialism against capitalism and imperialism.

The future belongs to the working class and its allies, the oppressed peoples. Karl Marx gave us the slogan: "Workers of the world, unite! You have nothing to lose but your chains!" Lenin, basing himself, as he always did, on the creations of the founders of scientific socialism and on thorough understanding of our world and its development processes, added to that slogan to update it for the age of imperialism—because the age of imperialism combined two things, the socialist revolution and the colonial revolution, into *one world revolutionary* front. Thus, Leninism modified Marx's slogan to proclaim:

"Workers of the world and oppressed peoples, unite! You have nothing to lose but your chains and a world to gain!"

Political Affairs. May, 1970

38   African Trends

An article by the widely syndicated columnist, Jack Anderson, reveals that the State Department is conducting a special bit of intrigue to take the wraps of restraint off U.S. relations with the state of Burundi—a campaign of cultural, educational and economic intervention to "warm up" relations between Washington and Burundi. Anderson indicates what's behind all this—he terms it "nickel politics."

He reports that a lode of nickel, worth something like $14 billion, was recently discovered in Burundi. Prior to this discovery, the United States—under pressure of world opinion had reluctantly given the appearance of disassociating itself from the Burundi government, which during the last few years has been engaged in a genocidal assault upon the minority people in that country. Some 200,000 of these people have been slaughtered, and another 100,000 put into exile. And so the United States imposed certain paper sanctions, in concert with other countries, against Burundi. But now all of those sanctions are down the drain. Not that the slaughter by the reactionary government there has ceased—but the $14 billion vein of nickel has been discovered, with certain prospects that there might also be oil.

And, as Jack Anderson points out, the United States Ambassador there calls for a complete change in Washington's attitude toward Burundi, saying that our government must encourage investments and corporate interests. And, states the Ambassador, "That is the function of our embassies overseas."

So, U.S. imperialism has geared itself to plunge in where old angels of imperialism no longer tread, seeking direct penetration into the heart of Africa via nickel developments in Burundi. Therefore, one can see an intimate relationship between the struggles of the peoples of Africa —not only to complete the process of liberation from U.S., British, French and Portuguese imperialism and neo-colonialism, but also to choose their path of internal political and economic development—and the struggle for democratic advance and against monopoly capitalism and ultimately for socialism in our own country.

If U.S. imperialism can find a pliant government to mimic the reign of the former exploiters and welcome U.S. corporate interests, not only will there be the possibility of loss of sovereignty for African states; there will also be a blood transfusion of wealth into the hardening arteries of the U.S. imperialists for reviving capitalism in its reactionary garb at home. Therefore, willy-nilly, we have a vested interest in terms of our own objectives for concerning ourselves with internal development in Africa.

U.S. corporations are already deeply committed to the exploitation of African labor and the robbery of African resources. In South Africa alone there is the massive presence of U.S. corporate interests, as well as concealed sums of U.S. investment capital. Among those busily taking and consuming labor power, extracting the natural wealth of these countries, are G.M., Ford, Chrysler and Chase Manhattan Bank. Some 350 subsidiaries of U.S. corporations are operating in South Africa alone. Alongside these U.S. corporate interests, participating in the robbery of the peoples of Africa, are British, German and Japanese corporate imperialists. A newcomer to this motley gang of economic pirates, political subverters of the freedom aspirations of Africa, is the state of Israel. Israel is becoming a special organizer of international capital, in collaboration with the government of South Africa, for penetrating and suborning the national independence and economic integrity of the various countries in Africa.

A really historic demonstration of the common bond between the anti-imperialist struggles in Africa and the struggle for deliverance from the Watergate society and monopoly rule in the U.S. took place on October 20-21, 1973 in Chicago. This was a conference of representatives from all parts of the United States in solidarity with the anti-imperialist movement of South Africa, and of Africa generally. This conference launched a new organization in our country, the Committee for Anti-Imperialist Solidarity with African Liberation, which already has a sizable constituency. Some 907 delegates from 28 states attended this conference and agreed upon a program designed to mobilize public opinion on the side of fighting Africa, struggling to throw off the last chains of imperialist domination.

Among the forces represented were unions, churches, student organizations, civic and social groups, as well as many outstanding personalities. One of the agreements of the conference was that participants would initiate a petition process designed to accumulate a million or more signatures, directed to the United Nations in general and the U.S. delegation and government in particular, demanding the ouster of South Africa from the U.N., and the seating of the new, independent government of Guinea-Bissau.

A very significant accomplishment took place in the U.N. in the last (28th) General Assembly. On the initiative of the Soviet Union and the other socialist countries, in alignment with the Afro-Asian bloc, there was adopted—for the first time in world history—a convention against apartheid, racism and discrimination. There was an overwhelming vote of approval for this instrument of international pressure. Among the four countries who abstained or voted against this anti-apartheid, anti-racist convention was the United States, in company with Portugal, Brazil and other fascist or neo-fascist countries. We have a special obligation to effect a change in the response of the American public and its representatives in Congress, in order to reverse this action and guarantee that this convention is ratified by our government.

This is a most remarkable document, which indicts with a bill of particulars all aspects of the crimes of racism as symbolized in the barbarous, genocidal regime of Vorster in South Africa. We should guarantee that this U.N. document—already adopted by some 70 parliaments of the world, with the Supreme Council of the Supreme Soviet of the USSR as one of the first to adopt it—becomes the property of the American people as a whole. A demand in the forthcoming elections must be for a Congress committed to voting for adoption of this convention against racism and genocide.

U.S. opposition to this U.N. convention is based not only on ill-will, cynicism and other imperialist attitudes toward Africa and the African peoples. It reflects also a determination to prevent establishment of a precedent whereby racism, discrimination and genocide against Black Americans and other oppressed nationalities can be handled under international law, brought under the sanctions of the world community of states.

A very interesting provision of this document gives an aggrieved person or people, victims of racism and apartheid, the privilege of entering an international law court—or any court in any country that has adopted this U.N. convention. What this means is apparent: Blacks, Chicanos, Puerto Ricans, American Indians and Asians, unable to get satisfaction in the courts of their own country against the barbarous practices of racism, discrimination and genocide, now have a precedent in international law for going to the courts of another country and bringing the offending government and parties before the bar of world public opinion. There are other implementing provisions in this convention, which sets up a permanent committee for controlling and policing the enforcement of this new charter of human rights.

Today in the U.N. there is a generally progressive bloc of African states. Together with the socialist bloc and the broader community of newly liberated Afro-Asian Middle-Eastern states, they constitute an effective forum of approximately 100 nations able en masse to confront, challenge and frustrate the will of U.S. and world imperialism, to prevent it from proceeding as though the world were its oyster.

Now there is a mighty Black presence in the U.N. that is in alliance with already liberated peoples, in the first instance the peoples of the socialist countries. This constitutes an important international diplomatic force on the side not only of African liberation, but of the freedom struggles of peoples in each imperialist country. And the consequence of this new reality in world politics—with Africa no longer an inert mass, the silent and dark continent—is an Africa coming into the sunlight of real politic, and becoming a force for changing the political complexion of the map.

What is the basis for this new development in Africa? It exists in the changed world relationship of forces. It is to be found in the existence in the community of nations of a powerful bloc of anti-imperialist socialist countries, with no vested interest in the robbery, exploitation and tyrannizing of peoples far from their borders who are concerned with raising the quality of life for their own people and who have a vested interest in promoting friendship and peaceful relations on a global scale. Peace in the world is a condition for national development and raising the standards of living within each of the socialist countries.

That is the credo, the governing concept, in the foreign policy of the socialist countries. Therefore, African peoples emerging from the prison of imperialist domination and oppression find a strong hand of fellowship in the world, a powerful voice in world diplomacy speaking in their interests, on their side; representing a reservoir of material aid and solid support for liberation in Africa. A great restraining force, more than an equalizer, now exists in the world—thanks to the strength of world socialism—against the aggressive proclivities of U.S. imperialism to frustrate or defeat the freedom, will, aspirations and strivings of people who are without, as yet, powerful industrial bases to defend themselves.

Indeed, thanks to the bastion of socialist strength—that is, of the working class in political power—there is no longer such a thing as a small and weak people. Every small and weak person, every community of persons, every small and weak nationality seeking its emancipation from tyranny, has now the opportunity to associate itself with a great power in the world, and therefore can confront the imperialist aggressors and exploiters with a power more than equal to their own.

How else could we explain the victory in Vietnam over the mightiest military armada ever assembled—the planes, the tanks, the battleships of mighty industrial U.S.A. How else to explain the ability of Guinea-Bissau, the liberation fighters under the leadership of the now martyred Amilcar Cabral, to have gone from a resistance movement to an established state power, though some parts of it are still occupied by the Portuguese colonialists. The new Republic of Guinea-Bissau has already been recognized by some 70 countries—but not the United States. Therefore, we have international obligations to perform in respect to Guinea-Bissau.

Thanks to this new world reality, on the continent of Africa a confident stride forward has been taken by the people: the overwhelming majority of people in Africa have accomplished the first stage in their revolutionary progress—the overthrow of the British, French and other imperialists.

Now, increasingly, in the complex of countries composing the African continent, the peoples recently liberated from colonialism are looking at the world, assessing their own experiences, and choosing, one after the other, a non-capitalist road of developing. Some are opting, consciously and deliberately, for socialism. What makes it possible for them to do so is the establishment of alliances, of many-sided economic, political and cultural relationships with the bastion of liberated peoples, with the socialist peoples—and finding that enlightenment of political science in the ideas of Marxism-Leninism, which indicate with the clarity of a torchlight who are the enemies and who are the friends of the people fighting for freedom. And, therefore, the peoples of Africa who have chosen a non-capitalist path of development in the direction of socialism, also seek broad alliance among peoples of whatever culture, among white peoples as well as Black peoples, on the basis of who is in struggle against imperialism. Because of Marxist-Leninist enlightenment, they recongnize that the main foe of national development and social progress within Africa, within each country, as well as the main and primary menace to solidarity with African independence, is the existence of ravenous, aggressive world imperialism—the capstone of which is U.S. imperialism.

Africa is not one uniform political map. It is a map of several shadings. Some of the African states, such as Ethiopia, have opted for capitalism, and have attempted to make it within the framework of capitalist relations. But Ethiopia, for one, has failed to meet the needs of its people. In some respects, in the area of foreign policy, Ethiopia pursues a generally enlightened line. But in domestic affairs, it has failed to follow a pattern of enlightenment, based on the experience of peoples who have succeeded in building a new life on the wreckage of old capitalist relations. Ethiopia sought to duplicate, to emulate, to repeat the pathways of capitalist development. And as a consequence, it has been unable to amass the resources to meet the hunger of the people for social development and progress within the country. It has been unable to advance beyond the first stage of struggle for freedom; that is, the establishment of state sovereignty. But even that state sovereignty becomes imperiled if a country doesn't move into the second stage of the social revolutionary process—that is, fundamental social change to satisfy the pent up needs of a long deprived and underdeveloped people.

By contrast, there is development of a notable character in Tanzania. There is expansive development in Egypt, Iraq, Syria, Mali, Congo-Brazzaville, because the main political decisions have been made by the democratic, progressive, forward-looking social forces within these countries. They have drawn the lessons of history; they have recognized that catching up to modern times in terms of meeting the people's accumulated social needs requires not a policy that enriches a handful—the bourgeois and landlord gentry—but a government policy reflecting the interests of the masses. Nationalization of industrial development and agrarian reform, cultivating a *genuine* cultural revolution, and extending to the masses the opportunity to participate in the process of the renovation of life is bringing about social development in these countries kept in stagnation for so many years by imperialist domination.

Africa presents a checkered picture of some three or four types of internal development, patterns of political and economic formation born out of the anti-colonial revolutionary process in the third world. What is emerging are patterns of democratic, non-capitalist development, and patterns of national democratic development leading in the direction of socialism. In their alliances, increasingly, the African countries are coming to recognize who in the world arena stands with them and who opposes them. Alliances are being solidified between the emerging African states and the socialist community.

What is the lesson of Africa to us? It is, as Amilcar Cabral and other outstanding revolutionaries on the African continent have shown, the concept that imperialism exists thanks to its ability to promote two things in the popular mind: racism among the ranks of white masses, and anti-communism—not only among the white masses, but in the ranks and leadership of the Black liberation movement. The key for people seeking freedom who would maximize their unity potential, is to rid themselves of the burden of anti-communism, which tends to isolate, segregate the Black liberation movements—whether in Africa or in the United States—from its logical allies, from bases of power which have already been achieved by the establishment of a world socialist sector. Freedom requires not only maximum unity of the unfree in the struggle for liberation. Freedom requires maximum alliance relationships, bonds of solidarity with all those who suffer under the yoke of the common oppressor, world imperialism.

These bonds between the African liberation struggles and the liberation struggle of Blacks in the U.S. are explored in all their significance and complexity by Henry Winston, National Chairman of the Communist Party, U.S.A. in his recent book, *Strategy For A Black Agenda*. (New York: International Publishers, 1973). This book has been welcomed here and internationally as an outstanding work in the service of the liberation of the African peoples, the liberation of his own people, Black Americans, and of liberation on a world scale.

In our country, to achieve unity among Black people, to strengthen the bond with and pride in Africa by dipping into the African inspirational resources, is not just a question of harking back to ancient Africa, the Africa of the great empires and kingdoms, of Mali and Ghana, when there were great kings and potentates and great cultural centers.

The basis of our ties with Africa are very current and very meaningful. They are a source of political solidarity and strength. The Africa of today, the Africa in struggle against imperialism, the bonds that link Black Americans to Africa, are the bonds not of blood—but the ties that flow from the struggles, the common struggles against the imperialist blood-suckers. This common struggle is the "blood tie" that binds Black Americans and Africans. It is also the tie that binds Black and white within the United States, and on a global scale, with Africa. All who join in the struggle against the common enemy, imperialism, are brothers under the skin, kinsmen one to the other. Solidarity is the requirement for waging a victorious struggle for national liberation and for the liberation of humanity from tyranny, war and impoverishment—these ugly creations of world imperialism.

We are also faced with the challenge of responding to the need for material solidarity with fighting Africa. Such international "dues" must be paid in order to achieve the maximum advantage for our own national liberation. Every form of solidarity must be extended to the African people in their struggle to throw imperialism, above all U.S. imperialism, out of Africa. Imperialism must be cut down to size, thrown out of the section of the world where it still sinks its fangs and drinks blood like a vampire. Imperialism must be thrown out of Africa as it was thrown out of Cuba. Solidarity with the African struggles will strengthen our working class and oppressed peoples in their battle with U.S. imperialism, helping us to prevail against it.

No one can speak of the struggle against world imperialism—of the mutual interests that unite the cause of African liberation and the liberation of Black Americans, and indeed of all our people, from racism and its consequences—without remembering the plight, the suffering, of the heroic people of Chile, who so recently made such a bold thrust to establish on the mainland of this continent a probe into the future, a democratic government that would create the conditions for further socialist development in the Americas. This government was intrigued against and bloodily crushed by the intervention of and financing from agencies of U.S. imperialism.

Solidarity with Africa also implies solidarity with Chile. Frederick Douglass said it 100 years ago—a blow struck for freedom anywhere is a blow for freedom everywhere. There is a oneness in the struggle against imperialism. We man a particular front. The people of Chile are fighting to overthrow the fascist junta, which they will surely do if we fulfill our obligations to them. The African people are taking the high road into modern times under their own banners, toward a new freedom, just as the peoples of the Soviet Union—who 54 years ago shook off the chains of imperialism—and the socialist world are marching into the future, pioneering a path that the rest of the world will follow.

The struggle is world-wide, with particular divisions, segments—and our front is a part of that world front. The struggle for Black liberation, for equality, for meaningful democratic opportunity for all of the peoples of our country, is a part of that struggle for the liberation of humanity.

Washington Heights Forum, New York City. March, 1974

39   Some Data on the Black Condition

The continuing gross inequality in the condition of the lives of some 25 million Black Americans has been given documentation from the most recently available data in a study by Dr. Harrington J. Bryce, director of research at the Joint Center for Political Studies in Washington, D.C.

Dr. Bryce's study is a polemical response to an article that appeared in the April issue of *Commentary* magazine by Ben J. Wattenberg and Richard Scammon entitled "Black Progress and Liberal Rhetoric." In their article Scammon and Wattenberg drew sweepingly optimistic conclusions about alleged near liquidation of discrimination and inequality on the basis of data compiled on the status of a narrow segment of less than 10 percent of the Black families of so-called "Black middle class" income categories. Using the same data from the U.S. Bureau of Census, Dr. Bryce proves that the claim that Blacks are nearing parity with whites in economic, social and political circumstances is but a wish, a hope and a caricature.

We have selected some of the findings and conclusions from the wealth of statistical data which he has assembled and analysed to profile the contemporary aspects of the Black condition in the United States of 1973.

In respect to family income and earnings: Black families' incomes fell behind white families' incomes by some $4,000 in 1971 as compared to $2,500 less than that received by whites in 1947!

Only 10.6 percent of Black families had incomes of $15,000 or more in 1971 while 26.4 percent of all white families had incomes of $15,000 or better. At the same time, 38.6 percent of Black families had incomes of under $5,000 in contrast to the fact that 16.2 percent of white families were in this below $5,000 income category.

Historically, the Black unemployment rate has been twice as high as the white unemployment rate. This two to one ratio holds currently. Black youth between the ages 16-25 experience four times more unemployment than white youth of the same age category. The unemployment rate among Black teenagers is 35 percent.

Dr. Bryce notes that—"Blacks remain under-represented in the high-wage occupations. In 1972 there were 35 percent fewer Blacks in professional occupations than would have been the case had Blacks had access equal to that of whites." They are 70 percent below their fair proportion in managerial occupations and sales forces. They are 30 percent below their equal share of jobs in the crafts and 21 percent short of their due share of clerical workers.

Although Black workers are 12 percent of all union members, in the craft unions which control entry into many of the high-wage blue collar occupations Blacks are only five percent of the membership of the craft unions.

One of every three Black families are compelled to live in unsafe and unsanitary slum housing. Seventeen percent of Black family households are without minimal plumbing facilities and this is three times the rate for white households.

Seventy eight percent of white youth finished high school in 1970, the percentage for Black youth is 56. One of every three college-age white youth was enrolled in college in 1970 as compared to one out of six for Black youth.

There is a 6 year difference between the life expectancy of Black as against white youth. Black maternal mortality is three times that of whites, as is the case of Black/white infant mortality.

By 1970, three of every five Black Americans in the United States lived in the central cities of major metropolitan areas. They make up more than half of the central city population in Washington, D.C.; Newark, New Jersey; Gary, Indiana; Atlanta, Georgia and Detroit, Michigan.

The Black population in the rural South is now only 3.9 million. Slightly less than half of the total Black population live in the South today. At the time of the 1970 census Blacks averaged 28 percent of the total population of the cities in the largest size category. Starting practically from point zero, Black people have made significant advancement in securing some political representation in elected governmental bodies during the past decade. There are now some 16 Congressmen, 1 Senator and 301 Mayors. The total number of Black elected officials—inclusive of many minor posts at the local level—still does not exceed 3,000, a figure which is about one-half of one percent of the total number of elected officials in the country as a whole.

There are some 58 Congressional Districts where the Black population represents approximately a third of the total, and with alliance and coalition arrangements with the working poor among the whites, the potential exists for the election of a sizable number of Black persons to Congress from these districts.

June, 1973

40   Dynamics of the Freedom Struggle

The condition of the Black masses grows more desperate with each passing day. Herded into the most blighted areas of the city ghettos and the rural slums, with one out of four heads of families unemployed and half of their youth without jobs or any prospects of employment in their future, Black Americans in large numbers are experiencing hunger and a rising death rate from the diseases of poverty.

The governments—at Washington, the state capitols, "downtown" or at the county seats—are responding to the angry demands of the jobless and desperate people with massive military and police concentrations and plans for waging a civil war against the poor communities of the Black Americans. The white workers are the Black people's objective allies. But most of the trade unions are in need of a progressive reconstitution of their leadership in order to be counted upon to champion the special needs of the Black people.

The old-line politicians largely dominate the scene and the voices of the masses are unheard. Marooned on islands of poverty and misery, in the midst of spangled cities flaunting affluence, millions of Black Americans face a desperate crisis of survival. Such is the situation confronting the least advantaged—the Black people. What is their way out? Where does the freedom route of the Black people's movement lead?

Freedom was the word most often heard on the lips of Black Americans during the decade of the 'sixties. Millions of the 25 million Black Americans took to the streets in its name during these years. The freedom struggle has projected many slogans and taken numerous forms. The variety of the demands which the Blacks fight for and the extension of the skirmish lines—from South to North, from coast to coast —reveals how widespread is its absence. Some of the specific immediate demands of the Black people encompassed by the freedom slogan can be stated programatically:

● Freedom is the right to have a full voice in deciding the affairs which govern the fate of the nation. It means Black citizens exercising the political power where they are "the many" and a just share of it where they are "the few."

● Freedom is a job at one's highest skill and the right to be trained and promoted in accordance with one's ability.

● Freedom is a good-sized home furnished as you need it to live as a family in a comfortable way.

● Freedom is an open door for one's children to get a first-class education in a top-rate, non-segregated school system.

● Freedom is all those other things which make one's neighborhood a fit place to live in: where the streets are kept clean, the community hospital is good, where there are playgrounds and parks and centers for young people's recreation.

● Freedom, above all, is the right to self-respect, to be treated as a human being; the right to dignity and respect shown toward one's color, race, people. The right to be one's self and still be treated as the equal of any other American. It is the absence of *racism*.

● Freedom is the right to community of one's own choice. It is the absence of segregation, of racially restricted and exclusive housing, jobs, clubs or what-not. Equally, it demands big-scale investments in the general rebuilding of the Black communities. It is a program to displace slum housing and reconstruct the material foundation of the poor communities of large Black populations.

● Freedom is security of one's person. It is the right to live free from arbitrary arrest, free from police terror and violence.

Such concrete aspects of a program for equality and democratic rights are encompassed in the concept of freedom, and appear to one degree or another in the programs of most of the organizations which together constitute the movement of the Black masses for freedom and equality.

In addition to such particular and urgent needs which the movement of the Black people put forward, it also joins the struggle in support of such general causes as that of ending the war in Vietnam and solidarity manifestations with other victims of imperialism in battle for freedom.

The freedom movement of the Black people has carried the main brunt of the struggle for social progress for the past decade. It has confronted some of the most reactionary bastions of ruling-class power. It has involved millions in the drama of its actions.

The deep commitment and mass courage of the Black freedom fighters who withstood the attack of police dogs in Birmingham and the shot and shell of machine guns and army tanks in Detroit testify to the iron resolve of the Black masses to continue the struggle without ceasing.

At the very time when the sympathetic pressure of public opinion throughout the country and the world was beginning to register some impact on the government and forced the beginning of a program to assist the most desperate of the jobless generation of Black youth, all interest was short-circuited and abruptly ended; funds for even minimal measures against poverty were diverted to expenditures for expanding the aggressive war against the people of Vietnam.

The *economics of the war* have wiped out the promises so lavishly made of a really sizable anti-poverty war at home aimed at reducing the disparity in opportunity between Black and white.

The *politics of the war* have spurred all the racist reactionaries in public life to come out for intensifying the repressive violence against the Black communities in the name of patriotism and war-time law and order on the home front.

An additional stimulus to the manufacture and dissemination of white supremacy racist ideas is presented by the need to rationalize the murder of the Vietnam people.

Capitalist society has become a sadistic torture chamber which grinds into the dust the lofty ideals, the creative potential, the hopes for happiness, the longing for brotherhood and freedom, indeed, the very lives of millions of people.

Nowhere on earth is the anti-humanist savagery of this historically outmoded system of capitalism more horrifyingly evident than in its treatment of the 25 million Black U.S. citizens. The values which the toil and creativity of this people have contributed to the formation, development and wealth of the nation establishes the objective and historical fact that they are a component part of the U.S. nation. It is one of the peoples of foreign origin which constitute the nation.

U.S. racism in doctrine and practice is a dreadful concoction compounded of prejudice and ignorance and was first administered on a mass scale to overcome resistance to the introduction and maintenance of slavery.

Slavery in the United States was a labor system based upon the capture and bondage of human beings from Africa, their shipment, sale and subsequent employment in the economy as human machines, work animals, sold and resold as chattel-commodities on the capitalist market. The apologists of the slave merchants and cotton capitalists shamelessly developed the doctrine of the inherent supremacy of people of white skin and the inherited inferiority of people of black skin.

Despite the terrible torture that the horrible hypnotic of racism has caused the nation—including the four years of Civil War—the monopolists are still able to use this ideological rot to promote race conflict among the exploited and convert it into profit.

Racism, prejudice and hatred against Black people are still counted upon by the capitalist rulers to "blow the mind" of the working class, to divert the anger of the white and Black exploited masses away from the exploiters and on to one another.

Racism is the ideological alley where the greed of Big Business and the lust of small merchants join in assaulting and robbing the Black communities.

Racism is the blinders on the eyes of the white working people which prevents them from seeing the threat to, and violation of, their own self-interest when discrimination is tolerated against Black citizens.

Black people were involved from earliest times in the rise and development of this American nation, and represent a historically determined component part of it. Nevertheless, because of the special forms of oppression and racial discrimination to which Black people have been subjected, it has also been alienated from the nation, forcibly kept from partaking fully of its rightful status as an equal member of the national family.

Notwithstanding the fact that Blacks communicate in the language common to the rest of the nation and have made major contributions to the economy and to the culture of the nation, the severe patterns of anti-Black discrimination and white racial exclusiveness have compelled them to be a people apart. They are set apart by identifiable features of their African origin, by barricades of physical segregation, as well as invisible walls of social ostracism and psychological rejection.

The cauldron of slavery's horror and segregation's aftermath were unique factors which fused a national consciousness that continues to be tempered in the fires of struggle for freedom. It is such singular historical and current experiences which contribute to and account for the special national features of the Black people.

While fighting to secure their full status as equal citizens of this American nation and, indeed, as a part of, and a form for, conducting that struggle, the Black people assert their identity as a distinctive people.

The particular national aspect of the American Black people has its distinctive cultural expression in a rich and growing body of literature and artistic creation. It is manifested also in the prideful reclamation of their history and in the popularization of esthetic taste and styles of African origin. This fight for self-determined standards and art forms appropriate to the tasks of giving cultural expression to the Blacks' own historical and contemporary experience and creativity, is an important part of the general struggle for dignity and freedom. At the same time, it enriches the culture of the nation as a whole.

The Black people, conforming to the nature of the capitalist society within which it develops, has an internal class structure. But the most important fact about the class stratification of the Black people in the United States is its overwhelming working class composition. Some 85 percent of the total population are of the working class. Another 8 percent are poor farmers and toilers in agriculture. There is an urban middle class stratum of professionals, teachers, and shopkeepers which represents 5 percent of the total. Less than 1 percent have a command of finances sufficient to qualify for the category of capitalists.

The principal class content of the Black people, therefore, is that reflecting its dominant class component—the working class. It follows, therefore, that in the long run, it will be the requirements, needs, aspirations and the leadership of personalities from the working class stratum of this people that will ultimately determine the program, goals, strategy and tactics of its freedom movement.

Suffering from national oppression and racial discrimination, as well as added economic exploitation as a consequence of the devices of discrimination, the Black workers know from their place in the production relations that it is not the white man in general who profits from the racist degradation and added economic exploitation to which he is subjected, but the white capitalists who are the common exploiter of both Black and white workers.

The conflicting tendencies and policies within the freedom movement are a reflection to one degree or another of the contradictory interests of the two basic class forces in the total society—the working class influence versus the capitalist influence.

Out of its factory experience the working class influence will express itself in an emphasis on building the movement to maximum strength, gaining allies from among the white masses, giving a democratic structure to its leadership, and elaborating a strategy—a longer-range plan, and associated tactics which do not contradict the strategic objectives but further their realization. The influence of the working class upon policy and leadership makes for planned struggles carried out in a well-organized and militant manner. Under its influence the movement reacts to spontaneous developments but it does not base its course upon them.

The capitalist class' influence within and upon the Black people's movement is reflected as policy that avoids struggle, involvement and appeal to the masses, and invites compromise without struggle and accommodation to the conditions that obtain. It often projects the prejudices and hatreds of the capitalists into the movement, especially in opposing alliances with white workers and in red-baiting.

Tendencies to excessive individualism, arbitrary and anarchistic decisions, underestimation of questions of organization, of tactics and alliances, of choice of forms of action appropriate to the circumstance are some of the negative inclinations of leaders who represent middle-class traits.

The influence of the non-working class forces on the direction of the movement may cause sections of it to raise slogans for separation and national exclusiveness as the form the Black people should adopt in seeking their freedom. An undifferentiated attitude of distrust and hostility toward all whites is also characteristic of these sloganeers.

The dynamic of the freedom struggle more and more discloses the fundamental unwillingness and inability of the monopolists to affect the kind of radical elevation called for to secure a fair and equal level of material well-being, economic and cultural opportunity for the Black masses.

Increasingly, the logic of the experience of the most conscious and thoughtful participants in the struggles of the movement will suggest the validity of the judgment of the Communist Party: that the road to Black freedom, to genuine equality and the self-fulfillment of Black Americans as a people, lies in the constant waging of battles for democratic reforms; but in so doing, to prepare the forces and establish the alliances within the framework of a great, popular anti-monopoly strategy that will open the way toward pursuing the struggle to its revolutionary conclusion—to the displacement of the racist exploitative system by a new and just society—socialism.

Memo to the National Program Committee,
C.P., USA. February 2, 1969

About the Author

James E. Jackson has been a serious student of Marxist-Leninist theory since he joined the revolutionary movement as a youth of 16. His work on problems of theory, as teacher and writer is a spin-off from an uninterrupted career of activism in the working class and national liberation movement which spans four decades.

Currently, he is the National Education Director of the Communist Party, U.S.A. and a member of its Central Committee and Political Committee.

He has been Editor-in-chief of The Worker newspaper; Regional Secretary of the Communist Party of the Southern states; and leader of the Party organization in the auto industry. For a long period he was the International Secretary of the Communist Party. In this capacity Jackson participated in many international conferences and traveled extensively abroad.

James E. Jackson is a Black American, born in Richmond, Virginia. He has academic degrees from Va. Union University, Howard University, Goddard College and Moscow University. In his early years, he was a prominent youth leader and one of the founders of the Southern Negro Youth Congress. During the late thirties he was the organizer and leader of a number of strike struggles, most notably in the tobacco industry.

During the anti-Soviet cold war hysteria and repression of the "McCarthy years" Jackson was indicted under the infamous Smith Act. He was a refugee from political persecution for five years.

Subsequently, the case of James E. Jackson versus the Government of the United States went for review to the appelate court where the earlier "guilty" verdict was reversed and he and his colleagues were exonerated of all charges.

A veteran of the anti-fascist war, Jackson served on the China-India-Burma front.

He is the author of *Negroes in Battle* (1967) and *The View from Here* (1963).